The Book on Fine-Grained Incremental Development

Slice the Problem
Grow the Solution

A Practical Guide to Fine-Grained Incremental Development

Bookstore / Preview Edition

Alistair Cockburn

The Simplifying Series

Humans and Technology Press

ISBN for paper: 979-8-9968976-1-2
ISBN for ePub: 979-8-9985862-9-3

v0.95b 260702-1123

Alistair Cockburn's "Slice the Problem, Grow the Solution"—originally designed to help human teams navigate complexity—has become a foundational "meta-strategy" for Agentic AI in software development.

-- Shunmugavel Mariappan

Cockburn's clarity cuts through complexity - a must-read for any Agile team serious about building what users actually need, not just what specs say.

-- Jawahar Prabhu Yenneti

What I like the most is your ability to make complex stuff sound so simple, and how the visuals help paint the whole picture.

-- Martin Alaimo

Table of Contents

List of Figures

Preliminaries

The series and this book

20% of the technique gets you 80% of the value, so why not learn a juicy twenty percent first and get running? Level up with other techniques that advance your skill.

The ***Simplifying Series*** delivers focused starter techniques for selected professions, designed to get you productive fast. Project management, software design, product management are entire careers, needing years of study. There is surely a starter kit in each case. That is what I have in mind for this series.

Incremental development. Many books say *do it*, but not many walk you through examples. This book collects examples from *Disciplined Learning, The Mini-Book on Use Cases*, *Hexagonal Architecture Explained*, my Elephant Carpaccio, and other writings to show you *why* and exactly *how* to do fine-grained incremental development in different contexts.

There is a section for executives interested in a quick read, another for business people, product managers and business analysts, another for project managers, and one for programmers. Hopefully each reader will find something of use.

AI changes a few things: Your steps will be bigger because it's so fast. But you can lose control of the result as it grows, so incremental development is still relevant for learning *what to build* as well as controlling the AI. (See *AI Hits* in the Epilogue.)

Let's go …

Alistair Cockburn
July 2, 2026

How to Read this Book

This book contains as close as I could find *everything* I have written on the subject over 30 years of decoding and attempting to explain my understanding. That means that you may need a guide to how to approach and process all these pages.

First, I put a "Snap Summary" in the immediately following pages. I want to be clear about the main message I wish to convey. You will find a 1-page summary of the book itself and a snap summary of each chapter, highlighting the point I really want to make in that chapter.

Please read these snap summary pages first, and see how many of those ideas you already know and have internalized. That will be your guide as to what chapters to open next.

Then, come back to that snap summary periodically to decide what chapters to open over time. I have no illusion that you would read this book from cover to cover in a linear manner, unless that is your preferred reading style.

Browse the table of contents and decide what your intention is in the next reading session.

Part 1 of the book contains a first pass over the background of the ideas, the core of the why and the how: particularly the idea of *decisions as inventory*, which is not an intuitive idea.

I have the idea that **various job specialists** will read different parts of the book and ignore other parts.

For the **busy executives** I made chapter 1 deliberately just one page and followed by short chapter on the key decision an executive will face: single delivery at the end of the project or staged delivery along the way. Even the busiest executive should be able to read the snap summary and the first two chapters before handing the book to someone else, or dipping into random chapters out of curiosity.

Part 2 of the book then addresses different job specialties:

- For the **business-side person**: splitting use cases;
- For the **programmer**: nano-incremental development of Hexagonal Architecture;
- For the **project manager**: tracking projects with burn charts and finding ways to show project progress and status to their sponsors, assuming fine-grained incremental development is being used;
- For the **product manager**: including Kano's subjective quality topics into feature prioritization and discussion of how to sequence features for feedback and value.

Part 3 is the long historical encyclopedia. Here you can see how close I got when I first started in 1992, and the big shift around 2008 when I discovered decisions as internal inventory. That changed my view of our work and allows these ideas to be used for initiatives in any industry, whether social or technical.

Finally, to summarize again at the very end of the book, I went through the chapters one by one and pulled out **key phrases** from each chapter, ones that you might not have noticed but I consider interesting to highlight.

Two things about the writing:

You will notice a lot of repetition, particularly in the images. This is inevitable, since this book is a compilation of all my writing on the subject, so of course that V-W curve shows up a dozen times. However, each time, there is a slightly different emphasis around its presentation, so you may find the slightly different twists illuminating.

Secondly, the chapters contain previously written articles and blogs. That means you may ask, "But why is the business-side person suddenly working with use cases?" and "But why is the programmer chapter only about Hexagonal Architecture?"

Even though the business-side person might be using numbered requirements, user stories, story maps, or AI-generated prototypes, the line of thinking they will need to follow will be the same. It happens that use cases illustrate the line of thinking really clearly, so I can show micro-incremental development right from the requirements stage.

Similarly, few programmers implementing Hexagonal Architecture will be already familiar with nano-incremental, acceptance-test-driven incremental development. Applying the programming rigor to a specific architecture allows me to show the code for both type-checked and non-typed languages.

To bring the old articles back to life, I added a ***Reflections*** section at the end of each chapter. If you are familiar with the ideas in the articles, take a look at those reflections, to see what I pull out for thought now, 20 or 30 years later.

The **Epilogue** is where you go if you

- Are impatient and you want to scan "important" sentences before you read the whole book, to see where you want to dip into for deeper reader. Or, perhaps after you read the whole book and just want to remind yourself of key phrases.
- Want to jump to the little post-script about AI and how that changes or doesn't change things.

Reminder: This is the *Preview Edition.* This version contains all the content I can find in the best order I can find *for now.* In the interest of getting this information into your hands, I am publishing the best I can manage right now.

Please find a way to give me feedback, not just typos, but places you were still confused or where you found the flow awkward. I will include those in a revision when they add up.

Best wishes, Alistair.

Snap Summary

Decisions define mental/social work

Almost all our work is *mental* work, which we aim to have a *social* effect. This work consists of nothing but inventing, communicating and deciding. *Decisions* are the building blocks of this work. With that preface, here are the lessons I hope you learn from this book:

1. Your organization operates from *decisions.*

   Your organization is a conveyor belt of decisions. Surprisingly, that decision flow is just like parts flow in manufacturing, so we can learn and borrow from decades of manufacturing lessons.

2. *Unvalidated decisions* are your enemy.

   Unvalidated decisions are those that have not yet proved themselves correct with the outside world. Your favorite initiative contains thousands to millions of them. They are your internal inventory. As they clog your system, your organization moves slower and mistakes get more expensive to fix.

3. Seek *bad news early.*

   The sooner you find a decision has a mistake, the more time you have to recover. And it's cheaper to change.

4. Think *small bites.* A bit at a time, the smallest possible.

   Get feedback on those *small bites* from the outside world. The outside world thinks differently from whatever you imagine. Put it out there. ASAP.

5. Work this way:

   Pay to learn.
   Grow business value.
   Trim the tail or Shine & gloss.

The mind map summary.

I had ChatGPT generate this different summary. I think some of you will find it useful. "I am the author and I approve this mind map" 😉.

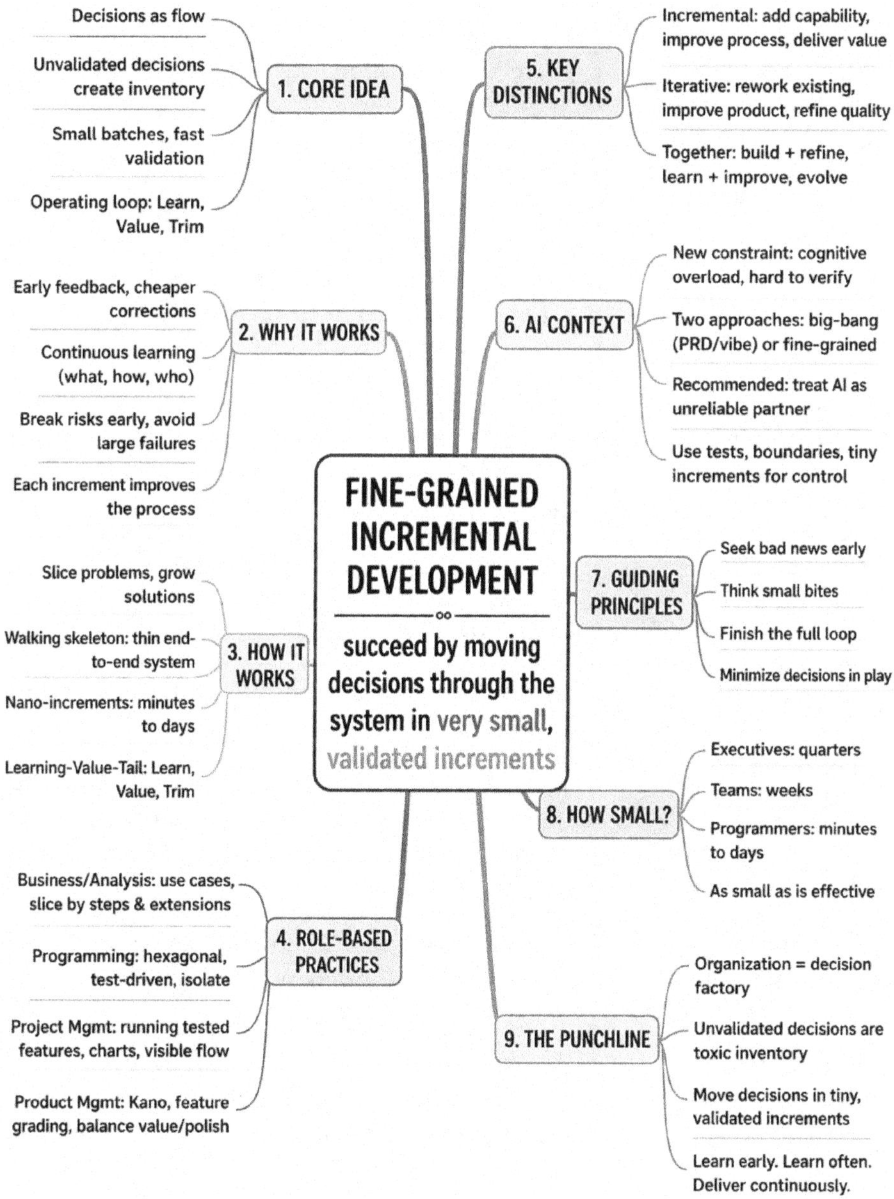

The punchline of each chapter

Chapter 1: **What**	Incremental means *add onto.* It improves the *process.* Iterative means *revise.* It improves the product.
Chapter 2: **Why: The executive's version**	Prefer staged over single delivery. It lets you capture value sooner, and find and fix errors sooner and cheaper.
Chapter 3: **Why Decisions Matter**	*Unvalidated decisions* are your internal inventory. The more they are stacked up, the slower your organization moves and the more expensive it is to fix mistakes. Find ways to move decisions through your organization in the smallest batches possible.
Chapter 4: **From slicing to growing**	We "slice" an initiative into smaller ones, but we "grow" the solution. Slice thinly when breaking down a large problem. Look for growth stages when growing the solution.
Chapter 5: **Disciplined learning**	Learn early, learn often. Validate or break decisions as soon as possible. We now have strategies to help do that.
Chapter 6: **The elephant carpaccio exercise**	This exercise shows both why to deliver soon and small, and how to do that, justified entirely from a business perspective.
Chapter7: **Why increments improve process**	You have to finish the gestalt round trip and find the boogeyman to improve your process properly.
Chapter 8: **The business person version**	Construct fine-grained growth stages from use cases while developing and deploying.
Chapter 9: **The programmer version**	Slice even more finely while programming to implement the *Hexagonal Architecture* in test-driven nano-increments.

Chapter 10: The project manager version	Visualize what is happening on the project with burn charts. Show status on complex projects with fox-and-rabbit charts.
Chapter 11: The product manager version	Slice your product features according to Kano's subjective quality elements. Fit those into the Learning-Value-Tail curve.
Chapter 12: How big should your slices be?	Smaller is generally better, but your mileage may vary, so learn how to choose.
Part 3: Learning over time (the articles)	It took me all these years to get to: Pay to learn/ Grow business value/ Shine & gloss or Trim the tail.
Epilogue: Key phrases from the chapters	Selected key phrases to summarize the whole book and each chapter. Also a short note on AI.

Part 1. What and Why?

In 1997, in *Surviving Object-Oriented Projects,* I captured the results of six years of interviewing project teams plus helping run a successful project.

Summarizing my findings, I wrote down four critical success factors and two prime failure indicators. Thirty years later they still hold:

CSF 1. Use incremental scheduling and staging.

CSF 2. Willingness to find and fix failing ideas.

CSF 3. A habit of delivering.

CSF 4. A good sponsor, project manager, and technical leader.

PFI 1. Absence of a delivery after 8 months.

PFI 2. Use of C++ in a commercial IS department.

Notice that incremental scheduling and staging is both a critical success factor, and a prime failure indicator in its absence.

That hasn't changed.

This book explores what happens when increments become finer and finer, from months to weeks, days, hours, and even minutes, down to the level of individual decisions.

1. What

Incremental development defined:

By incremental development, I specifically mean a

> **staging and scheduling strategy** in which the various parts of the system are developed at different times or rates, and integrated as they are completed.
>
> It neither implies, requires nor precludes iterative or waterfall development, those are rework strategies. The alternative is to develop the entire system with a "big bang" integration.

Incremental development helps you improve your **process.** Each time around the process, you get to change and improve your work habits.

Iterative development defined:

By iterative development, I specifically mean a

> **rework scheduling strategy** in which time is set aside to revise and improve parts of the system.
>
> It does not presuppose incremental development, but works very well with it. An increment may actually ship, whereas an iteration is examined for modification.

Iterative development helps you improve your **product.** Each time around the process you get to change and improve the product itself (and maybe some of your work habits)

(First defined in "The Impact of Object-Oriented Programming on Application Development," 1993)

[Yes, I know many other people have written other definitions of these terms. That's why I'm writing this book. I'm fixing that for you. 😊]

Incremental means ***add onto****. It helps improve the* process. *Iterative means* ***revise****. It helps improve the* product.

---

2. Why: The Executive's Version

Prefer staged over single delivery. It lets you capture value sooner, and find and fix errors sooner and cheaper.

Consider two strategies:

In Strategy I, "single delivery," you save up all your team's work to deliver the entire system at the end.

In Strategy II, "staged delivery," you deliver a subset of the system early and grow it over time.

<u>In Strategy I,</u>

- <u>you don't earn any income until final delivery</u>. If the project is delayed, so is your income. Your investment pot is tied up until everything is done;
- the day after you deliver, <u>your brand-new call center gets swamped with calls about errors</u>. If you delivered to multiple states or multiple countries, all 20 or 50 zones call in to report the same error. If your system is a critical-use system, such as food and medical aid, your staff is quite possibly unable to deliver due to the support center being swamped;
- you are likely to discover that <u>the world has shifted since the project was originally funded</u>, so that what was the correct thing to build at the start no longer matches what the world needs.

In Strategy II,

- <u>you start earning money from the moment of the earliest delivery</u>. Your investment pot gets some relief as income grows, reaching the point of being "self-funding project" earlier;
- <u>you stage the load on your call center</u> so that you can discover mistakes in legal compliance and user design with fewer calls.

If there is a service disruption due to those errors, the number of end users affected is smaller;

- you get to discover mistakes in your business model early and with less damage, plus you get to follow changes in the world as you continue delivering the stages.

Strategy I holds your organization hostage to all errors until it is too late to do anything about it.

Strategy II allows you to shift and adjust in real time, earning money as you go.

In short, there are no advantages to operating with Strategy I. It may be the "typical", "standard" or "traditional" way of working, but we have learned better ways by now. That's what this book is about:

- Gain value earlier.
- Discover and fix errors earlier.

There is a cost; well, two, actually:

1. Rework: After delivering, your team will have to revise some of the things they developed in order to incorporate new features and deal with new audiences. Although unnerving to beginners, experienced executives call this "business as usual."
2. Support competes with new development: You have to support and repair the early releases while developing the later ones. This is annoying and must be factored into the cost of staged delivery.

Staging versus single delivery, the view from the call center

Here is a story about two state-wide projects that used the two strategies. For obvious reasons, I can't name the states. We'll call them states A and state B.

Both projects were for the Department of Health and Human Services in their respective states. They provided welfare payments, food, medical assistance, and so on. Both projects were complete rewrites. They were both years overdue and well over budget, as is fairly common. Both planned for a single delivery at the end of development.

I was called in by state B's new Director of Health and Human Services to help look at the system she was inheriting. The primary leaders of the project were present, obviously concerned about what I was likely to say or recommend.

The key moment of the meeting, to my mind, happened when they defended their strategy of not delivering anything until the entire system was completed, by comparing their project with state A's.

They said that the government of state A had gotten annoyed with all the delays and cost overruns of the new system and cut funding for it. Therefore, they argued, it was important to keep the entire system development in one piece, so that it would be too important for the state government to cut its funding.

(I confess, this was an interesting argument for me to hear!)

Given how far along in development state B's project was at that time, it made no sense to re-evaluate their system architecture or project plan – those were both outside the scope of the new Director's competency and authority. Plus, they were too far along to change those things. The only option left to consider was the question of single or staged delivery.

If they continued as they were going and replaced all the new services at once, some of their offices would be shut down as errors and questions surfaced in all offices on the same day. This would hit the small offices in rural locations particularly hard. The recipients would come to the office and find the staff unable to use the new system, unable to provide them critical aid.

The alternative was to deploy the services in stages, so that the errors would come in a trickle instead of a flood. Some services would still work if others were broken. The support center would be able to keep up with the calls and the change requests.

My recommendation to her was to leave everything as it was, except roll out in stages instead of in a single delivery.

I'm happy to say that she did that. I called her a year later to asked her how it went. She just said: "It worked."

Notice that that story only refers to the second of the three factors I listed at the beginning — the early errors found in single or staged delivery.

The flow of money and self-funding projects

To anchor the discussion, let's imagine a situation in which you are developing a system to be used in 50 states in the USA, or perhaps 20 countries in Europe, or both.

Often, when motivating an idea, people look at how income should grow after release – they focus on positive return on investment (ROI). It is more interesting, however, to look for when money coming in equals money going out – the moment at which the project becomes "self-funding." This is interesting because it frees up your investment pot for other initiatives.

Some serial entrepreneurs work only in this way: They fire up an idea and the moment it becomes self-funding, they cast it loose and move onto their next idea.

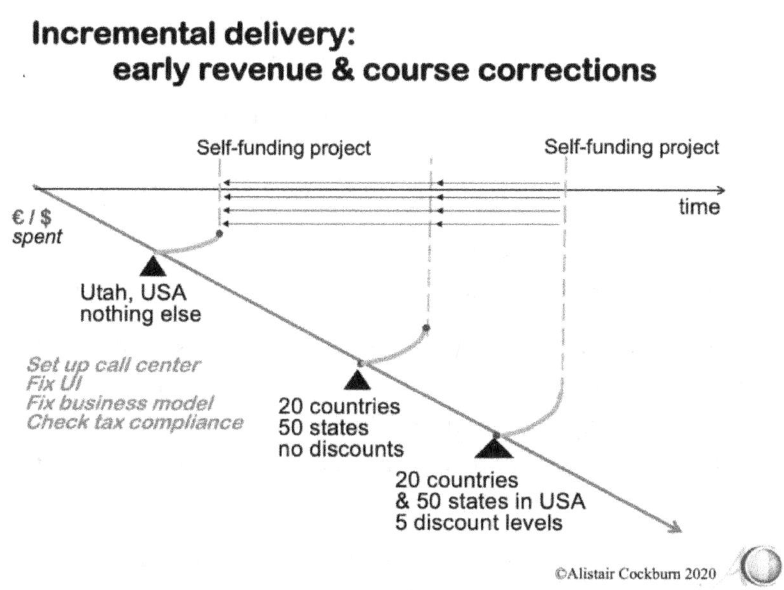

Figure 1, Chapter 2. Self-funding project moments with staged delivery.

Figure 1 shows the shift of that "self-funding project" moment as we find earlier moments for the first income-producing delivery. The descending red line shows money being spent during development. The rightmost upward curve shows the result for a single-deployment strategy: Income only starts when the total system is deployed.

In this sample problem, we have two requirements: one is offering discounts, the other is handling taxes. Which should we prioritize to develop first?

Let's be pessimistic for a moment and suppose the project runs out of funding before the project completes. If we had decided to work on discounts before taxes (a natural thing to do, since discounts are calculated before taxes are applied), then running out of funding means that we have nothing at all. We can't deploy without tax compliance.

However, if we complete tax compliance before starting to work on discounts, then even if we run out of money, we at least have something legal to deploy. We have a system.

Surprisingly, an optimistic view produces the same recommendation: Once we have implemented taxes, we can deliver and start earning money! The discounts can be added over time.

Therefore, in the graph, I show implementing all states and countries before implementing any discounts.

This is one of a set of possible strategies blending tax- and discount calculations. The discussion is around how to manage both risk and income in the case of running out of money.

For the sake of keeping the graph simple, I choose implementing all states and countries first before touching discounts. In a real business situation it might be better to do a few states and then a discount or two to test the waters before continuing with the other states and countries.

The next question is, how many states do we implement before the first delivery?

For exactly the reasons mentioned earlier, it is still better to deliver to just *one* state or country to begin with, than to all of them.

Delivering to just one state lets you

- start earning money right away. To the main point I wish to make here, it moves that moment of being a self-funding project as early as possible;
- set up the call center and check tax compliance as described earlier;
- adjust your business model and track consumer changes.

That's the financial argument motivating delivering in stages and to one state to start with, rolling out to the others in stages.

Improving your business model

To the final topic: We live in a rapid-changing world. The odds that you guessed correctly what your users and customers would need, and also how the world would shift over the duration of the project, are slim, probably zero.

Delivering to just one state, and then one more, incorporating the other states and the discounts a few at a time, allows you to track changes in the needs and wants of your customers and users.

* * * * *

That's a quick sketch of the argument of the book. The following chapters develop the idea that *decisions* are the actual internal inventory in mental/social work, and what that means for development strategies for initiatives of any kind. *The Elephant Carpaccio Exercise* examines our example system in more detail, showing not only staged rollout, but also fine-grained incremental development internally.

Reflections and Key Points

If you only remember one thing from this book, it is:

"Small bites"

Throughout the book we'll look at how *decisions* become your internal inventory in mental/social work, and how unvalidated decisions create drag on your organization. The fewer the better. Hence, "small bites."

In this chapter, we looked at only one choice for you to consider:

- Save up and deliver everything at the end in a single delivery, or deploy in stages over time?

We saw that the longer you wait to deliver something, the more that those unvalidated decisions block both value and feedback.

So: Deliver something small and soon.

- Gain value earlier.
- Discover and fix errors earlier.

Do you remember the key points?

In Strategy I, you don't earn any income until final delivery, your brand-new call center gets swamped with calls about errors, and the world has shifted since the project was originally funded.

In Strategy II, you start earning money from the moment of the earliest delivery, stage the load on your call center, discover mistakes in your business model early.

Serial entrepreneurs fire up an idea and the moment it becomes self-funding, they cast it loose and move onto their next idea

---

Prefer staged over single delivery. It lets you capture value sooner, and find and fix errors sooner and cheaper.

---

3. Why Decisions Matter

Unvalidated decisions are your internal inventory in mental/social work. The more they are stacked up in your organization, the slower your organization moves and the more expensive it is to fix mistakes. Find ways to move decisions through your organization in the smallest batches possible.

"What engineering has in common with manufacturing and why it matters," presents the crucial idea that in mental work such as design, *unvalidated decisions* are your *internal inventory*. It was originally published in 2007 in *CrossTalk*, the Journal of Defense Software Engineering.

What Engineering Has in Common with Manufacturing, and Why It Matters

Engineering – software engineering in our case – is remarkably like manufacturing, once we shift to view the unvalidated decision as the unit of internal inventory. The parallels with manufacturing allow us to borrow from results in manufacturing theory to understand how to better structure our software processes, and the teams involved.

It is generally considered frivolous to compare engineering – software engineering, in our case – with manufacturing. Manufacturing consists (so the argument goes) of making the same thing over and over, while engineering is about making something different each time. In software engineering, the design is the hard part, production is the easy part, often as easy as pressing CDs or publishing onto the internet.

Once we shift to considering *decisions* as the items being handed from person to person, gathered into larger and larger assemblies, then suddenly, there is a very real parallel between design and manufacturing. This is useful to us because manufacturing has been heavily studied over the last hundred years, and we can learn from their lessons.

In what follows, I shall talk about *software* development, but it should be clear that the same argument applies to every team design activity, including theatre, publishing, engineering, and much of business.

Waiting for decisions

We start by recognizing that in team design activities, people wait on each other for decisions.

Figure 1 shows a simplified view of the dependencies between people in software development – it is missing the feedback loops, in particular. Figure 2 shows a more complete mapping of the decision dependencies, with some typical feedback loops. The feedback loops complicate matters, but don't change the basic results.

In Figure 1, the dependency of one person on another is shown with a large gray arrow. The person on the head of the arrow is waiting for or being handed decisions from the person at the tail of the arrow. A small pyramid represents the actual decision being passed from one person to another.

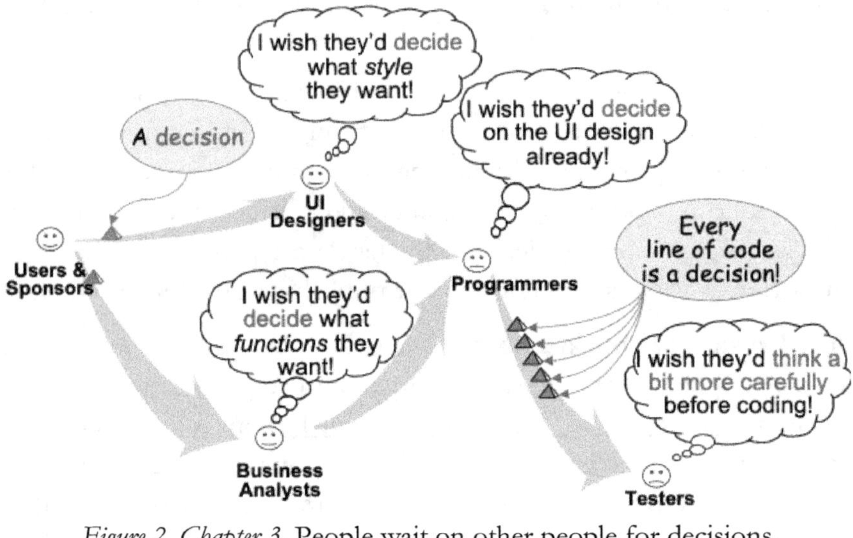

Figure 2, Chapter 3. People wait on other people for decisions.

In *Figure 2*, we see

- business analysts and user interface (UI) designers waiting for users and sponsors to decide what functions and design styles they want,
- programmers waiting for business analysts to work out the business rules, and UI designers to allocate behavior to different pieces of the user interface,
- testers waiting for programmers to finish their coding.

A nice thing about considering individual *decisions* as connecting people is that we can move away from stereotypes about how a company's process or decision-making activities *ought* to look like, and instead focus on what it *actually* looks like – what decisions actually get made by which people, who is really waiting for whom.

There is no ideal software process any more than there is any ideal manufacturing process. Each company has its own strong-minded people, who make a disproportionate number of decisions that might, in other companies, be made by people in other roles. Each company has its own shortage of UI designers, programmers, testers, or even sponsors, which causes its process to have a certain characteristic shape – people working overtime, or perhaps sitting idle because other people can't get their work done fast enough. Each company has its own reasons to have a large, external test department, or perhaps no test department at all.

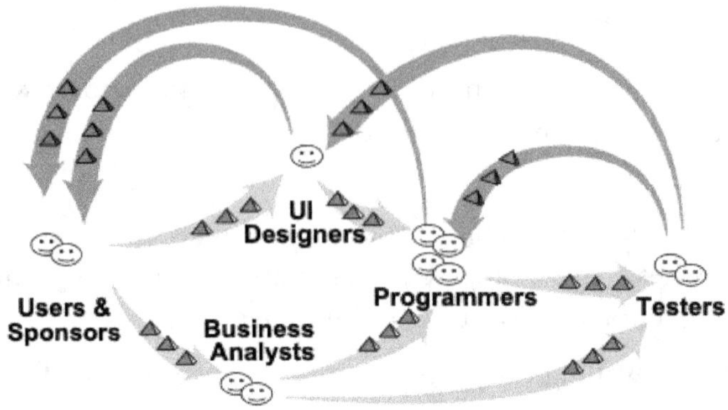

Figure 3, Chapter 3. A more complete view of a decision-dependency network, showing feedback loops.

Different bottlenecks, different processes

In any organization, we can find a backlog of decisions stacking up at some particular work group. That stack creates a *bottleneck*, limiting the speed of the overall team.

Bottlenecks are of great concern in manufacturing, and have received much study. The obvious thing to do is to increase the capacity of the bottleneck group – hire more people, or better people, or get better tools, and so on.

Sooner or later, however, the organization hits its limit as to what it can do to improve the speed of the bottleneck group At that point, what comes into play is the process definition itself.

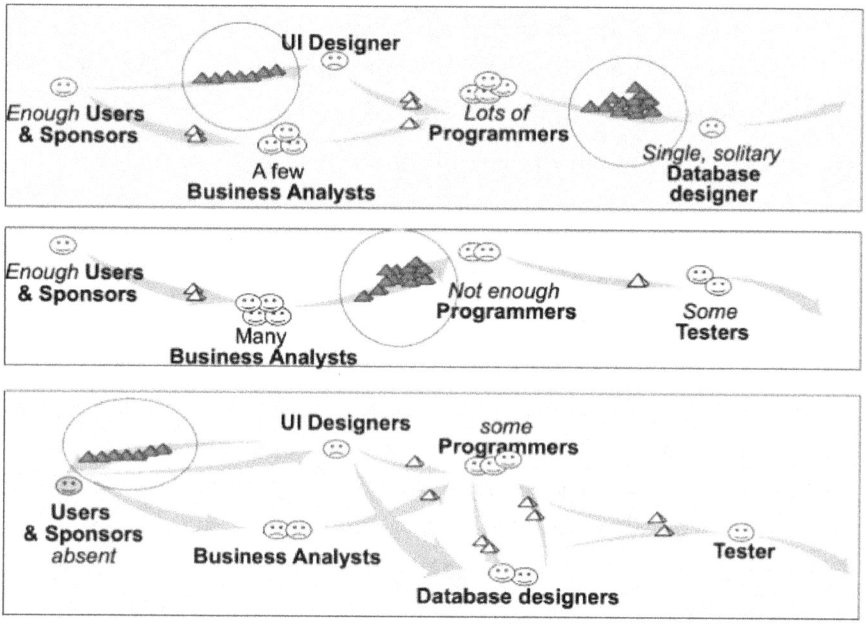

Figure 4, Chapter 3. A team's optimal process and strategies vary with its decision-dependency network.

Figure 4 shows three different, but fairly typical organizations.

- In the first (top) organization, there are not enough user interface and database designers to keep up with the work. We see decisions stacked up at their work centers.
- In the second (middle) organization, there are not enough experienced programmers, and work requests stack up in front of them.
- In the third (bottom) organization, the users and sponsors are notably missing from the discussion. What happens in these organizations is that the business analysts and UI designers end up making the business decisions, and then sending those decisions (or running products) back to the users and sponsors for comment. The picture shows those requests for review stacking up in front of the users and sponsors.
- The third (bottom) picture also shows the programmers and database designers sending decisions back and forth to each

other. Both groups need to come to agreement on the domain model and how that will be represented in the code and in the database.

There are two points to draw from these pictures:

- First, they should be using different processes;
- Second, these drawings help us to see how those processes should be different.

The organization at the top, assuming that they can't or won't hire more UI and database designers, should look at ways to have programmers and business analysts pick up sections of the UI designer's and database designer's work. Even assuming that UI design work is specialized, parts of that work can be automated, carried out by assistants, or handled by programmers.

In the second organization, the reverse is more the case. The programmers, being few and inexperienced, might need to have much of the problem "digested" for them as much as possible. In a case that I participated in, we recommended that the business analysts write quite detailed use cases (not containing the user interface, but containing the business rules more explicitly than we otherwise might), and also the layouts of the data needs, plus discussions of different business scenarios.

The business analysts then sat with their respective programmers as they started on each use case, and discussed the use case, the scenarios, and the data. They left the paperwork with the programmers, and made themselves available for discussions and tutorials as needed.

The process in this second organization was aimed at minimizing the trouble the programmers had to undergo to understand the problem at hand. This is quite different from the process in the first organization.

In the third organization, the process might call for prototypes and early samples to be produced and put in front of the users and sponsors. Since those people have the least availability, the material should be as fully prepared as possible. Also, since close collaboration between the programmers and database designers is required, those teams should be seated together, or at least have frequent meetings and joint design reviews.

The purpose of this article is not to make these recommendations, which any good manager or consultant would be likely to spot, but to show how they come from mapping and considering the bottlenecks in the flow of decisions through the organization.

Lessons from manufacturing

To complete the mapping to manufacturing, we use the *unvalidated decision* as our unit of internal inventory, or "work in progress" (WIP). Each decision that has been made but has not yet been validated by someone (the sponsors, the testers, the marketplace) is still "pending", still waiting to show its quality.

Move inventory out

The first lesson that we draw from experiences in manufacturing is to keep work-in-progress (WIP) down. This is as important in software development as it is in manufacturing, since every decision that is pending costs the organization money.

<u>The value of decisions decays over time</u>:

- Each "requirement" is a decision based on a business climate; when the business climate changes, the decision may become incorrect. If the software isn't yet earning value for the company, the requirement is waste.
- An "architecture" is a decision based on technology and business. If the technology changes before the software is earning value for the company, those decisions are waste.
- Each line of code is a decision based on requirements, domain, technology and aesthetics. If anything causes it to become obsolete before the software is earning value for the company, it is waste.

To the extent that it is not earning value in the business, each decision loses value and quality with time. The more decisions stuck inside the pipeline, the more decaying "inventory" the organization is carrying.

Inventory stacks up quickly. Assume for reference an organization that is so fast that when a new requirement arrives, they can implement and deploy it by the next morning:

- The company with a 1-day turnaround has about 1 day's worth of inventory lying around the office.
- The company with a one- to two-week turnaround has about 10 days' worth of inventory lying around the office.
- The company with a quarterly delivery system (assuming they deploy from fresh requirements every quarter) has about 100 days of inventory lying around.
- The company delivering once a year from fresh requirements has 365 days of inventory around them.
- The company delivering a 3-year project has 1,000 days of inventory (decaying) around them.

The message, in software as much as in manufacturing, is: *get the inventory out the door and earning value!* Find ways to shorten the pipe.

Move small amounts, continuously

The second lesson to draw from manufacturing is to reduce the size of the transfer batch between working groups. That is, move small amounts, continuously.

Figure 5 shows two ways of transferring work from the programmers to the testers.

In the first case, the programmers hand over 100 lines of code (each week, let's suppose). The testers get a regular weekly arrival rate of about 100 lines of code, and have to integrate and test them against the rest of the system and against the known defect log.

The actual size handed over will vary, of course, and the actual length of time needed to work through the new code will also vary. That variance is very important.

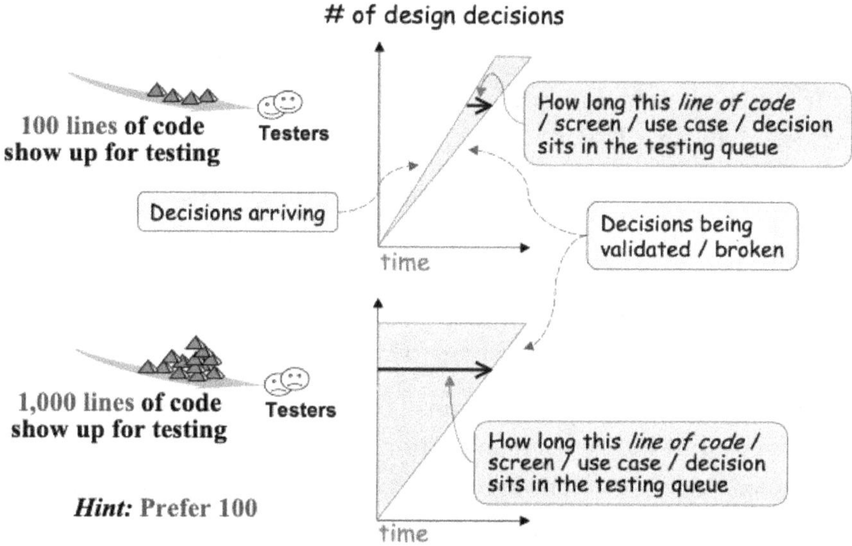

Figure 5, Chapter 3. Systems run more smoothly with small transfer sizes.

The lower part of Figure 5 shows the programmers handing about 1,000 lines of code to the testers (each quarter, that would be, to keep the rate of production about the same as in the upper picture).

The problem with the lower picture is that all 1,000 lines of code show up at one time. The responsiveness of the testing group suddenly becomes much more variable, with the large arrival of an unknown number of bugs of varying sizes.

Equally bad, when they start handing over bug reports back to the programmers, the programmers suddenly see a large spike on requests on their input queue coming from the testers (see the arrow in Figure 2, from the testers back to the programmers). The programmers are now juggling two input queues, requests for new features and requests for bug fixes.

Manufacturing lines have experienced and studied all the above, and concluded that these sorts of feed systems run best when *small* amounts of work get handed from one group to the next. The ultimate goal is to hand over just one part from one group or person to the next.

Toyota pioneered this idea in its lean or just-in-time manufacturing lines. They aim for *continuous flow*, the flow of just one piece of material from one person to another (what to do when a queue backs up is the subject of another lesson we'll see).

It is not clear exactly what *continuous flow* might mean in software development. Some decisions affect large parts of the system, and some decisions can't be validated for a long time. However, the experiences in manufacturing are backed up by both mathematical models and experiences in agile software development.

It is rare to find development teams able to deploy fresh requirements every week, but I have been able to find a few teams who both deploy weekly *and* have a low enough defect rate that they get only one or a few requests a day. On one team I talked with, a person was assigned each day, on a rotation, to handle any incoming requests, whether bug reports or requests for small enhancements. That person would stop other work, do the work and redeploy the system before rejoining the main group. The average time to redeployment was half a day. With such a small, steady flow of requests on the feedback queue, the team was able keep from being diverted from their main assignment.

Cross-train people

The lean and agile manufacturing literature contains the recommendation to cross-train people at adjacent stations. The idea is that when a small bubble of inventory grows at someone's input, the neighboring person, having a spare moment, steps over and works it down. In this manner, small variances in work flow can be evened out and not disturb the organization's overall flow.

We see this in software development, when programmers help testers, user interface designers and business analysts, or when business analysts help testers. Unfortunately, programming is a technical enough activity that UI designers, testers and business analysts are unlikely to be able to help the programmers. Programmers can help other programmers, though. We see front-end developers, middle-ware developers and back-end developers helping each other in some companies when one of the groups has a sudden bump in work.

Extend the network

All of the above ideas are good – so good, in fact, that a company using them soon finds that their bottleneck lies somewhere in their supply chain, whether their sponsors, their subcontractors, or their distributors. These companies start to draw the queuing or decision-dependency network for the larger system in which they sit, and start including their supply chain partners in their discussions.

Toyota is well known for working with its suppliers. Less well known are cases of software development groups doing it. The same team I referred to earlier, having the the daily programmer rotation for fixes and enhancements, also wrote automated acceptance tests for their subcontractor's parts of the system. They reasoned that their time was better spent writing automated acceptance tests and catching bugs on arrival than debugging and finding those same faults in the integrated system when their supplier's code broke it. The supplier was, of course, surprised but delighted to find they didn't have to write the automated acceptance tests.

The lesson from Toyota and the other companies who are streamlining the wider network is: *the wider the network of 'we', the faster we all go.*.

Who's writing about this?

Once you see the mapping between manufacturing and team design activities, suddenly a lot of literature becomes available.

Toyota's production system, also called The Toyota Way, Toyota Production System, and lean manufacturing, is widely documented. *The Toyota Way Fieldbook* [1] is a good place to start.

The application of lean manufacturing principles to design work is described in *Managing the Design Factory* [2]. The Poppendiecks have applied lean manufacturing principles to software development [3, 4]. *Agile Software Development* [5] contains an experience report from a software product company (Tomax) that is including its customers directly in its dependency network.

Goldratt wrote about bottleneck stations in manufacturing [6] and then widened the discussion to constraints in general (*theory of constraints*) [7]. David Anderson applied the theory of constraints and queue size to software projects [8]. I have written about strategies for dealing with bottlenecks that have reached their capacities [9].

Summary

It is not immediately obvious that software development teams can learn from manufacturing. However, once we map the network of dependencies between people in a software development organization and make the shift to think of *unvalidated decisions* as comprising the "inventory", then the parallels become startlingly clear.

We learn 6 lessons from the parallels:

- Drawing the decision-dependency network helps us see the bottleneck stations, where decisions-to-be-made are piling up.
- From the different decision-dependency networks in various organizations, and their varying bottlenecks, we can see how the optimal process varies from organization to organization.
- *Move inventory out*: Decisions decay over time, so it is important to find ways to shorten the pipeline from arrival of a request or decision to the deployment of the system.
- *Move small amounts,* continuously: Transferring large batches of inventory (decisions in our case) between workers causes unpredictable variations in the organization's output. It is better to move small numbers of decisions more often. This reinforces the idea of incremental development, with the smallest increment size possible.
- *Cross-train people*: When people can help each other across specialties, they can move quickly to eliminate small bubbles in

each others' input queue, thus smoothing the organization's output.

- *Extend the network*: By widening the network included in the dependency analysis and queue-size reduction, a company can smooth its own input stream and simplify its working.

References

1. Liker, J., Meier, D. *The Toyota Way Fieldbook*, McGraw-Hill, 2005.
2. Reinertsen. D., *Managing the Design Factory*, Free Press, 1997.
3. Poppendieck, M., Poppendieck, ?, *Implementing Lean Software Development: From Concept to Cash*, Addison-Wesley, 2006.
4. Cockburn, A., *Agile Software Development: The Cooperative Game, 2nd Edition*, Addison-Wesley, 2006.
5. Goldratt, E., *The Goal*,
6. Goldratt, E., *What is This Thing Called the Theory of Constraints?*
7. Anderson, D., "Managing Lean Software Development with Cumulative Flow Diagrams," May 2004, BorCon 2004.
8. Cockburn, A., "Two Case Studies Motivating Efficiency as a Spendable Quantity", Humans and Technology Technical Report HaT TR 2005.00 [https://web.archive.org/web/20140329205947/http://alistair.cockburn.us/Two+Case+Studies+Motivating+Efficiency+as+a+%22Spendable%22+Quantity].

Reflection and key points

Reflection

That article was published in 2007. Reading it 20 years later, I find my favorite sentence is this:

> *"If the software isn't yet earning value for the company, the requirement is waste."*

I have since changed how I talk about it. Try this:

> *Keep the number of unvalidated decisions to a minimum, moving the smallest number of decisions through your organization possible.*

- Large internal inventory makes it hard to change direction.
- Large internal inventory makes for late discovery of mistakes.
- Lumpy flow plus rework make it impossible to predict when the final product will come out.

The problem of changing directions, Detroit vs. Toyota

Large internal inventory makes it hard to change directions.

In Detroit in the 1950s and 60s, the baseline assumption was, "someone will buy this car." Car parts could be stacked to the ceiling as long as the expensive sheet-metal pressing machine was busy 24 hours a day.

Internal inventory was fine.

But imagine, now, a hit movie in which the hero drives a different car. The factory can't change to meet this hot new demand, because it is stacked full of unfinished car parts.

Japan after the second world war didn't have money for internal inventory. Toyota perfected single-piece or just-in-time flow, where internal inventory is kept to a minimum. Leaving aside other aspects of lean manufacturing, having small internal inventory meant they could change the factory cheaper, faster, and easier than Detroit.

The equivalent to an unfinished car part in mental/social work is a decision that is waiting to validated (or broken). You can't know if the decision is a good one until it is delivered and in use.

The problem of late discovery of mistakes

Everything an organization produces is the reification of a decision. Even something as simple as a press release: *That* you decided to publish it, *when* you decided to publish it, the audience you had in mind, and the specifics you decided to include.

Every product, every public announcement, makes decisions concrete. Millions of them, all stacked up inside your organization waiting to deliver value or be shown to be incorrect.

This screen snapshot is my favorite example of how the world isn't kind to our brilliant ideas.

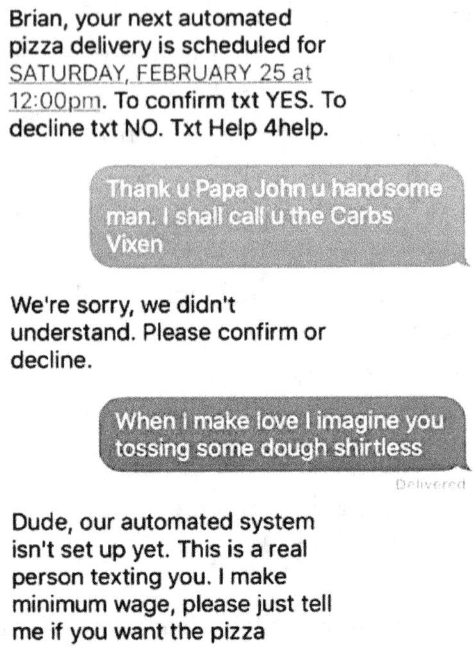

When you're done laughing, consider that screen in the context of decisions: Someone (in the pre-AI era) had the bright idea to write an automated response system to talk with customers.

That is one decision. They poured a few hundred thousand dollars (and decisions) into building it.

The moment it is released, some smart-aleck messes with the system in a way it can't respond to.

Using "usual," old-school approaches, it would have been too late to tune the system to respond to this customer; "Late bad news," as we say. However, in this case, the company was smart enough to *not* develop the expert system, but to have a person role-play the script, for exactly this reason.

The more decisions stacked up blocking delivery just means the later you'll get your bad news and the more work you'll have to do to back up and revise it.

Big batch flow and rework make for unpredictable deliveries

There was a time it was considered efficient to move a big stack of parts from one work station to the next: *Big batch transfer.* Toyota mastered the art of single-piece flow and showed the many benefits of *small batch transfer.*

Big-batch transfer is even worse in mental work.

In manufacturing, they put a lot of energy into making sure they don't have to do rework on the items they produce. That effort pays off in obvious ways.

In mental work, however, it is impossible to avoid rework. People make decisions, refine them, review them, and change them, as illustrated in *Figure 3, Chapter 3*. A more complete view of a decision-dependency network, showing feedback loops..

There is no way around this. Your strategy, your system design, your user interface design, your database design, your tests, everything, is going to get scrutinized and changed.

Suddenly, we have two issues exacerbating each other. The big-batch transfer makes movement lumpy and the timing unpredictable. Combining that with constant revision means that you *cannot say when the final product will come out.*

This is such a significant topic that it is the subject of the next chapter, "Disciplined Learning."

In product development, your product requirements document contains your first large batch of unvalidated decisions.

Consider a common, 300-page requirements document for a software system. Very carefully thought out and reviewed, it contains something like 50 decisions per page for 300 pages, or 15,000 decisions – none of which have actually been validated or can yet be validated. They have been thought through, but until they hit the users, you can't know if they are correct and appropriate, or not.

In former times, and in many places still, that 300-page requirements document is treated as gospel and as the basis for all on going work. It is passed to group after group, to user interface designers, database designers, back-end designers, front-end designers, test engineers, and others, each of whom will make thousands more decisions based on those ones.

Problems are stacking up here:

- Every decision in the requirements document gets compounded by thousands of work-hours put in developing it. Each error in that document costs an enormous amount if left undiscovered until the final, big-bang delivery.
- The organization fills up with more and more decisions, decisions that no one can know are correct or wrong until the whole system ships, at which point it's very expensive to start making changes.
- Exactly when the system will come out is unknown. It depends on when all the critical errors that can be found before delivery are actually found and corrected.
- If the market shifts, the organization is locked up in partially completed work. It can't shift to keep up with the market.

Large decision inventory and your master plan

Now look at your plan, or whatever plan you have in front of you. How many decisions do you have stacked up in there? What are the odds they are all correct? How soon can you detect the flaws? How many unvalidated decisions will you have stacked up inside your organization when you find one and need to change direction?

Unlike in manufacturing, we can't get to just *one* decision in flow at a time. However, we can work toward *smaller* packets of decisions that get validated or broken *sooner*, so that we have more time to repair them, and can change direction more quickly and with less cost.

It is impossible to overstate the importance of *decisions-as-inventory*. Look for more on this in Chapter 5, *Disciplined Learning*.

Do you remember the key points?

"people wait on each other for decisions"

"There is no ideal software process any more than there is any ideal manufacturing process"

"decisions stacking up at some particular work group. That stack creates a *bottleneck*, limiting the speed of the overall team"

"these drawings help us to see how those processes should be different"

"To the extent that it is not earning value in the business, each decision loses value and quality with time"

"Move inventory out, Move small amounts, continuously, Cross-train people, Extend the network"

"If the software isn't yet earning value for the company, the requirement is waste"

"Large internal inventory makes it hard to change directions"

"Large internal inventory makes for late discovery of mistakes."

"Lumpy flow plus rework make it impossible to predict when the final product will come out."

"The equivalent to an unfinished car part in mental/social work is a decision that is waiting to validated (or broken). You can't know if the decision is a good one until it is delivered and in use."

"In mental work, however, it is impossible to avoid rework"

"Every decision in the requirements document gets compounded by thousands of work-hours put in developing it."

Unvalidated decisions are internal inventory in mental/social work. The more they are stacked up in your organization, the slower your organization moves and the more expensive it is to fix mistakes. Find ways to move decisions through your organization in the smallest batches possible.

---

4. From Slicing to Growing

We "slice" an initiative into smaller ones, but we "grow" the solution. Slice thinly when breaking down a large problem. Look for growth stages when growing the solution.

We need to take a small detour here to talk about how language and metaphors shape our thinking. We'll build two metaphors: slicing down from large to small, and growing up from nothing to large

"Slices" is a commonly-used word, but it calls to an incorrect analogy, so I want to take some time to talk about it, give it some framing, and also provide an alternative analogical word: "growing," as with a plant.

Slicing

The business person wants an elephant. It is too big to develop and deploy all in one go, so they ask to have it developed in *phases.*

Phases mean there will be a complete but delivery of some useful subset of the desired system. Each phase when delivered is done and complete. Having completed Phase A of the project, they then embark on Phase B, running it as a separate project, with separate funding and possibly different contractors. This is incremental development and staged delivery, with increments that take months to years. In terms of "slicing an elephant", this would be like getting a whole leg or so. (Yes, there is something wrong with this metaphor; you may already see it.)

In this book, we are after finer and finer slices.

Let's say, to humor the metaphor a bit, that if you deliver something useful every quarter, that would correspond to a thick Texas steak.

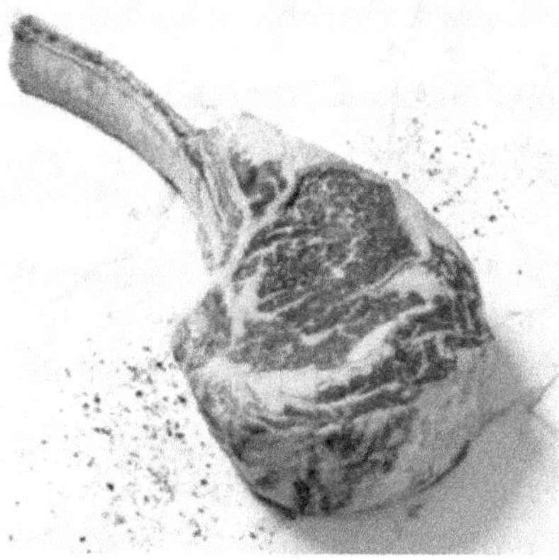

If you could find something of value to deliver every month, that would be like Japanese *sashimi*.

What we will chase down are slices so fine that they are like Italian *carpaccio*, meat sliced so thinly you can almost see through it.

Vegetarians make carpaccio of zucchini 😊.

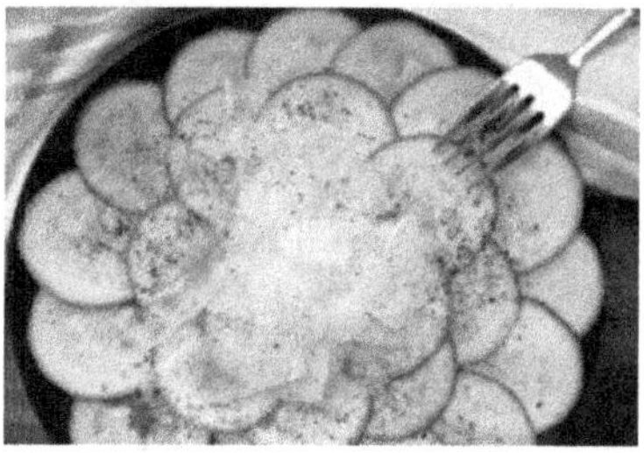

What we want to learn, is how to take any problem and slice it in a way that everything we do shows some externally visible growth of the system.

But there is a problem with the slicing metaphor:

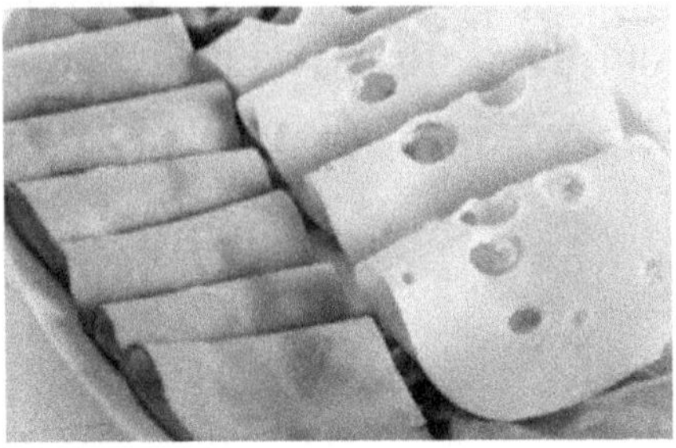

People hear the word "slice" and think of a slice of bread, cheese, tomato, or ham in a sandwich. If they are working on the ham section (in software terms, the user interface, the application code, the database, etc.), the moment they finish that slice of ham, they think they are done.

But having just a slice of ham doesn't give us a sandwich, any more than having just a user interface gives us a running application. Thus, each person claims, "I'm done," only to find out later that the pieces don't work together. They are missing the integration, putting the sandwich together so the customer can enjoy it.

To address this common problem, when we ask for a "slice," we demand that all the layers be integrated, so that integrating them is part of being "done."

What we are after is not a slice in a sandwich, but a slice of layer cake. When you cut a slice of layer cake, it's a vertical slice, you get all the layers, integrated and ready to eat. For a software system, that means the user interface, the application code, and the database.

There is a second problem with the slicing metaphor: Imagine (apologies for the image coming up) putting an elephant through a giant slicer. You won't get miniature elephants, you'll get skinny slices of tail for a long while, then suddenly a rump! And a vertical section of leg … nothing that resembles an elephant.

So, this language – *slicing* – although useful in thinking of how to cut down a large problem to smaller ones, can lead listeners astray.

Skateboards and Cars

At this point I have also to punch a hole in the old but incorrect analogy of the progression: skateboard → scooter → car.

Your client comes in and asks for a car.

One way to do incremental development for a car is to first design and build the wheels, then design and integrate the frame, then design and add the body, and so on until we have the car.

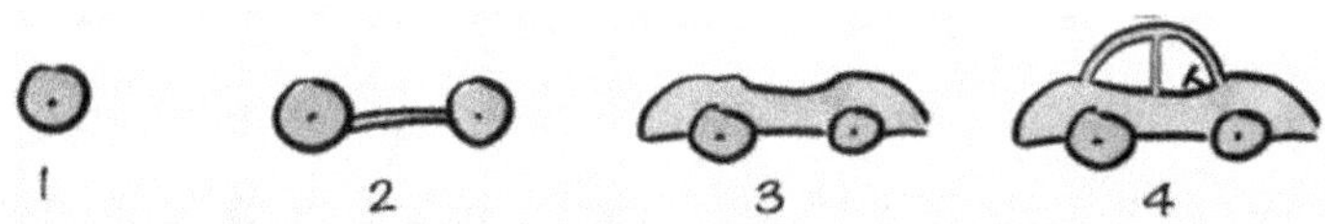

This "staged integration" makes sense in many situations, as with designing and building an airport terminal.

> ***I was lucky enough to interview someone who designed airport terminals as a profession. I knew he couldn't do much with the iterative side of design, so I asked him if he at least did "early integration" of the sections to surface nasty surprises early. Indeed he did and it served his purposes well.***

However, we can apply both *incremental* and *iterative* strategies in software development to get better results.

Someone came up with the skateboard analogy in the early days of agile development. It is wrong, very wrong, but you may still get this presented to you, in which case you will spot the flaw immediately.

The idea is if your client asks for a car, you first make them a skateboard to see how it goes. You take the feedback and include that in a push-scooter and deliver again. From there you progress to a bicycle, then a motorcycle, and finally the car they wanted from the beginning.

A faulty analogy: skateboard → scooter → bike → motorcycle → car

As any client will tell you, if they want a car and you show up with a skateboard, you'll be fired. They want a car. There isn't enough learning from using a skateboard to feed into the design of a car. This analogy should never again see the light of day.

In the early 2000s, Jeff Patton beat me around the head and shoulders for months with the car example until I got the point.

His point was, you can't evaluate a car until you have a car. Nothing else suffices. What Jeff taught me that I couldn't work out on my own was that in the early version of the car,

- you do need a steering wheel, but not power steering;
- you do need brakes, but not an antilock braking system;
- you do need an engine, but not a turbocharger;
- you do need lights (maybe), but not fog lamps;
- and so on.

It must always be a *car*, even if it is a very simple one.

Fortunately, Joe Justice already showed us how to do this with his *WikiSpeed* project(s). He did exactly what Jeff Patton described, starting from the simplest legal car, making changes until he ended with a race car. I encourage you to read up on it. See:

[https://en.wikipedia.org/wiki/Wikispeed]

[https://www.forbes.com/sites/stevedenning/2012/08/01/transformational-leadership-in-agile-manufacturing-wikispeed/]

Joe Justice (in red) and an early WikiSpeed car.
Photo credit: brewbooks near Seattle, USA - WIKISPEED, CC BY-SA 2.0, [https://en.wikipedia.org/wiki/Wikispeed#/media/File:WIKISPEED_-_Flickr_-_brewbooks.jpg]

Growing

A better metaphor is *growing* the system.

The exec walks in and asks for an elephant. Now, although you may think about how to slice it to a smaller problem, when you work, you start from zero and build upwards: You *grow* the system.

This applies to virtually every industry, to construction as much as to software.

> *Two outside staircases needed replacing. Each was in a corner of a hill with complicated placements. It was impossible to model just how to make them work. I asked the contractor to start with a plywood version, so that we could easily change the wooden structure and work out the exact shape.*
>
> *He did such a good job with the back steps that we immediately replaced it with stone. It needed only a final fine-tuning.*

I asked him to make the front staircase so we could take it apart and try out different landings. I walked up and down it in different shapes until I was comfortable with the feel.

To make the final version, he laminated plywood to the outside of the frame, then to the insid. At this point, he had the exact curve he had framed up, and the sturdiness we needed.

In terms that we will use later, he created a Walking Skeleton and then restructured that to make the final product.

One does similarly in working with *papier mâché* (paper soaked in glue).

To make a *papier mâché* sculpture, you first put in place an armature or skeleton of the shape ("That's not much of an elephant!"). You add layers of paper and glue, making a continually "better elephant" (or whatever), until you can paint and decorate it at the end

(Photo credit Alison Schwebach, YouTube v=Ud9sqhTB9Ao)

We finally get to the growing analogy. I need this because I want to talk about *growth stages*, specifically the first shoot, the first bud, etc.

With these analogies and metaphors on hand, consider that the sponsor walks in and asks for that elephant. It is too big to do all at once. So look for *growth stages*, things that are directionally like the elephant, always getting to a better elephant.

Reflections and Key Points

Reflections

"Slice the problem" to strategize how to maximize early delivery and growing value. Then "grow" the solution, starting from nothing. Thankfully, no elephant ever gets "sliced". We first create a baby but real elephant, then make that a better, fuller elephant over time.

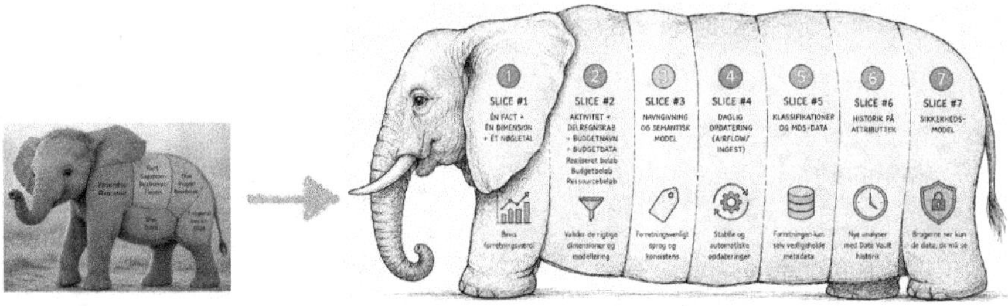

The "elephant plan" from an project, courtesy of Anne-Marie Gebbink.

Did you catch these key points?

"having just a slice of ham doesn't give us a sandwich, any more than having just a user interface gives us a running application. When we ask for a *slice*, we demand that all the layers be integrated."

"if they want a car and you show up with a skateboard, you'll be fired. They want a car."

"A better metaphor is growing the system."

"first put in place an armature or skeleton; add layers of paper and glue, making a continually 'better elephant'."

"look for *growth stages*, things we can show or ship, intermediate stages that are directionally like the elephant, always getting to a better elephant."

We "slice" an initiative into smaller ones, but we "grow" the solution. Slice thinly when breaking down a large problem. Look for growth stages when growing the solution.

---

5. Disciplined Learning

Learn early, learn often. Validate or break decisions as soon as possible. We now have strategies to help do that.

Here is the 2014 article originally published in *CrossTalk*, the Journal of Defense Software Engineering.

> ***Disciplined learning upgrades project planning from failure-avoidance to success-seeking. Not "fail early, fail often," but "learn early, learn often," it updates agile development and risk management. Disciplined learning is a rich, creative and rewarding endeavor in use in small pockets of excellence.***

This article describes how to use disciplined learning to deliver better.

The following are three examples, notable as they are from small and large projects, and fixed- and floating-price projects.

- The first project, developing a medium-sized web site, involved only the web site owner and the programmer. Neither the delivery date nor cost were fixed. After some months of work, the somewhat frustrated web site owner declared he wanted the site launched "soon". As they had been working with the disciplined learning approach, they trimmed functionality and "prettiness" back aggressively and repeatedly until a system much smaller than originally envisaged was deployed, to the satisfaction of the owner.
- A company often bid small, fixed-price contracts of three- to six-months involving three to eight people. The sales team typically committed to more than the team could deliver. The development teams tended to miss both deadline and scope, working overtime but often still accruing penalties at the end of the contract.

One team lead worked in the manner described in this article. Knowing he would run out of time, he developed the most critical features first, thinned out the less critical features, and left the least important features to the end.

When the contract period ended, it was clear to the customers that they had gotten *most* of what they wanted and the parts left out were the least significant. This produced the least overtime, the smallest penalties, the highest customer satisfaction and the greatest likelihood of receiving a follow-on contract.

- A company with a rich product line had several thousand developers in half-a-dozen countries. Under normal circumstances, when they called for full integration on a particular date, every team worked overtime and jockeyed for position not to be the one most behind schedule. The integration date kept slipping as team after team failed to complete their work on time.

Had this company used the disciplined learning approach, each team would have in place the essential elements needed for the integration, with only tail elements left unfinished. The business sponsors could decide whether to deliver slightly less on time, or slightly more a bit later.

Disciplined learning is neither obvious nor for the faint of heart. However, it is in active use by teams in various disciplines, who manage to deliver success in difficult circumstances.

Strategy 1: Being just hopeful

To highlight the difference disciplined learning provides, consider as a reference *Figure 6*. This figure illustrates a common way of working in which integration or delivery occurs at the end of a long period of work without integration or delivery. It is not necessary to be working in a waterfall fashion to fit this picture, so the curve need not be ascribed to waterfall. It is a simply a common behavior.

The figure shows time on the horizontal axis. The dotted line shows project costs increasing steadily over time. The solid line shows that some learning occurs while the project teams work. However, the major surprises and learning come with integration and delivery.

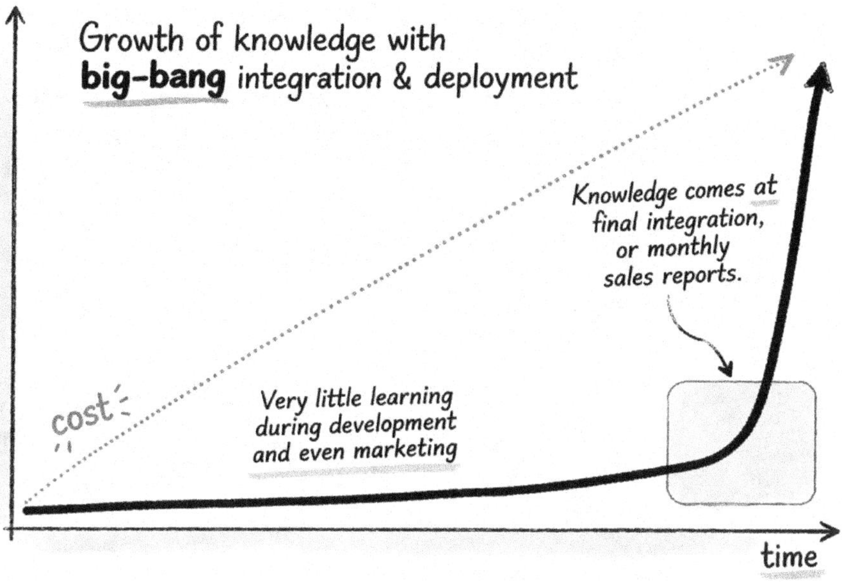

Figure 6, Chapter 5. The typical "late-learning' strategy.

In *Figure 6*, learning comes late in the project, after most of the cost has been accrued and decisions have been made.

What we want is a way to learn earlier in the project, when changes can be made with lower cost and greater safety.

Strategy 2: Disciplined learning

A development team has four critical things to learn:

1: What they should really be building, never mind what they thought they should build at the start.

2: Where their technical ideas are flawed.

3: Whether they have the right people on the team, and how those people might best work together.

4: How much it will cost to develop.

Those are all learned when the parts are integrated and when the consumers finally give feedback on the result. In *Figure 6*, this arrives too late to benefit the project.

The disciplined learning approach is to apply the "broken" learning curve in very small doses, deliberately and often, so that each step provides information that can be used to adjust the four categories of learning. The payoff is a fine-grained ability to steer the final delivery in time, features and quality.

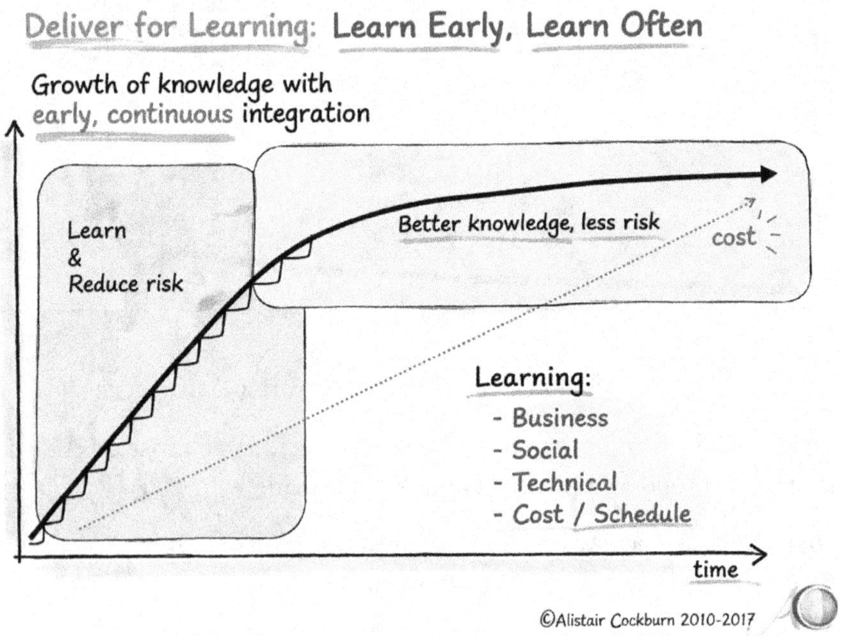

Figure 7, Chapter 5: Learn Early, Learn Often.

Figure 7 illustrates:

- Time is again on the horizontal axis, with a dotted line showing project costs increasing over time.
- The thin solid line shows knowledge increasing rapidly at the start of the project, slowing toward the end. The aim is to have "no late surprises", or "all bad news early". Executed well, the project gets easier and safer over time.
- The thick green and red arrows show business value growing in uneven spurts as time is spent *learning* what might go wrong as opposed to building straight business value.

It is not as though intending to get this curve automatically produces the desired effect. Bad news can show up any time on any project. The intent of the strategy, however, is to minimize surprises late in the project.

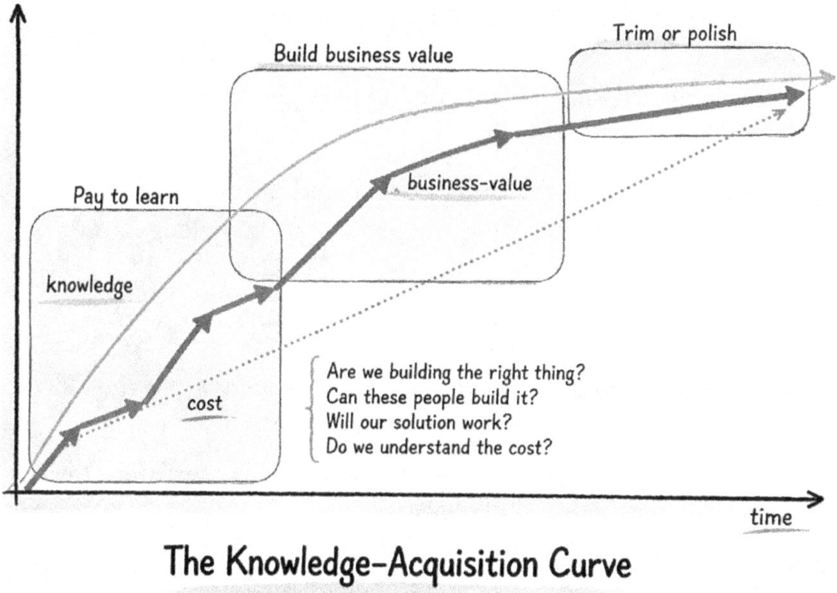

Figure 8, Chapter 5. Applying the sequence: Learn – Value - Tail.

Figure 8 illustrates:

- Time is again on the horizontal axis, with a dotted line showing project costs increasing over time.
- The thin solid line shows knowledge increasing rapidly at the start of the project, slowing toward the end. The aim is to have "no late surprises", or "all bad news early". Executed well, the project gets easier and safer over time.
- The thick green and red arrows show business value growing in uneven spurts as time is spent *learning* what might go wrong as opposed to building straight business value.

It is not as though intending to get this curve automatically produces the desired effect. Bad news can show up any time on any project. The intent of the strategy, however, is to minimize surprises late in the project.

The small arrow segments of different shades show the growth of business value, sometimes rapidly as attention is given to business value as a priority, and sometimes slowly, as attention is given to learning activities as a priority.

The difference between the thin gray line and the arrows illustrates the difference between maximizing the growth of knowledge and that of business value.

The three boxes show three periods in using the strategy:

- In the first period, learning is pursued aggressively, to identify needed changes as early as possible.
- In the second period, delivery value is given greater emphasis, mixed with continued learning.
- In the third period, attention is given to what can be omitted at the discretion of the business, the "tail."

The difficult and interesting part of the approach is artfully blending experiments to learn with incrementally growing business value. The sections that follow describes strategies for learning in the four categories and creating a project plan.

1: Learn what to build

The most important and also the most difficult question is: Will people like, buy and use what we're building? If not, what would they like, buy and use?

Normally, this question gets answered when it is too late. Recently, however, strategies have come into usage that move this learning forward. Although simple, the strategies require discipline, patience, and a willingness to change course based on the results.

Sample strategies are:

- Paper prototyping
- Ambassador user
- Early delivery
- Empty or manual delivery

Paper prototyping [2] and its related strategies come from the user-centered design community [3], and involve nothing more complicated than putting a mockup of the product into the hands of the consumer, who reacts to these early design thoughts. Prepared at low cost, early in the development cycle, these prototypes allow the development team to change their minds about how to proceed.

An "ambassador user" is a friendly user to whom the team can deliver an incomplete but growing product. This user usually breaks the system within moments, giving valuable feedback from his or her (limited) perspective. The difference between the "ambassador user" and "paper prototyping" is that the ambassador user is encountering the actual system as it grows, not a mockup of the system.

"Early delivery" indicates a true deployment of the system with reduced capabilities. The intention is to learn, first of all, what is incorrect with the product as envisaged, but possibly more significantly, how the presence of the product changes the users' thoughts about what should be built in the first place. "Early delivery" recognizes that once people start using a system, their habits, needs and desires change, often in unpredictable ways. Delivering a thinned version of the system early allows the team to gather input on those questions and to adjust the priorities on what should be developed.

The above are all standard, if frequently ignored, techniques, found in the regular literature.

Two strategies have emerged in the last decade within the lean startup community: Empty delivery and manual delivery (my terms for them).

- The "Empty Delivery" strategy [4] is suited for online products. Initially, with no implementation behind the façade of a click, all that is detected is whether anyone clicks on a link or accesses a feature. Measuring these clicks, a team can identify which features are drawing the most attention, and tune the project plan to develop those ones first. The system evolves in the direction of maximum draw.

- In "Manual Delivery," a product or service is delivery manually, even when that may seem preposterously expensive and inefficient [5]. Since the people performing the service can change their behavior intelligently on every single delivery, they can converge to a service offering that is much more appreciated by the customers. The increased cost in these first deliveries is recaptured by offering a product or service that the customer base really desires.

2: Adjust design decisions

Mistakes in design come from

- choosing technology that doesn't work as advertised,
- misunderstandings and mistaken assumptions between people,
- mistakes and omissions in design.

These are discovered and repaired using four strategies:

- Walking skeleton
- Micro-incremental development
- Spikes
- Story splitting

The *Walking Skeleton* strategy [6] calls for the team to connect a thin path through the architecture. This simple system builds morale and surfaces the first round of technical surprises.

Once the system is thinly connected, the infrastructure and functionality teams each add onto their part of the system. It is not uncommon to see the infrastructure team redesigning the skeleton during the project. This restructuring is one of the costs of using the strategy.

Micro-incremental development is when teams integrate their work every day, half-day, or even every hour. The shorter the time between integrations, the faster they find mistakes and the lower the cost of changes. Since they are less likely to change the same part of the design at the same time, they may not need to check out and branch the design, making integration easier, faster, and less error prone.

A *spike* [7,8] is a small, disposable piece of work created to explicitly address the question, "Is there an obvious flaw in this approach?" It is used to flush out interface mismatches as well as various performance and scaling problems.

The difference between a spike and ordinary incremental development is that ordinary incremental development is conducted using full production conventions, with the assumption that the work will be used in the final product.

A spike must *absolutely not* be used in the final product; it is throwaway work. Because the work is throw-away, it is always done in the most rapid manner possible, with the sole purpose of learning about the question at hand.

Story splitting [9] is a technique that allows learning to be moved forward in the schedule for work that otherwise belongs later in the project. An example of this might be final conversion of the database. The work is spit into a spike for learning and a production piece.

The purpose of the spike is to learn how to address whatever difficulties might lie ahead. The production work is left until the appropriate moment in the schedule.

3: Learn to work together

Failure to deliver is sometimes due to not having skilled people on the assignment. However, it can also be due to them not learning how to work together. Tom DeMarco and Tim Lister refer to a team as being "jelled" [10] when they have learned to work well together. Three strategies help create a jelled team,

- Early victory

- Walking skeleton
- Simplest first, worst second

The Early Victory [11] strategy is based on the work of sociologist Karl Weick [12], showing that achieving results helps people come to trust each other more, raises morale and helps them perform better.

Walking skeleton, already described, produces an early technical victory to the team and to the sponsors, and it also provides a chance to correct mistakes in team composition and improve intra-team communication.

The "simplest-first, worst second" strategy [13] is contrary to the usual recommendation in the agile development world, whose usual agile advice is to build the highest business value first. That strategy makes good sense once the team is functioning well, social risks have been reduced, and the team is capable and confident of being able to deliver whatever is of the highest business value. However, many conversations need to take place before the team has reached that point. For this reason, it is sometime useful to build something simple to start with just so the team can adjust social habits in good time before the difficult parts of the project are reached.

4: Learn how much it will cost

Two strategies help with learning the cost of a project:

- Core samples
- Microcosm

Tim Lister told the following story at a conference [14]:

> *A man wanting a pool built in his back yard calls in three contractors to present estimates. The third contractor, instead of presenting an estimate, tells the homeowner he will drill and core sample the ground, and will charge the man for that.*
>
> *The homeowner complains, saying that the first two contractors didn't charge him for core sampling. The contractor responds that he has no idea how the first two contractors could submit a*

bid, since they don't know what sorts of rock layer lies under the lawn, but he couldn't possibly put in a bid without having that information.

The homeowner now comfortable with the third contractor, hires him for the work.

To create core samples with a development project, a team might identify parts of the system the development of which is not obvious and develop very small elements within those areas. They will identify what sorts of surprises lurk below the surface and understand how difficult the work will really be. Carefully selecting such "core samples" allows the team to develop a more reliable cost-, time- and resource estimate for the project.

Core sampling is the miniature version of the more general "Microcosm" strategy [15], in which a mini-project is run for the sole purpose of establishing a sound estimate. A full Microcosm project can be set up to test the productivity of a new development team (think off-shoring, in particular), as well as to test the learning speed of staff with new technologies, to benchmark the productivity of expert versus ordinary or new developers.

Whereas a core sample effort is intended to take hours to days, a full Microcosm project may take weeks to carry out, and should therefore only be used for larger development efforts.

Finer-grained: Splitting features

Figure 7 makes it appear as though only the project has a learning period, a value period and a tail. In fact, *every feature* being developed has them.

The learning period for a feature involves learning what the customer really wants, how much it costs to develop, what the team needs internally to be able to work well, and what technical surprises lurk inside the feature request.

Many features need little or no learning period. However, for features with notable risk profiles, as the database conversion example above or features with critical user acceptance criteria, it is appropriate to make a separate entry in the project plan for the spike.

Similarly, many features are not important enough that tuning and improving the delivery quality need be broken out into distinct line items in the project plan - "adequate" is good enough for delivery. However, some features are so important that distinct schedule entries might be allocated to revising and polishing them to reach top quality - optionally, depending on how the schedule looks closer to the end.

Creating separate schedule entries for the spikes and tail allow the team to manage risk, value and quality criteria in a fine-grained way, as described further below.

The punchline: Trimming the tail

The surprise to many people is that a team can arrange for a certain set of features to be at an "adequate" level of wonderfulness in good time before final delivery, and then spend the remaining time polishing those feature that are deemed more important than the others [16]. If time is short, they can cut back on (or trim) the tail, to deliver early or on time [17].

The financial benefits of Incremental development are well presented in Software by Numbers. [18]. A project may become self-funding if it is delivered to users part-way through development, lowering the financial load on the sponsors.

Equally valuable is the ability to *not* develop certain aspects of the system, to cut back on features and quality. You might trim four aspects of a system:

- Features
- Feature details
- Usage quality
- Internal quality

You drop an entire feature. A car (for example) might not need a sun roof. The first iPads did not have phone modems.

If not an entire feature, you might trim an aspect of a feature: Given that your car must have all of the basics (such as brakes), it might not need brakes with antilock braking. A computer system might require searching capability, but not auto-completion or auto-correction.

Recognizing that really smooth and easy to use features take a lot of work, you might choose to skip improving usability for selected features.

Finally, you can trim internal design quality and correctness. The question is how much internal quality is needed for the delivery in question.

If development has proceeded incrementally, attending to the learning areas, then the team can deliver

- early, with reduced features or quality;
- on time, with either full or reduced quality, depending on where development stands at that time; or
- later, with enriched features or quality;

-- *at the choice of the sponsors!*

Under usual project circumstances, the only choices are to delay or work overtime. The third, "trim the tail" option, is available for those who have worked in this more disciplined fashion.

Creating a plan

Disciplined learning calls for merging learning steps from the four categories with incremental growth of business value.

The quality of the plan is sensitive to the ability of the planners to identify and merge the learning needs and the upcoming possibilities for income. As lessons are learned and new risks and opportunities spotted, the plan will need to be updated.

At the periodic re-planning meeting (weekly, bi-weekly or monthly), the various leads and experts share their thoughts about the experiments needing to be done to reduce risk or learn about the four categories. They also decide on the features or elements that will incrementally grow business-value.

One way to capture their thoughts for discussion is to fill in a project map, as shown in Table 1.

The project map has four columns. The first holds the name of a feature, feature cluster, or non-feature work element (such database migration). The second holds the learning or risk work that needs to be done for that item, the third the incremental steps for business value, and the fourth the tail aspects that might get delayed or trimmed.

Separate entries are created as needed on each row. Some rows might, of course, have empty risk or tail entries. Features might be combined into a single row to make the table easier to work with. Table 1 shows a simple project map, to illustrate.

The project map does not dictate in what order to execute each entry, it only shows the presence of those items. The job of the project steering group is to traverse the project map in such a way that at the end, when time runs out, the maximum possible was delivered.

Feature or Work Element	**Learning (Risk)**	**Value**	**Tail**
Shopping cart	Test 1 payment to bank Test fraud alert Discount formulae	One item in cart Multiple items in cart	Return to shopping place with cart intact
Search	Cost of full-text search	Search by sub-string in titles Search by sub-strings in full text	Search returns "other people like this" entries
Data migration	Show that script-migration works	Convert database	---

Table 1. A simple project map showing risk, business value and tail elements.

Conclusion

Disciplined learning with trim-the-tail is one of the few approaches equally available to very small and very large projects, fixed-price and floating-price projects. It is not for the faint of heart, however, as it requires discipline, creativity and constant correction.

The payoff is the ability to get a team working together, discover early what is needed, deliver it early in order to create a self-funding project, and trim the tail at the end to meet inelastic deadlines.

References

1. Jeff Patton, "Unfixing the Fixed Scope Project: Using Agile Methodologies to Create Flexibility in Project Scope", in Agile Development Conference 2003, Proceedings of the Conference on Agile Development, 2003, ACM Press. [https://dl.acm.org/doi/10.5555/942789.942822 ACM paywall]
2. http://en.wikipedia.org/wiki/Paper_prototyping
3. http://en.wikipedia.org/wiki/User-centered_design
4. "Searching the internet's long tail and finding parrot cages", http://www.bbc.co.uk/news/business-11495839
5. Eric Reis, The Lean Startup: How Today's Entrepreneurs Use Continuous Innovation to Create Radically Successful Businesses, Crown Business, 2011.
6. http://alistair.cockburn.us/Walking+skeleton
7. http://c2.com/xp/SpikeSolution.html
8. http://agiledictionary.com/209/spike/
9. http://alistair.cockburn.us/The+A-B+work+split
10. Tom DeMarco and Timothy Lister, Peopleware: Productive Projects and Teams. New York: Dorset House Publishing Co., 1987.
11. http://alistair.cockburn.us/Advancedpmstrategies1-180.ppt
12. Karl Weick, The Social Psychology of Organizing, McGraw-Hill Humanities/Social Sciences/Languages; 2nd edition, 1979.
13. Alistair Cockburn, Crystal Clear: A Human-Powered Methodology for Small Teams, Addison-Wesley, 2005. Also online in "Individuals" at http://alistair.cockburn.us/ASD+book+extract%3A+%22Individuals %22
14. Lister, Tim, keynote at Agile Development Conference 2010.
15. http://alistair.cockburn.us/Project+risk+reduction+patterns
16. [http://www.agileproductdesign.com/downloads/patton_embrace_uncertainty_optimized.ppt]
17. [http://alistair.cockburn.us/Trim+the+Tail]
18. Mark Denne and Jane Cleland-Huang. Software by Numbers: Low-Risk, High-Return Development. Prentice-Hall, 2003.

See online : [https://web.archive.org/web/20140329201317/http://alistair.cockburn.us/Disciplined+Learning]

Reflections and Key Points:

Rereading this article, I found the most surprising part was this:

> *Every feature being developed has a learning period, a value period and a tail.*

In 2019, David Bland and Alexander Osterwalder published a very comprehensive catalog of techniques around "what *should* we be building?" Read *Testing Business Ideas: A Field Guide for Rapid Experimentation.*

Did you catch these key points?

"Upgrade project planning from failure-avoidance to success-seeking. Not 'fail early, fail often,' but 'learn early, learn often.' "

"A development team has four critical things to learn:
What they should really be building,
How their people might best work together,
Where their technical ideas are flawed,
How much it will cost to develop."

"attention is given to what can be omitted at the discretion of the business, the 'tail.' … Trim the tail."

"Every feature being developed has a learning period, a value period and a tail."

"Disciplined learning with trim-the-tail is one of the few approaches equally available to very small and very large projects, fixed-price and floating-price projects."

Learn early, learn often: Break or validate decisions as soon as possible. We now have strategies to help do that.

---

6. The Elephant Carpaccio Exercise

This exercise shows both why to deliver soon and small, and how to do that, justified entirely from a business perspective.

This is the exercise I run whenever I have even just two hours with a company. I invite *everyone* in the company to participate, business as well as technical specialists, top executives to staff employees. Everyone needs to see, hear, and feel this exercise to get a proper sense of both *why* and *how* to work in fine-grained increments.

The exercise can be done on a spreadsheet or with programming. If the room is full of non-programming people, use spreadsheets. If there are enough programmers to partner up a business person and a programmer, have them program it together. For some business people, this is often the only time in their life that a business person gets to see code getting written.

As one business person said after watching their programmer typing like mad: "I never imagined there could be that much typing and nothing happening!"

The slicing is the same for spreadsheets and programming aside from the first slices of programming. After those, everything is the same.

I encourage you to not only read the problem and the breakdown, but to do the full exercise, so that you feel it under your fingertips. Treat it like a *kata,* something you do over and over until it's automatic.

The problem is really simple:

Imagine you are working on some part of a sales system where your part is to calculate the price of an order.

To keep this problem simple, the customer will only order one type of item, so you don't have to capture the item's name or catalog number. They will enter just the item's price and the quantity.

They will get a discount based on the order value, and they will pay tax based on their location and the discounted order value.

Your assignment is to show them the final price they will pay.

This problem is literally the smallest assignment I can construct that people will still honor. I will tighten the constraints on it a bit more just to keep your work tightly constrained.

The difficulty with the problem is not in making the spreadsheet or the program. I assume that anyone practiced in spreadsheets or programming can manage it. The difficulty is in coming up with at least ***fifteen*** growth stages to develop it in.

How many slices or growth stages do you see so far?

The Problem Statement in Detail.

The sponsor walks in and says, "I want a price calculator for 50 states, with 5 discount levels."

For my version of the exercise, I use only five states and five discount levels, because it is just complicated enough to illustrate the point I'm after. In practice, there would be 50 states. If you are in Europe, imagine a similar system for all the European countries.

Here is the tax table:

State Taxes:

NV : 6.85%
UT : 4.85%
TX : 6.25%
AL : 4.00%
CA : 7.25%
... add more if you like ...

The problem so far is too simple to be interesting. To complicate it just enough to be interesting, let's add discounts. That is, we'll discount a certain percentage based on the value of the order.

Here are the discount break points:

Orders under $1,000 → no discount.
From $1,000 but under $5,000 → 3% discount
From $5,000 but under $7,000 → 5% discount
From $7,000 but under $10,000 → 7% discount
From $10,000 but under $50,000 → 10% discount
From $50,000 and up → 15% discount

The formula you need to implement is this:

Order Value = Price * Quantity
Discount Amount = discount[Order Value]
Discounted Order Value = Order Value – Discount Amount
Taxable Value = Discounted Order Value
Tax Rate = Tax Rate For State [State Code]
Tax Amount = Taxable Value * Tax Rate
Final Price = Taxable Value + Tax Amount

That's the assignment.

Now for the hard part. Don't work out that calculation in one big crunching formula, but *grow* your spreadsheet or program in at least **15** growth stages from nothing up to the final complicated formula! For most people, that is not obvious.

The Warmup Question.

Let's set up our discussion with this image. The top half shows value growing over time, the bottom half shows money getting spent along the way.

Figure 9 shows the requested elephant: 50 states with 5 discount levels.

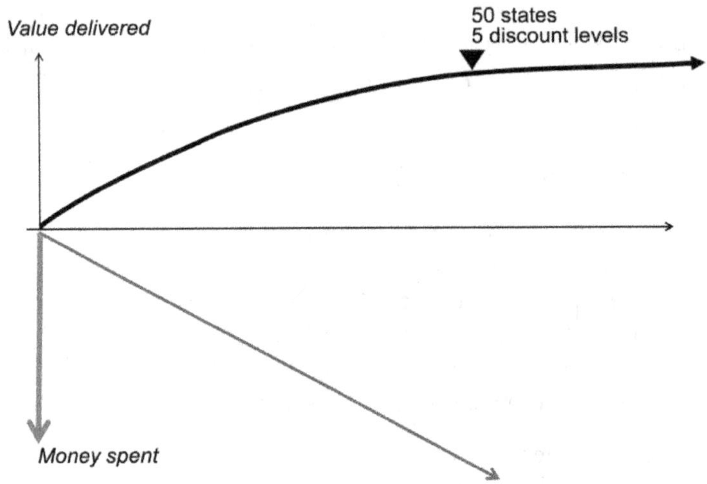

Figure 9, Chapter 6. The assignment with financials set up.

Before we get into the slicing, we need to address this question:

Which do we program first,
the discount calculation or the tax calculation?

The argument for programming the discount first is that it is simple and matches the order of calculating the final answer: discount first, then add taxes.

But here's where the first plot twist shows up. Let's play the pessimistic scenario and the optimistic scenario and see what happens.

The pessimistic scenario: What happens if we run out of time or money and have only implemented the discount part?

Then we have nothing – the project is a total loss of the sponsor's money. If we implement the tax part first, then at least we will have something we can ship, it will just be missing discounts. Hence: implement taxes first, discounts as there is time and money.

From the optimistic point of view, the answer is even clearer: Once we have the taxes implemented, we can ship and start earning money!

Let's mark this on the graph (*Figure 10*). Let's drop down the line from the originally requested milestone, call it milestone A. That's when money starts to flow in. The sponsor is interested in that moment when the money gained matches the money spent, or when they get a "positive return on investment."

However, there is an even more interesting moment, namely, when the money coming in equals the money going out – that's when the project is *self-funding.*

This is a magical moment, because it means the sponsor's investment pot can go to funding a new initiative. I know entrepreneurs who work this way: They run an initiative until it is self-funding, then let it go on an independent path while they start their next initiative.

Figure 10 and *Figure 11* show how that "self-funding project" moment moves forward when we implement the taxes first.

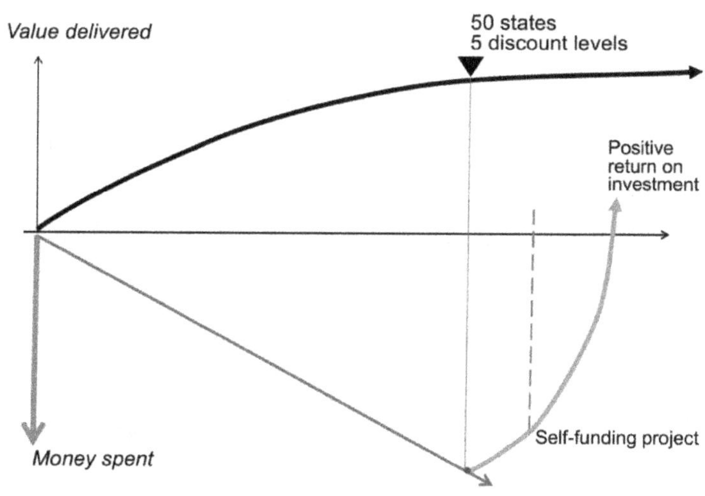

Figure 10, Chapter 6. Planned income growth after final delivery.

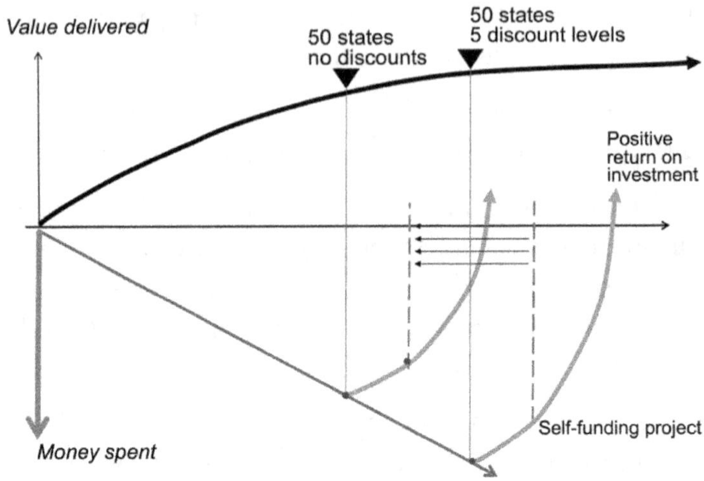

Figure 11, Chapter 6. Income growth after early delivery with no discounts.

To anchor my learning goals, in my classes I play the role of the pointy-haired boss intent on his money. I fire anyone who programs anything about discounts before delivering all of the states with tax calculations.

"Don't get between me and my money!"

will be our guiding theme in this exercise.

The First Riddle Solved.

At this point, someone sees the pattern forming and says, "Yes, but you don't need to deliver to all 50 states – You can start earning money after delivering to just *one* state" (*Figure 12*).

This is a significant observation. Two things happen when we deliver to that first state:

- We get to start earning income, bringing that self-funding moment earlier.
- We have to set up the call center and start repairing the things that were wrong.

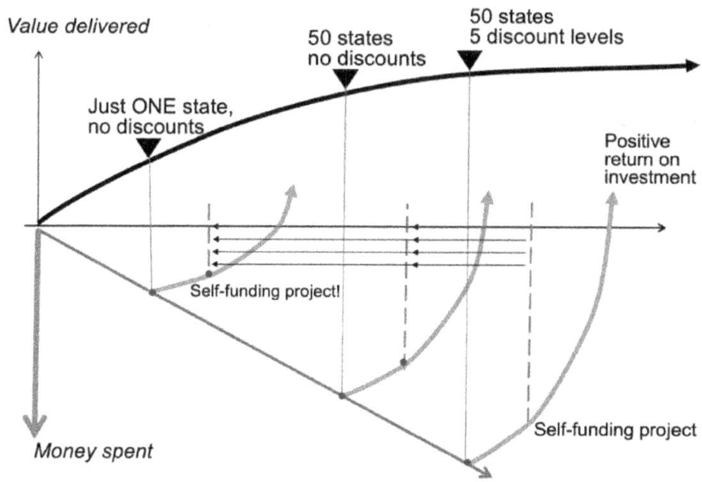

Figure 12, Chapter 6. Income growth after minimal early delivery.

This is the point missed by most developers. They are thinking, "*While my fingers are in here, I might as well type in all the states and discounts.*" However, the cost of typing, even revising those tables later, is small compared to the cost of setting up a call center, and much smaller than the cost of shipping a mistake to 50 states and having them all call in reporting the same mistake.

Nobody these days deploys to all 50 states at one time, it would be madness.

Companies these days deploy to the smallest segment of the population possible, to minimize damage from any mistakes.

In that first delivery, you have to do the following:

- Set up the call center for the moment you deploy.
- Check the user interface (Do people use it the way we think they will?).
- Check tax compliance (Are we legal?).
- Update the business model (Is this having the effect we hoped for?).

Those are much more significant than revising the state tax tables.

We continue this line of thought to build our strategy:

Every state gets a separate delivery. First Nevada. Then Utah. Then Texas, and so on. Those thinking ahead will notice that 50 is a lot of states, so we will probably deploy to one state at a time for a while, then two states, then five states, then ten states. 50 makes for a lot of states. The number of states we choose at any moment is based on the damage we foresee.

Of course, we also start making money sooner if we only deploy to one state: *"Don't get between me and my money!"*

Therefore, in my workshops, teams get fired if they deploy to more than one state at a time. Even just typing a second entry in the tax table counts as locking an unvalidated decisions into the system. Fired.

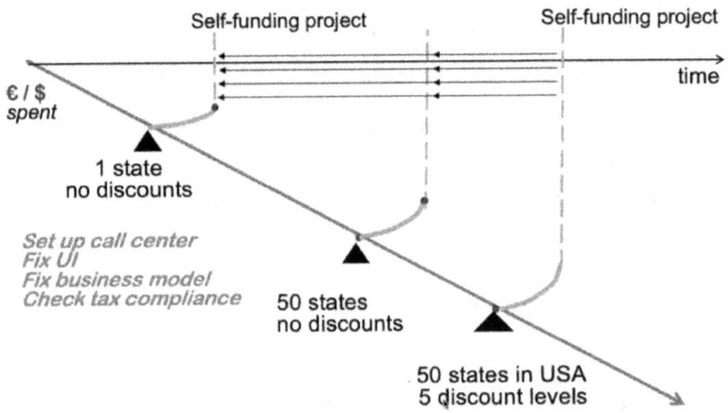

Figure 13, Chapter 6. Deliver to one state first.

Figure 13 shows the financial model at this point. It's looking much better than the first one.

The formulas below show the calculations. Notice how much simpler this system is than the original, and it's already an elephant – a baby elephant 😊.

Order Value = Price * Quantity
Taxable Value = Order Value
Tax Rate = Tax Rate For State ["NV]
Tax Amount = Taxable Value * Tax Rate
Final Price = Order Value + Tax Amount

Now we see the answer to the first riddle:

Make a full deployment at every moment there is something new to deploy, starting from the first tax calculation.

Stage the Discounts.

We repeat this line of thinking with the discounts. It's not quite as drastic as with the taxes, but still:

- How do you know that five is the correct number of discount levels?

You don't and you can't. On a real project, you would deploy one discount level first and see what happens. Based upon that, you would decide whether to add a second. Eventually, you will choose the number of discounts and their amounts that work for you.

In other words, deliver each discount level separately and watch how it works.

That means that you will have one deployment for every state and one for every discount level.

For the exercise, I ask for only five states, just to keep the exercise under control. Thus, we have ten deployments in total, the five states and the five discount levels.

For the sake of playing the greedy boss and anchoring the learning, I fire any team that types in more than one line in either the tax or the discount table without first deploying and testing their answer. You'd be amazed at the number of teams who do that, and also the number of teams that give the wrong answers for the calculations.

Figure 14 shows the deliveries to states first without, then the discounts. They are marked as delivery milestones.

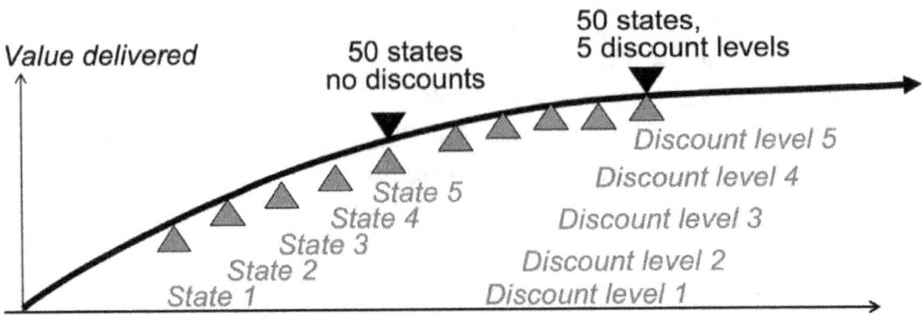

Figure 14, Chapter 6. The actual deliveries.

The Second Riddle is the Most Surprising.

Some people notice right away that once we decide on the above strategy, then we can actually deliver to Nevada without ever asking for the state code.

This moves the moment of first delivery forward as well as the self-funding project moment.

Additionally, it allows us to

- set up the call center,
- check the user interface,
- check for tax compliance, and
- check the business model.

All this without touching any of the complexity of the calculation!

The calculation now looks like this:

```
Order Value = Price * Quantity
Final Price = Order Value * 1.0685
```

Stunningly simple, already earning money and solving problems!

To be honest, I didn't see this to start with. But once someone mentioned it (it has been spotted by both business people and programmers), I saw its value and now require it in my classes.

Programmers, in particular, object to this delivery, because they don't want the *rework* of having to go back and change the formula after they have already typed it in once.

I hope you can see that the cost of retyping the formula is small compared to the value produced by the early delivery, not only the earlier flow of income, but also the result of setting up the call center and checking the user interface, tax compliance and business model.

Oh yes, I fire any team that bothers to take as input the state code. It not only wastes time and energy, it introduces the possibility of extra errors and adds more unvalidated decisions to the system.

So it's more than just *"Don't get between me and my money!"* It violates every aspect of optimal development.

Five Notes on the Second Riddle.

Note 1: This first delivery is technically called the Minimal Viable Product (MVP). Many people misunderstand or misquote the term MVP, so let me clear it up:

- The delivery must be a *Product*, that is, it is a real delivery, offering real value. It is not just an experiment, a prototype, or a survey.
- It is *Viable.* That is, it could exist on its own in your product catalog.
- It is *Minimal.* That means you can't deliver anything smaller and have it still be a Viable Product.

It is easy to spot when it is a *Product* and likely to be *Viable* imagine, but it is very hard to see what is really *Minimal.* Even I tend to include too much in my first delivery.

That takes us to the second note:

Note 2: People practiced in these techniques will not start as I did in this exercise, trying to slice the whole elephant down to the minimal delivery That turns out to be too hard to get right. Instead, they work from the bottom ("growing" the system) and ask:

What is the smallest useful thing we can deliver?

Asking this question tends to give a smaller valid answer then slicing from the whole elephant.

Even junior-level, actually, especially younger people will say:

"How about we just fix the tax rate and ship to one state with no discounts?"

They do this without even thinking about the early income or the call center. It's just the simplest thing they can deliver.

People with experience work this way naturally and identify very small elephants they can deliver very soon. A particularly striking example of this was the story told to me about installing RFID tags at a major retailer. I include that story at the end of this chapter.

***Note 3*:** That MVP allows you to change your business model at the earliest possible moment.

Remember, unvalidated decisions are your enemy. Your business model is the biggest unvalidated decisions you own, and earliest one you make. The longer it hangs around, the more expensive it is to change. Hence, that ridiculously simple MVP is your best friend.

Let's play this out…

A person starts a business delivering goods ordered online (imagine specializing competitor to Amazon or Door Dash). They start delivering in Utah and discover for whatever reason that staying in Utah is much more interesting than spreading to different states.

They change their business model to stay in Utah, which means they will never use that tax table! Oh, the database designer gets mad no one uses their beautiful tax table! (Of course, in my exercise, they got fired.)

Once you see this way of thinking, look how heavy it is to list the states you *imagine* you will deploy to and the list of discount levels you *imagine* you will use. Typing those into your spreadsheet or program before you actively need them is filling your system with *unvalidated decisions* and future drag.

It turns out that

"Don't get between me and my money!"

is not such a bad guide, after all.

Note 4: Both business people and developers hate rework. However, I was educated by my first project sponsor:

> ***"Of course we'll have to revise the system. Once you consultants leave, the very next day some business event will force us to revise the system. But in the meantime, we have this system running and delivering value. That's just business as usual."***

What I wish to highlight here is that the rework we will encounter in this exercise and this strategy is paid for by the value obtained by the early delivery.

I never shy away from discussions about rework. I hope readers of this book learn to dialog with both business and development people to work through which proposed rework will be adequately paid for by early business value, as opposed to those that won't. Personally, I have never had difficulty having this discussion with any business executive, they understand the concept well.

Note 5: You will need to re-deploy to Utah once you decide to go multi-state.

You deployed to Utah, set up the call center, fixed some bugs, improved the user interface and checked your tax compliance. Once you decide to go multi-state, you will need to:

- Change the UI to collect the state (only UT to start with!)
- Change the program to look up UT in the tax table (which only has one line in it, of course).

- Re-deploy to Utah again, to make sure that the system is still tax compliant and the new UI works.

All of this falls into the discussion of rework we just had.

Figure 15 shows the updated graph with first state hardcoded, plus the rework, included redeploying to Utah once the state input field gets added.

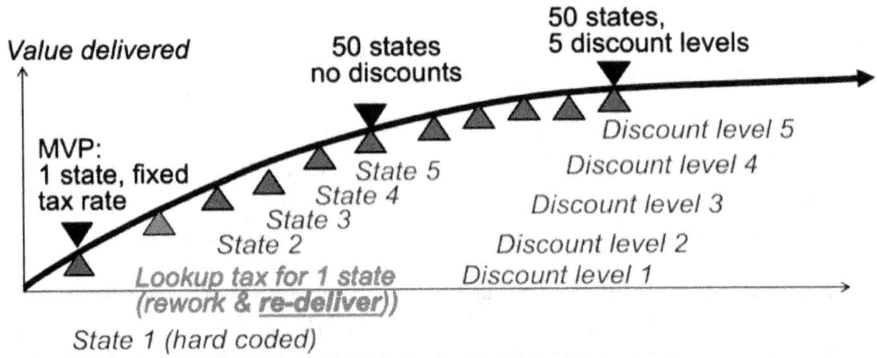

Figure 15, Chapter 6. Delivery with a hard-coded tax rate, deferring collection of the state code, and re-deploying to Utah.

Oh, in case you didn't already see it coming, anyone who bothered to collect that third input, the two-letter state code, got fired. They did unnecessary work, put unvalidated decisions into the system, and *got between me and my money.* 😊

The Final Riddle: Growing the Business Rules.

We have 11 growth stages of our little app so far, each one resulting in a full delivery:

- The first with the fixed tax rate,
- then redeployment to that state,
- then the four other states,
- finally the five discount levels, each getting is own deployment.

What else can we slice or grow?

We have only looked at full deployments so far. Now let's shift to internal demos.

Each demo will show that we have increased the capability of the system, even if it is not ready for deployment.

I can't overstate the value of these *demo* growth stages. Many of the problems we tackle these days are really complicated, so it is useful to show *that* we are making progress and not stuck somewhere. It also allows the business to notice simpler requests they could make that could still deliver value.

Here are the business rules we need to implement in this problem, in development sequence, along with the deliveries. Demos are in dark gray italics, deliveries in black:

1. Capture and show Price (P)
2. Capture and show Quantity (Q)
*3. Order Value (OV) = P * Q*
4. Taxable Value 1 (TV') = Order Value (this will be reworked)
5. Tax Rate 1 (TR') = 6.85% (this will be reworked)
*6. Tax Amount (TA) = TV' * TR*
7. Final Value (FV) = OV + TA. Deploy that first delivery
8. Capture and show State (S)
9. Revise Tax Rate (TR''): lookup TaxRate[S] *(rework re-deploy)*
10-13. Step through the other four states.
14. Discount Rate (DR) = lookup DiscountLevels[OV]
*15. Discount Amount (DA) = OV * DR*
16. Discounted Order Value (DOV) = OV – DA
17. Revise Taxable Value (TV'') = DOV *(rework 2)*
(Tax Amount & Final Price are automatically corrected with this change. Deploy)
18-21. Step through the other discount levels.

In the end, we had 10 demos and 11 deployments.

Each of these steps, trivial in this tiny application, are likely to be sizable in your real application. Some are worth a demo to the business, while others might only be done by the programmer to keep their steps small and under control. (Think about AI hallucinations here.)

Figure 16 shows the final view of our system development for this exercise, showing the value growing over time. I draw this in the workshop and ask the teams to follow this development exactly.

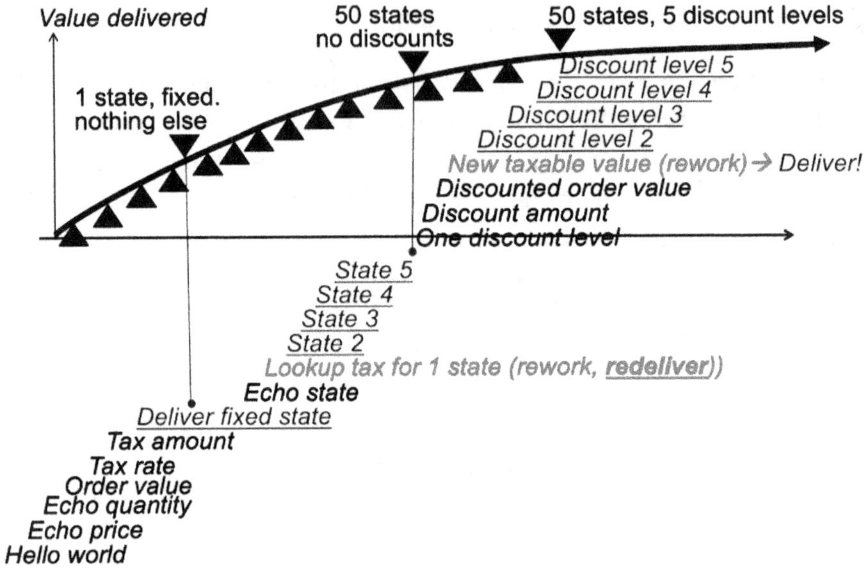

Figure 16, Chapter 6. Final spec of the development sequence.

Discussion.

The point of this exercise is to show

- the *why:* The fine-grained increments provide deliveries that provide early value while checking business concerns and demos along the way for safety;
- the *how:* Select simplified business rules for early deployments and internal demos to show business rules growing.

In real life, your step sizes will vary depending on the technology you are using, the ease of deployment and roll-back, what your end users can stand, and your personal preferences. This exercise steps through the smallest steps possible to showcase the thinking involved.

The RFID Story.

I end this chapter with a true story, which I am happy to repeat elsewhere because it is so important:

> *A large, international merchandise chain decided to put RFID tags in all their products. (RFID, or Radio Frequency Identification tags, are the little tags they use to track inventory movements, and also to catch you if you walk out of the store without paying.)*
>
> *They would have their suppliers buy the RFID tags from them to put them into the products. The system to be built was to let all the different suppliers order RFID tags for all the products they carried. This was going to be a fairly large project.*
>
> *The development team asked who their biggest supplier was, and what item they supplied the most of.*
>
> *Their first delivery was a screen with just* <u>one</u> *button, to order 1,000 RFID tags of that exact item from that supplier. If the supplier needed 8,000 tags, they pushed the button eight times.*
>
> *They developed and deployed that system to the supplier in ONE WEEK!*
>
> *After that, they asked what that same supplier's second most ordered item was, and added a second button.*
>
> *Then they repeated that scenario with a second supplier.*
>
> *At this point, they had a working and delivered system that supported multiple suppliers and multiple items. From there, they expanded their system to all the suppliers and inventory items.*

The lesson is that the seemingly overly-simple suggestion, delivering to one state with a fixed tax rate, is not at all silly – it is actually a delivery of great value.

Reflections and Key Points

Reflections

For years, I wasn't clear what an MVP (Minimum Viable Product) really was. Running the exercise for years and comparing with any other project I saw, it became clear to me the value of this MVP idea.

It must be out in the world, trying to earn its way with all competing ideas. If it earns good money, that's great, but its real purpose is to answer the questions all the previous tests couldn't:

> *Can this team deliver a real product, and*
> *will the customers buy and use it?*

Nothing but a real delivery with real use answers these most important questions.

Did you catch these key points?

"do the full exercise, so that you feel it under your fingertips."

"when the money coming in equals the money going out – that's when the project is *self-funding*."

"You can start earning money after delivering to just one state", and set up the call center, check the user interface, tax compliance, and your business model.

"the cost of retyping the formula is small compared to the value produced by the early delivery."

"That MVP allows to change your business model at the earliest possible moment."

"I never shy away from discussions about rework… discuss which will be adequately paid for by early business value."

> *This exercise shows both why to deliver soon and small, and how to do that, justified entirely from a business perspective.*

---

7. Why Does 'Incremental' Help Improve Your Process?

You need to <u>finish the gestalt round trip and find the boogeyman to improve your process</u> properly.

In 2026, I posted this meme on social media, with the intention to put it on a mug:

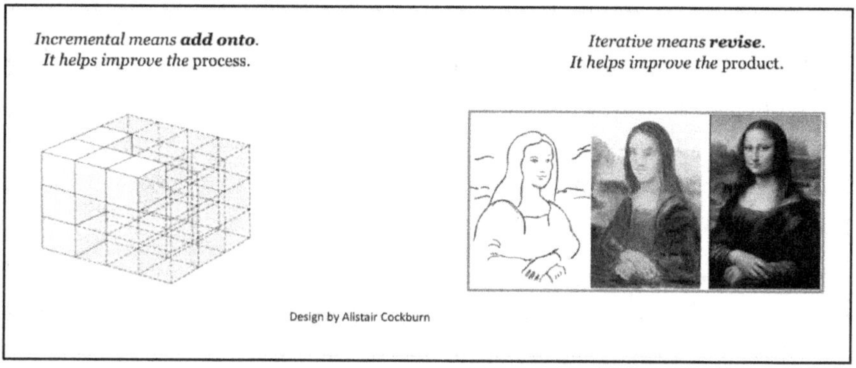

Figure 17, Chapter 7. The incremental vs. iterative meme for the mug.

Many people couldn't see how incremental helps improve the *process* while iterative helps improve the *product.*

Investigating, I found that the insight came from my interviews and experiences in the early 1990s. Few people were lucky enough to have similar experiences, so the meme is less obvious than I thought.

- First, it depends on your actually *doing* incremental and iterative development with early access to users, staged delivery and reflection workshops. You can't get the benefits without those.

That turns out to be somewhat rarer that I could wish. So, I'll run the back story for you. Hopefully it will become clear.

- Secondly, the answer involves the ***gestalt round trip*** and the ***boogeyman***, which again, most readers today are unlikely to be familiar with.

So, first I introduce Grady Booch's *gestalt round trip*, and my use of the *boogeyman* concept. After that, I include the long description that introduced this meme back in 1997, *Surviving Object-Oriented Projects.*

Grady Booch's "Gestalt round trip"

Somewhere around 1992 I heard Grady Booch talking about the need to conduct a *gestalt round trip.*

He was saying that you can't really understand your process until you go through it, and not just part of it, but all of it. Only after you deliver can you see how your requirements gathering process did or didn't feed well into your design and test work. Maybe you didn't write enough detail or maybe you put in too much. You can't know until you go through all the steps of the process.

After you see it all together, you can see the relationship between the elements. You don't get this if you only go through any other single part of the process. You need the whole.

It was a valiant try on his part, but most of us didn't understand what he was saying or how to use it. I had a vague understanding, but couldn't see how to apply it. I spent years asking the question:

> *How do you schedule a gestalt round trip?*

I did work it out in the end, with the V-W staging that you've seen all through this book. I wrote it up in detail in *Surviving Object-Oriented Projects* in 1997.

The "Boogeyman"

In *Surviving Object-Oriented Projects*, I was looking for a way to explain that <u>any part of your process that you don't go through fully is likely to contain a problem that you can't foresee</u>.

This insight came from many project interviews, but highlighted in what one project manager told me:

> *The project manager wanted to do a trial deployment of the upcoming system to find any problems that might be lurking.*

> *However, the corporate process was strictly linear, so they were not allowed to do any deployment activities until the one and only final deployment.*
>
> *He managed to get process variance from his executives*
>
> *When he went to deploy, he found that what should have been a few-day process actually took several weeks. (I don't recall what problems he ran into, it doesn't matter to us, just that they were surprises.)*
>
> *With that information in hand, he was able to revise the deployment process to get it into a suitable time frame.*

Let me repeat this:

> *Any part of your process that you don't go through fully is likely to contain a problem that you can't foresee.*

To anchor this thought, I recalled the childhood idea of the "boogeyman," a terrifying manlike creature that would come and steal you away in the night if you didn't obey your parents.

Only after I started writing about it did I work out that the boogeyman is What You Don't Know You Don't Know (WYDKYDK). And sure enough, if you don't exercise some part of your process, you don't really know what problem is lurking there. WYDKYDK is the very real boogeyman on your project.

As the book extract explains:

> *"if you follow this project setup, you will find out where he is hiding, and be able to deal with him. The early parts of your project have two goals, and one of them is to find the boogey-man (learn WYDKYDK). If you do not take care of this, he will indeed jump out at you when you least expect it."*

This is what gives rise to the phrase "Incremental development helps improve the process."

Surviving Object-Oriented Projects (1997) captured all my project experiences from 1991 through 1997, including the project interviews and the successful two-year project on which I was the lead consultant.

In what follows, I offer a short summary to help motivate the meme, followed by the long explanation I wrote then, which is as valid now as 30 years ago.

Summary:

Increment 1

The purpose of the first increment is to:

1. Establish an architecture for the software,
2. Deliver feedback to the project sponsors and users,
3. Develop good patterns of programming and designing,
4. Find the boogeyman and learn WYDKYDK.

Increment 2

The purpose of the second increment is to:

1. Repair the major mistakes discovered in the first increment,
2. Establish or tune the software architecture,
3. Create a process and teaming that works for you,
4. Settle on good development habits.
5. Deliver more function to the users.

* * * * *

Now here is the full extract. Yes, you have seen all these figures several times by now. I hope you find they make sense at this point.

Increments and Iterations (from Surviving Object-Oriented Projects, 1997)

Increments are so important that we should become clear as to what they are, and are not. Here are three questions to consider.

- What is the difference between "increments" and "iterations"?
- What is the purpose of doing increments?
- What is the purpose of doing iterations?

The short answer is:

- Increments let you fix or improve the development process.
- Iterations let you fix or improve the quality of the system.

Although both are necessary to produce a good system, increments are usually necessary just to survive.

Increments and V-W Staging

Incremental development is a *staging strategy* in which portions of the system are developed at different times or rates, and integrated as they are completed. It does not imply, require or preclude iterative development or waterfall development, which are rework strategies. The alternative to incremental development is to develop the entire system as one lump deliverable.

The phrase "incremental development" does not, by itself, indicate which deliverables are developed incrementally and which are developed *en masse*. Often, requirements are done *en masse*, with design and deployment done incrementally. Project Ingrid even created requirements incrementally.

The rewards of doing of incremental development are great. They are:

- **Education** - People do not know what they are heading into when they start a project. Incremental development lets them go through the entire development cycle once, and use that newfound knowledge immediately.

- **Discovering what you don't know you don't know** (WYDKYDK) - You think you know what you are up against, but your project has surprises in store for you. The increments let you find out early, rather than late.
- **Fixing the way you work** - Finding out early what the surprises are gives you a chance to change your way of working. Each increment boundary is a chance to improve everything you do.

Staff, techniques and tools change on every project. A person who has not been through the entire process really does not know why they are gathering requirements in your particular way, or how well they are doing. They do not understand the analysis, or design, or documentation, testing or delivery tasks. Going through the entire process gives them an "aha!" or feeling of comfort about how the project works. This is what Grady Booch calls the "*gestalt round trip*". It lets them start the next round of development with an understanding of what is going to come, and how the early activities affect the later activities.

If you can manage it, put your new staff on a very small, two- or three-week development assignment, just so they can experience the entire process. Several project groups have told me they have adopted this as a standard way to get newcomers comfortable with the development cycle and development process.

Most project leaders are confident at the start that they know how to do the project. However, the development processes in most projects do not work very well at the start. The discrepancy between the two is that the people do not know what it is that they do not know about this project. They are in for a surprise. Where will the surprise occur? No one knows. That is why delivering the first increment is so important. This first increment is covered in more detail below, in *The Project Increments.*

Even after the first increment, there are surprises in store and things to fix. Incremental development allows you to find, fix and improve those things every few months, before they cost you too much.

The drawings that follow are a schematic rendition of incremental development.

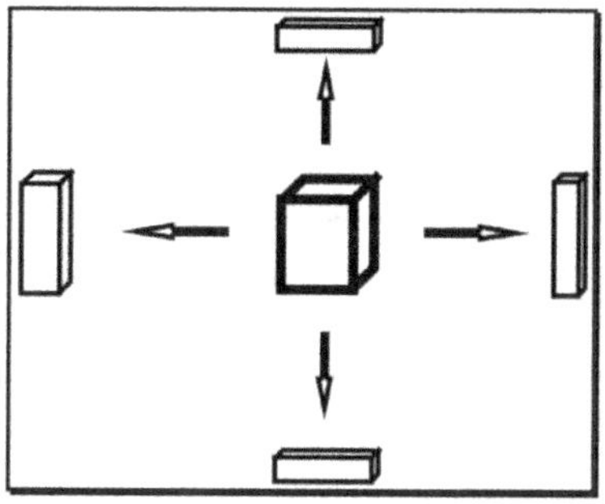

Figure 18, Chapter 7. Incremental is integrating in stages.

Figure 18, above, shows a box in the center, the portion of the system being built in one increment. The other four boxes are sections that will have to be integrated with the center one later on.

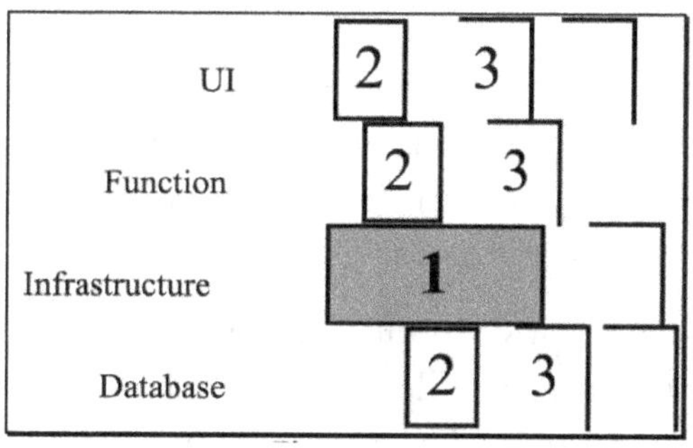

Figure 19, Chapter 7. Develop parts of each layer in each increment.

Figure 19 shows the sequence in which parts of the system are built. Time flows across the diagram from left to right. The figure shows the infrastructure being built in the first increment. The second increment might be started in parallel: the user interface (UI), the system functions, and the database. After they are all deployed, using the infrastructure, a second set of functions may be deployed. The infrastructure will then be extended.

The figure illustrates that all four parts of the system will be under development at the same time, and all will continue to grow over time. The pieces are integrated into the total system as they are completed.

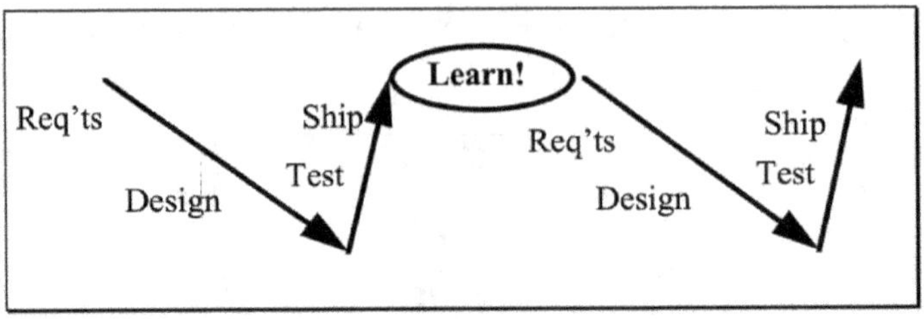

Figure 20, Chapter 7. Incremental development in linear time.

Figure 20 shows how incremental development fits onto the project time line.

Once again, time flows from left to right across the diagram. One increment follows the other, usually at 2-4 months per increment. Within each increment, the well-known activities of requirements, design, test and ship follow each other (I show how to modify this shortly). At the end of each increment, you set aside some time to learn what to improve on the next increment. This time may be as short as 2 to 4 hours in a group discussion, or it may go several days as you try to invent new approaches to your existing problems. Hold the meeting, however short it has to be, as that is where you get leverage on development.

Wait a minute! Isn't that waterfall development being shown in *Figure 20*? Among object-oriented developers, this is considered a terrible accusation, and so we must deal with it fairly.

The diagram illustrates a simple fact of life: you cannot ship any part of the system until you have tested it, you cannot test it until it is designed and built, and you cannot design it without requirements. That particular sequencing of activities is simply a fact of life for any part of the system; I call it the *validation-V*.

The validation-V holds whether you use increments, iterations, rapid prototyping, or waterfall development. "Waterfall" development is when there is only one copy of the V, no matter how long the project is. Incremental development requires having a series of V's, so that lessons from one V feed forward into the next. Because the connecting V's make a W, I refer to this form of project segmentation as *V-W Staging.*

V-W staging is a general strategy which subsumes incremental development, iterative, spiral, and prototyping strategies. It provides a way for the project manager to:

- uncurl the spiral of spiral development so that the activities lie flat against the project time-line,
- arrange prototypes and iterations without sacrificing the notion of continuous progress,
- derive effective progress indicators based on delivered function rather than "phase deliverables",
- manage subcontractors on delivered increments instead of phase deliverables,
- get the value of "*gestalt round-trip*" without having to study Zen.

In V-W staging, different parts of the system are put through the validation-V at different, specific times. The V's can be arranged to overlap, or sit within one another.

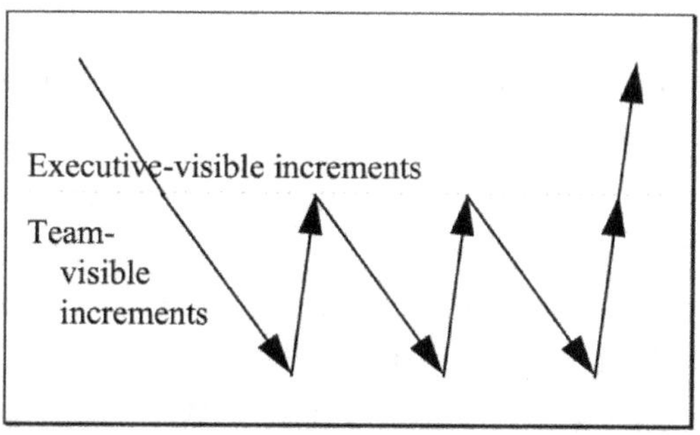

Figure 21, Chapter 7. Separate team- and executive-visible increments.

Suppose your highest-level management has given you 10 months to create each segment of the system. Ten months is a long period to hold everyone's interest. You decide, therefore to split the 10-months into three increments of 4 months, 3 months, 3 months, respectively. This is illustrated in *Figure 21*.

Each increment produces a chunk of the system you could deliver if you chose to. You get continuous staging of your system, which raises morale, lets you fix process problems (including antagonistic developers), and gives you dependable progress measures. The increments give you assurance that you will be able to show your executives the system segment at the end of 10 months - the period they may consider as one increment.

V-W staging also gives you a handle on managing multiple teams in parallel.

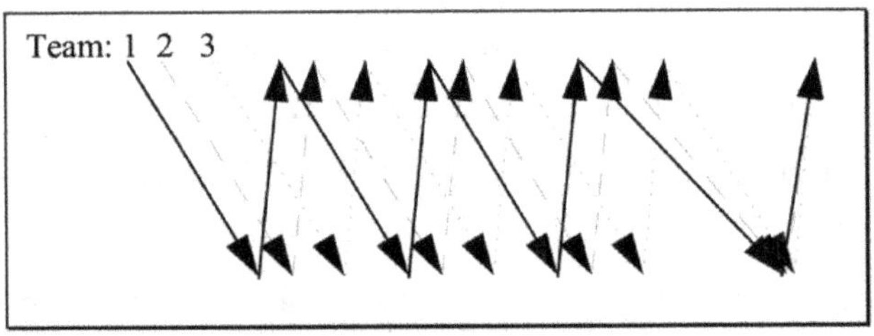

Figure 22, Chapter 7. Multiples teams synchronizing their deliveries.

One person from a 150-person, multi-year project told me that each team defined their increments on a two-week grid. Each increment could be 2, 4, 6, 8, or 10 weeks long, as needed. Based on the dependencies between the teams' deliveries, they worked out a schedule and an owner for each newly integrated version of the system. A team only participated in the creation of the new version if their increment ended on that 2-week boundary. Thus, the V's needed by the various teams differed in length, as their problem required, and the project manager had the interesting task of managing the dependencies and integration activities. A multi-team V-W is shown in *Figure 22*.

I know of one project which successfully used increments 1 week long! They worked in an environment in which priorities were constantly changing. To keep up with the changing priorities, they broke all work into one-week chunks. Each Monday morning, they met to arrange their work assignments for that week. While this situation is extreme and a bit confronting for most developers, the technique did allow them to track the company's needs and get the necessary software out.

Most project teams say they feel comfortable with increments 1-4 months long. There is overhead with picking up and putting down work, which causes them to prefer the longer increments.

One Line Summary:

Increments let you improve your development process.

Iterations and V-W Staging

Iterative development *is a rework scheduling strategy in which time is set aside to revise and improve parts of the system.* It does not presuppose incremental development, but works very well with it.

The phrase "iterative development" does not, by itself, indicate how many deliverables get revised, or when the revision happens. You have great freedom in choosing whether to revise requirements or only design, whether to treat the revisions as separate increments, or embed them within the increments. Iterative development does not mean that there is a free-for-all with no delivery targets, and you should not accept arguments that say it does.

Iterations are difficult to schedule because you recognize that your knowledge is inaccurate, without knowing exactly what.

The rewards of doing iterative development are that you:

- **Reduce risk.** You think you heard what your users want and need - but did you, really? Your team assures you that the new technology will handle your work load - but will it really? Iterative development gives you a chance to schedule a first look at key parts of the system without having to ship it. In many cases, that saves you from an embarrassing first shipment, or even a non-shipment.
- **Improve quality**. Even if you are close to correct on the algorithm or user interface, it is fairly inexpensive to add two

weeks during initial development, and get the algorithm, design, or user interface tuned properly before shipment.

- **Improve communication**. Scheduling a pre-release look at the system lets the users, executives and other teams see what your team is doing.
- **Ensure that you are delivering what your clientele can use**. Sometimes people ask for a feature not knowing what it will mean to get it. Often, they can only tell if that is really what they need when they see it. Iterative development lets them ensure that what they request is what they can really use.

You want to reduce risk when you are using a new, key algorithm, when you are trying a new technology such as objects, client server, or networking, when you are using a new vendor, when you have new staff, when you are trying a new process. You may not know the performance of your database. You may not really trust the users who are giving you your requirements. You therefore deploy the system in an early release, and let people examine it.

You feel confident in your staff, so you don't need to plan rework time into the schedule, you think. How confident are you? What is your fallback strategy should you discover just before delivery that the response time through the network and database is unacceptable? That the users really do not like the system?

The "system integration" period is a time when faulty assumptions come to light. It is, however, an expensive moment to discover mistakes, and planned to make working things come together. It is less traumatic to plan a period to discover the ways in which the system pieces do not fit, and to schedule a rework period after that to get them to fit.

Quality will certainly improve if you set time aside to evaluate what you have done and redo parts of it. Almost certainly you need this improvement at the user interface. Not only are you unlikely to get the screen optimal the first time, experience shows that you are unlikely to get the functions of the system right the first time. People giving requirements just forget to say some things, or say them with an unknown bias, or the people listening miss something, or hear with an unknown bias.

Quality improvements also come in the infrastructure. Both algorithms and technical design get better over time. The improved architecture will be easier to learn and more efficient. Object-oriented frameworks are designed to support variation, but it is almost impossible to guess correctly just what variation will be encountered. For framework development, therefore, revision should be planned.

Early examination is a two-edged sword. You reduce risk by finding out early whether your design is adequate. This saves you failing to ship or shipping a defective system. On the other side, you add risk by permitting the discovery that you need to rework something. The added risk is a worse schedule delay than you anticipated.

The drawings that follow are a schematized rendition of iterative development.

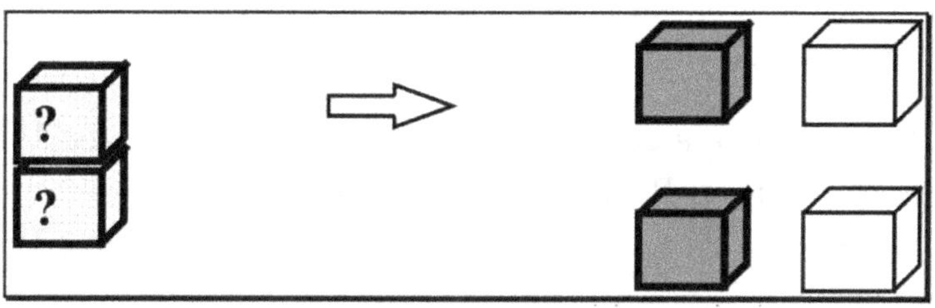

Figure 23, Chapter 7. Iterative development is improving content of existing modules.

Figure 23 shows on the left two portions of the system being developed incrementally. They are dotted to show that they are relatively complete. They contain question marks to show that there is some open question about them. They have been developed according to schedule. The next stage in the schedule calls for them to be evaluated, so the question marks can be removed. The right part of the figure shows them reworked, ready to be fit in with the next portion of the system.

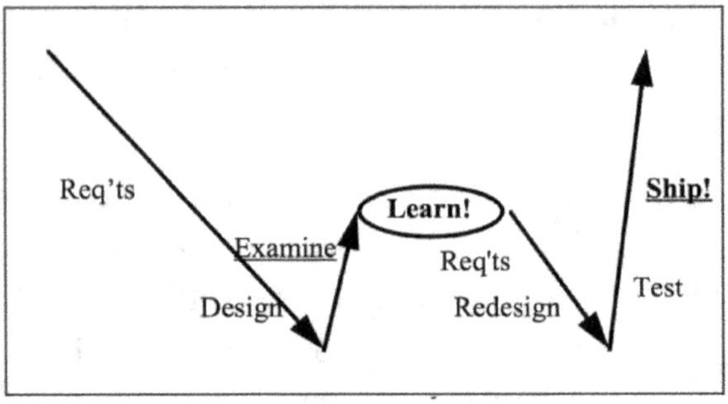

Figure 24, Chapter 7. Iterative development in linear time.

Figure 24 shows the iterations unrolled, using the V-W staging notation.

As usual, requirements precede design, which precedes testing. Testing, in this case, means examination. After examination, the sequence is repeated until the risk is low and the system is ready to ship.

Both incremental and iterative strategies provide a chance to reduce ignorance and improve. Incremental lets you improve your process. Iterative development primarily lets you improve your product. They work well together.

Iterative development certainly does cost more time - than delivering a low-quality system. Planning the iterations allows you to predict and control those costs.

One Line Summary:

Iterations let you improve the quality of your product.

Combining Increments and Iterations

Increments and iterations do not require each other, but they work well together. A useful strategy is to create, for the end-user functionality, 4-month increments, each with 3 iterations (see *Figure 25*). The infrastructure has its own increments, but it will have iterations that span the function increments, because feedback to the design of the infrastructure comes from delivering functionality. Here is how it works:

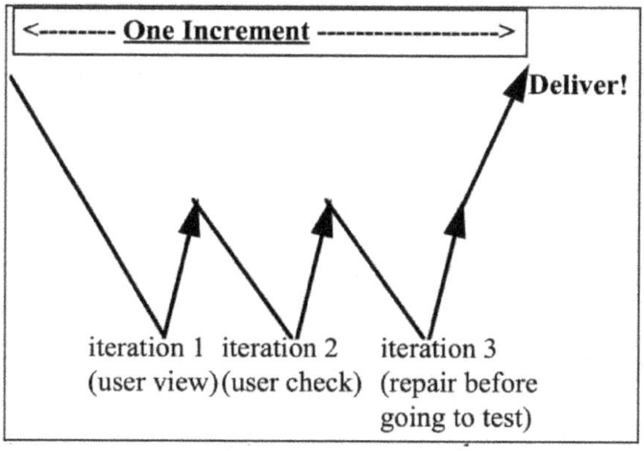

Figure 25, Chapter 7. Iterations fit within an increment.

Ask what the users really need to have first. Ask what they must have second, third, and so forth. Combine user needs with the technical dependencies to determine what must be in the first release, or increment. Choose the smallest acceptable amount of functionality for the first increment. The architecture and first iteration of the infrastructure belong in the first increment.

Within each increment, allow a period of quiet time for design to happen. As soon as there is a design of the screen and screen flows, show them to the users and learn how closely the design seems to meet need. This is the first, "shallow" iteration of the user function. Build that function as well as is known how, then show the working system to the users. This is the first "deep" iteration. At this point, plan on having surprised users and developers. They thought they have communicated well, but now they find how they managed to misspeak and misinterpret.

Do a second deep iteration, and show the newly working system to the users. This shows that the necessary corrections were made and catches remaining small errors. The third and final deep iteration results in putting that portion of the system into system test.

There are two particular dangers to iterations:

- Prototypitis
- The Death Spiral

Prototypitis is a well-known and distressingly common ailment in which the development team never stabilize their design or interfaces, but simply rework a prototype in the hope that it will eventually become a product. *Project Manfred* fell into this trap. Prototypitis can befall a project of any size. I have seen it on a 200-person project.

The response to prototypitis is incremental development *with delivery*. Have the development team commit to a delivery. Nothing sharpens the mind like having to deliver in two to four weeks. If the design is mildly insufficient, it can be improved on a subsequent release. If it is badly insufficient, that will show up. Even if delivery has to be cancelled, the key issues will become apparent and you can address them.

The death spiral is less well known, but attaches to iterations through the worries of the management. The death spiral runs like this:

1. Management asks for a schedule. Team creates one.
2. Team develops iteration 1.
3. Management gets worried, asks for a schedule. Team creates another.
4. After the pause to create a new schedule, team starts working on iteration 2.
5. Management gets more worried because the pause stalled development. They ask for a new schedule.

...and so on. The project dies because there is never enough time to make progress on the design.

There are two parts to getting out of the death spiral, both of which fall under the general strategy *Someone Always Makes Progress* (**Risk Reduction Strategies**).

The first is a "timebox". During a timebox, your permit no interruptions to the development, whether to change requirements or ask for future schedule estimates. The timebox gives your team a period of protection for some progress to be made. The other part is the strategy *Sacrifice One Person* (**Risk Reduction Strategies**). When a schedule needs to be made, the team draws straws or otherwise selects one person to create the new schedule, while the rest of the team keeps making progress.

Getting out of the death spiral is as difficult as ending prototypitis. Take both seriously.

* * * * *

Here is an Eyewitness Account by Luke Hohmann, taken from his book *Journey of a Software Engineer*, with permission from Prentice-Hall. This account relates how he shifted people from a single-V model (waterfall), to a multiple-V iterative model. He does it by giving them permission to be wrong at certain times in the project.

"<u>Burn Some Pancakes</u>" (Luke Hohmann)

> *In one assignment I had to find a way to change the development process of a team of developers. As you can guess, prior management enforced an extremely strict waterfall model. In a waterfall process, you are expected to create complete outcomes from each process before moving to the next. The only problem was that my predecessor had elevated the practice of waterfall development to an anal-retentive art: developers were expected to produce nearly perfect outcomes! As I tried to change their overall development process from waterfall to an iterative one, I encountered extreme resistance. In the past, the staff learned if they did not practice waterfall they would be punished. How could I change their attitude? The only thing I could think of was to introduce them to the burnt pancake process model. Burnt pancakes?*
>
> *I am not the best cook in the world, but every now and then I like to make pancakes. The trouble is, I always seem to make the skillet too hot for the first pancake. By now, I have accepted the fact I will, with a high degree of probability, burn the first pancake, throw it out, fix the temperature, and start again. To encourage my staff to get an initial system completed, I would ask them to "burn some pancakes" (i.e., create an initial system), with the assurance I wouldn't "eat" (i.e., judge) the first pancake. At first, they responded tentatively. The idea became quickly adopted when they learned I meant what I said: I would not judge them on incomplete outcomes.*

> *Within a few weeks they had fully adopted the approach, making it a part of the culture of the group. When asked for an outcome, staff members would respond: "How edible does it have to be?" If I responded with: "fairly edible", they knew I was looking for a rather complete outcome. On the other hand, if I responded with: "completely burnt", they knew I just wanted to briefly assess their activity to ensure they were headed in the right direction. In no way would they be judged on the outcome. Soon, the entire team was talking about pancakes, and productivity started to improve.*

Following Luke Hohmann's lead, I introduced the burnt-pancake model into a project where there was extreme sensitivity to being wrong or producing an incomplete system. I also found it to work well. The burnt-pancake model is a way of managing expected "accuracy" on a project, which is useful while getting started with iterations (see **Managing Precision, Accuracy and Scale**).

One Line Summary:

> *Use iterations within increments to reduce risk.*

Your Project Increments

This section shows a Production project as a first increment, a second increment, and a succession of next increments. The first two are different, the rest should look fairly much the same. Each increment is approximately four months long.

The S.W.A.T.-type project and Investigative-type project have different timelines, but were both discussed in enough detail in the earlier parts of the book. A Committed-type project can be modeled on the Production project plan.

In the sections that follow, I reintroduce the fearsome being that some of your parents scared you with as children - the "boogeyman". According to the old story, the boogeyman is a terrible person who hides in dark places. When you are not behaving yourself, he will jump out and carry you off to some horrible place. Where in normal life the boogeyman is apocryphal, on a software development project he is real

- he is What You Don't Know You Don't Know (which I shall abbreviate WYDKYDK).

Although the boogeyman is indeed waiting for you on your project, if you follow this project setup, you will find out where he is hiding, and be able to deal with him. The early parts of your project have two goals, and one of them is to find the boogeyman (learn WYDKYDK). If you do not take care of this, he will indeed jump out at you when you least expect it.

Increment 1

The purpose of the first increment is to:

1. Establish an architecture for the software,
2. Deliver feedback to the project sponsors and users,
3. Develop good patterns of programming and designing,
4. Find the boogeyman and learn WYDKYDK.

There are many possible ways of running a successful first increment. This one builds on the earlier descriptions of teams, incremental development, methodology and staffing. I also state the intentions of the plan, so that when you choose to do things differently, you can protect the intentions.

The target is to deliver a functioning base architecture for the software, with one, small piece of functionality.

Split people into two teams:

- The architecture team
- The training team

The architecture team. The architecture team consists of your best designers. They will do three things, which will hold the project together over time.

- They will design the "large design" of the system, and how critical details get handled, all of which I shall refer to as the architecture of system. It includes partitioning across platforms and functions, the philosophy of handling errors, the philosophy of handling persistence, the philosophy of handling user interface commands. These things must be known for a group of developers to reinforce each other with their different work styles, as opposed to competing with each other.

- They will both design and build a base infrastructure, the "plumbing" of the system. The infrastructure contains the object-oriented frameworks that carrying user interface commands, transaction completion, error notification, searching, and so on. It is built and tested.
- They will design, build and deliver a few of the end user functions. This has two uses. First, it ensures that their architecture works. They will find and repair any flaws in their design faster than anyone else. Second, it establishes a pattern of programming for other programmers to follow. Your other developers will see how these, your best designers, design and write code. They will use these designs to establish their own design habits. Most probably, they will copy the sample code and modify it to their need. Let there be good code for them to copy!

The training team. The training team consists of a mentor for every 5-10 novices. Their purpose is to spend the first increment becoming fluent in object design and programming, and to deliver a very small piece of function. The mentor should spend at least an hour each day working individually with each trainee.

The training team will go to several weeks of classes, where they will learn the language, OO design thinking, and the tools. They may spend another 2 weeks working on a small problem from start to finish, to get the feel of an entire cycle.

Finally the training team will be given a relatively simple section of work to do. The mentor will work with the architecture team to set up design and coding templates that can be copied. They can get started, but will almost certainly have to make changes along the way to accommodate the changes in the templates as the architecture team makes fixes.

The intentions. If you set up the first increment differently, try to preserve these intentions:

1. Develop a strong statement of how the system is put together. This "architecture" provides coherence as the project staff changes.
2. Develop acceptable templates for designing and programming. Most developers find it easier to work from existing code from than to develop afresh. Setting good templates in,place early allows novices to learn faster, and everyone to work faster.
3. Deliver something to the users. It may not be much, but it shows the project sponsors that the team delivers, and it shows the users what they are getting, allowing them to make better suggestions on the next cycle.
4. Work through a full cycle of development. This provides the learning effect described in **Incremental Development**. The second increment will go more smoothly once everyone knows what the full cycle looks like.
5. Find the boogeyman (WYDKYDK). You simply cannot know, as you start, where your big problems will be. Will it be that the users are constantly changing their minds? That the developers cannot follow standards, or will not document? Or that the error rate is very high? Or that the test-fix cycle goes on forever? Or ...? Going through the entire cycle through delivery lets you examine every component of your process and discover the ones that needs attention. Finding the boogeyman is a critical success factor. Find him early, and develop a response. If you do not find him within the first 6-8 months and take steps, he will jump out at you later, at some unexpected and critically bad moment.
6. Develop the habit of delivering. The habit of delivering is a second critical success factor. It anchors in everyone's mind the very important notion that "this team delivers". The presence of that

thought or its opposite determines what the project team thinks it can do.

Two stories.

We already studied *Project Ingrid* (**A Study Project**).

It failed its first increment: it exceeded its schedule, had poor morale and no apparent chance at recovery. However, they had only failed at one increment, and were able to detect this failure after only four months. They found their boogeymen: their staff, their teaming structure and their process. In fact, their boogeymen were everything except the project management and the incremental work plan. They recovered the project by revising staff , teaming and process.

Project Ingrid delivered on the second increment. They learned they could deliver, and learned how to deliver. At the end of the second increment they were on sound ground.

Project Winifred started off badly, too.

The first increment was delivered, but reduced in function. There was no architecture to speak of, quality, communications and morale were both low. Their delivering established that they could deliver, setting the foundation for the eventual success of the project. They also discovered their boogeymen: the absence of architecture, absence of a technical leader, and a long Quality Assurance / Test cycle.

On the second increment, they created an architecture concurrently with adding function. They delivered on time again, this time with slightly higher quality and morale. By now, the team was clear that they could deliver their system. They found other boogeymen, which included an overly rigid process unable to handle shifting requirements. However, there was not much question they could adapt to solve these problems.

Over the increments, the architecture improved, the design and code quality improved. They found various problems on the different increments and were able to change much of the way they worked. In their case, persistence became a habit. If they had not put out the first, "bubblegum" release, it is quite likely that the project would have been canceled.

I include these two stories to impress on you the importance of actually completing and delivering the first increment.

One Line Summary:

Establish the architecture, deliver one function, find the Boogeyman.

Increment 2

The purpose of the second increment is to:

1. Repair the major mistakes discovered in the first increment,
2. Establish or tune the software architecture,
3. Create a process and teaming that works for you,
4. Settle on good development habits.
5. Deliver more function to the users.

Pause and learn. Review the first increment. This may take half a day. Remember that the boogeyman was what you didn't know that you didn't know. What unforeseen things kept you from performing the way you thought you would? What mistakes did you make? To get your project to succeed, you may have to change some of your closest-held wishes and beliefs. While I was a programmer, I thought project managers, project plans and object diagrams were all useless. Obviously, I have changed those beliefs by now. Some managers believe they must have all the requirements and time estimates before they can step into the project. Those managers fail until they change their beliefs. Before your second increment is your best chance to locate possibly faulty habits and try one some new ones.

If you feel forced to change something you hold dear, consider all the new strategies as "hypotheses." By doing this, you reserve the right to change back or change to another approach. That attitude alone may save your project.

Review these aspects of the project:

- *Process.* Most large project have too much paperwork, which slows down the communication, flexibility and learning. What can you do in the process to let learning propagate faster through the teams? What paperwork can you drop? Some projects have too little paperwork, with the result that one team's decisions do not get communicated to the people who need it.
- *Team structure.* Why are decisions not getting communicated between teams? Do you need to put people together who are apart? Perhaps you have teams which fight against each other. Consider creating teams around function if they weren't before, or around design components if they weren't before, or making them cross-functional.
- *Standards.* It is quite common at this point to discover that there is too much diversity in design styles and programming styles. Get the technical leaders together to settle on writing, designing and programming standards. Think about how you will get the standards followed.
- *Linkage to the users.* Did you really deliver what the users need? How often did real users come and see the system? Most projects need to strengthen this aspect.
- *Architecture.* The first increment's architecture often is built on wishful thinking. What do you know now that you did not know then? Decide what your new architecture should be.
- *Training.* What do you now know your staff needs to know? Usually, this is the time to set up some more training.

Move on. Everything that was true about the first increment is true again, except that now you are starting with an architecture and people who know what they didn't know the first time. Deliver again, to develop the pattern of delivering regularly. It will become a habit. This second increment is the start of your way of working successfully.

One Line Summary:

Pause & learn, revise & persist.

Increment N

By the time you reach the Nth increment, you have the habits and patterns of success. There are only two dangers to watch out for: falling asleep and overexpanding. If you have paid attention to this book, you will not fall asleep, but rather, your project will get more efficient over time.

Project Ingrid was so successful that it was cloned, split, copied and distributed. The original 24-person team grew to over 100 people spread over several locations. The techniques that worked so well on the single-site project did not work when scaled up that way.

Which moves us into a later chapter, larger projects and more people.

One Line Summary:

> *Always recall how you became successful.*

Back to 2026

I hope you get the point by now:

- Until you actually deliver something, you have not exercised your entire process, and troubles will still be hiding (the *boogeyman*).
- Only after you deliver can you accurately reflect on how the different parts of your process interact (the *gestalt round trip*).

That is, only after you deliver something to real users can you see your process in its entirety and decide what to change for next time.

This is the basis for saying "Incremental development helps improve the process."

Of course, all this requires you to actually sit together after the delivery and reflect on exactly this topic. I take that for granted, since it became the cornerstone for all my work in 1992. However, not many teams actually reflect on their process deliberately, so for them, delivering doesn't obviously link to process improvements.

On the other hand, every demo and delivery gives you feedback on the product. Thus, "Iterative development helps improve the product." That should be self-evident.

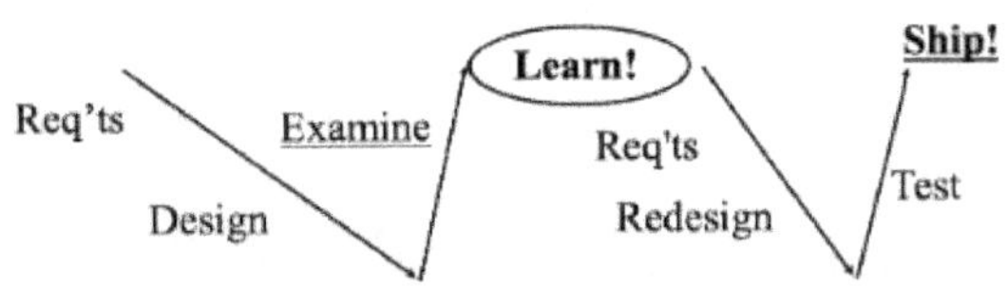

Figure 26, Chapter 7. V-W staging with an iteration and an increment.

This V-W picture should become its own meme. The first V shows one run through the development process to produce a demo or prototype. It does not go into production. Thus, the learning that happens is about the *product*. "Iterative development helps improve the product."

The second V shows a second run through the development process, possibly changing the requirements themselves, and continuing into production, going through the deployment process. It is at this point that gaps and overlaps in the entire process become visible.

Thus, the learning that happens is about the *process.* "Incremental development helps improve the product.

Here's the mug 😊

Figure 27, Chapter 7. Incremental and iterative: The mug.

Part 2. How

8. The Business Person Version

Construct fine-grained growth stages from use cases while developing and deploying.

This chapter is adapted from "*The Mini-Book on Use Cases*," where I show how to construct fine-grained growth stages from a system specified with use cases.

You don't need to know what a use case is to learn how to grow business requests for evaluation and delivery. Once you see how to do it with use cases, you can apply the same thinking to whatever you use to make your large-scale view of what is being requested.

Preamble: What and Why Use Cases?

A use case is a written description of all the interactions needed for a user using your system to achieve a goal they might have.

Buy a product ← (The goal of the primary actor)
System: Order Processing System ← (The system under discussion)
Primary Actor: Clerk ← (The primary actor)
Goal Level: Sea level ← (Goal level: kite / sea / fish)

Main success scenario:
1. Clerk identifies customer, item, quantity. ← (Action steps: typically 3-9 steps full sentences showing who takes the action, & their goal)
2. System accepts and queues order.

Extensions:
1a. Low credit but 'preferred' customer: ← (Condition needing different action)
System gives them credit anyway. ← (Action steps to handle that condition)
1b. Low credit & not "preferred":
Clerk accepts only prepayment.
2a. Low on stock & customer accepts rain-check:
Clerk reduces order to available stock level.

Figure 28, Chapter 8. A use case with its parts labeled.

Figure 28 shows the structure and an example of a use case. The use case captures the user's goal as its title, then goes through all the steps the user and the system take individually and together to accomplish that goal. All alternative and failure possibilities are considered and collected as alternative scenarios or extension fragments attached to the main success scenario. It even includes interactions system has with other systems as needed for that goal. It is a full spec of the behavior of the system with respect to that user goal.

The power of use cases is:

- They capture all the usage pathways your development team will need to consider;
- They are easily read, understood, and passed around the organization.

Being both readable and complete is a rare combination, so they are my favorite way to capture the behavior of a system.

Here is the use case we will examine in detail in this chapter. It is a substantial use case that will take multiple iterations to implement, and therefore benefits from fine-grained incremental development.

Register for Courses

Student using Course Enrollment System, User-goal level

Main success scenario:

1. Student requests to construct a schedule.
2. The system prepares a blank schedule form.
3. The system gets available courses from Course Catalog System.
4. Student selects up to four primary and two alternate course offerings.
5. For each course, the system verifies that the Student has the necessary prerequisites and adds the Student to the course, marking Student as "enrolled" for that course in the schedule.
6. The Student indicates the schedule is complete, and the system saves it.

Extensions:

1a. Student already has a schedule:
System brings up the current version of the Student's schedule for editing instead of creating a new one.

1b. Current semester is closed and next semester is not yet open:
System lets Student look at existing schedules but not create any.

3a. Course Catalog System does not respond:
The system notifies the Student and the use case ends.

5a. Course full or Student has not fulfilled all prerequisites:
System disables selection of that course and notifies the Student.

Notice, in particular, sentence 3 in the main success scenario: "The system gets available courses from Course Catalog System." This is an example of the system under design needing information from another, existing system. We refer to an external system our system needs to interact with as a "secondary actor." The person or system with the goal that drives the use case is called the "primary actor."

Avoid Decision Inventory While Capturing Use Cases

The following is a generic incremental growing strategy for capturing use cases in parallel with development, so that you don't build up decision inventory too early.

The theme here is to keep constructing a broad, coarse-grained view that allows you to narrow your focus on the next thing to expand. What we are after is a way to spy trouble spots early without going into too many details too soon, to let you steer your decision-making energy to fit the risk.

Here are the generic 7 steps:

Step 1.

> Write down in a paragraph to half a page the purpose of the system, who it should please, its reason for existing.
>
> This is your touchpoint for everything that follows. It keeps you centered. Yes, of course you can change it. At half a page, it is the shortest description of your system and the easiest to update.

From the perspective of decisions, it contains the smallest number of decisions needed to describe your system. You decision inventory has officially started.

Step 2.

> List all the primary and secondary actors that will interact with your system.
>
> This list is not likely to change much. Together with your short statement of purpose, this helps you direct your energies.

From the perspective of decisions, this is the first expansion of unvalidated decisions. This list is the first one you will scan for both early value and for potential trouble spots.

Step 3.

Brainstorm and list the main sea-level goals your primary actors will have. This is the first draft of your *"Actor-Goal"* list. You will, of course, modify it over time, so it is handy that it is in the shortest, most readable and easiest-to-modify form.

Stare at your actor-goal list carefully. This is the list of services your system will offer the outside world. Trim it to the few most important, most critical ones to develop and deploy, whether for early value or because you suspect there is a risk hiding in there somewhere. That risk could be around development, deployment, or in acceptance by the users.

Make sure the lead developers also work on this list. Have them highlight those that they sense will give them development trouble. You may want to develop a bit of those ones early, just to manage the development risk.

I once saw an executive and senior product manager work over their actor-goal list for several weeks as they looked through all the possible next stages of their initiative and tighten their focus.

Step 4.

Write a high-level (kite) use case that covers all those early and critical sea-level use cases. One or two should be sufficient.

Hunt for failures and extension conditions to your kite-level use case. Those will indicate something about the complexity in your system that you otherwise might not think about yet.

What you just did is to create a broad, coarse-grained view of the system as a whole. It is the smallest set of decisions that allows you to

- view the whole system in a way that lets you scan for value and for trouble and
- minimizes your decision inventory at this point.

This is what we are after: the least writing, the fewest unvalidated decisions, the easiest to scan, that allows us to find value and risk.

Step 5.

Choose some sea-level use cases to investigate closely. Expand them one at a time in two steps:

- Write the main success scenario carefully.
- Brainstorm and list *all* the conditions that could cause *any* different behavior.

List the conditions, but *don't* dig into their handling just yet. Listing the conditions is well worth the energy at this point, as well as being rather fun and easy. Working out how to handle those conditions is hard, tiring, and best left for later, in a just-in-time manner.

In terms of energy and decisions, it takes a *lot* of work to write down the condition-handling business rules. Days, to weeks, sometimes. Don't do that until you need to. When do you need to? That's why you and your tech lead are scanning these sketches.

Step 6.

Review your work with business and tech experts. Select the extensions to expand in detail, the use cases scenarios and extensions to develop for early value and early risk mitigation.

Step 7.

From here on, you are in a game of repeating step 6 forever:

1. Add scenarios to add value.
2. Expand extensions to discover complicated or hidden rules.
3. Do these in time to have them ready for the programmers.

From here on, you are in a game of peeking ahead at what you *might* need, detailing things you think will cause trouble or deliver value. You are balancing three things:

- Careful exploration of the business value. Tune what you write, develop, and deploy to what will be used and valued.
- Careful exploration of risk and complexity. Keep looking ahead at failure conditions, because those often cost disproportionate amounts of work to handle.
- Careful control of the energy expended in writing. It costs a lot of energy to write a request for software, whether you are writing use cases or any other form.

In the end, you will have to describe, the developers will have to program, and the testers will have to test every possible situation. You just don't need to do it all at once.

Gather Requirements & Control Risk While Developing and Deploying

A totally finished set of use cases captures all scenarios with all extension handling. However, if you write them all at once, you have spent a huge amount of time creating a terrible stack of unvalidated decisions, blocking early delivery of value and filling your organization with internal inventory.

In most cases, you don't have to write, develop, or deliver them all at once. For certain fixed-price / fixed-scope contracts you do, but even there, look for creative ways to reduce your decision inventory before you start developing (to get feedback and find errors).

For the purpose of this chapter, I will assume that you have permission to expand the use cases in parallel with developing what you already have written. That is, you have completed step 6 of the previous sequence and have something concrete and valuable to start developing while continuing with step 7 in parallel.

I would just like to note that this is where use cases meet project management. It is not about what a use case looks like when it's done that is important, but how the use case and other requirements decisions evolves along with your conversations with the users, the developers and the business model.

Find the Walking Skeleton.

We will draw heavily on the concept of a *walking skeleton*, which forms the armature for our papier-mâché sculpture (see Chapter 4: *Slicing versus growing*), our first *growth stage.*

> *A Walking Skeleton is a tiny implementation of a process or system that supports a small end-to-end function.*

The idea of *walking skeleton* applies everywhere, from your business process to your use cases, to individual business rules, to your technical system. Having a *walking skeleton* in place allows you to grow your system in very fine slices, really very much like adding very thin papier-mâché sheets to that armature of the elephant.

In the case of our use cases, the kite-level use cases describe your overall business processes. Choose the thinnest path through the top one you want to develop – that will make for the *walking skeleton* of your business process.

Then take the thinnest path through the most important sea-level use cases you will develop. That will make the *walking skeleton* of the use case.

When you get to a complicated business rule, find the thinnest meaningful subset of it. That will make the *walking skeleton* of the business rule.

Your development team will be doing something similar on the technical architecture: What is the thinnest connection of technical elements needed to deliver a round-trip transaction in the system? That will be the technical *walking skeleton.*

Everybody needs to think this way, from the sponsoring executive, through the business experts to the development team. Working this way allows you to minimize your internal inventory of unvalidated decisions, while delivering value the soonest and finding things to improve the earliest possible.

You can read more about the *walking skeleton* concept here: [https://web.archive.org/web/20140329201356/http://alistair.cockburn.us/Walking+skeleton]

Okay, enough talk Let's walk through two examples in detail.

A Simple Example: Buy a Candy

Let's start with something simple. Our elephant is nothing bigger than a candy machine: just big enough to see the *walking skeleton* and some very thin slices to lay over it.

Here is our elephant:

"Buy a candy"

System: Candy machine *Primary Actor:* Customer *Goal Level:* Sea

Main success scenario:

1. Customer selects candy. Machine shows price & allows money to be put in.
2. Customer puts in the money.
3. Machine drops the candy and the change.

Extensions:

1a. No more of that candy:
    Machine shows "Empty" and doesn't accept money.

1b. No change available in the machine:
    Machine puts up "Exact change required."

3a. No change available in the machine:
    Machine drops the candy but no change.

We start by asking ourselves: what is the *least* we can develop that will produce a functioning machine?

Thinking about the lessons from the Elephant Carpaccio exercise, we are looking for something that is too simple to put into use but which still connects the parts of the machine to show the baby system working. This is one of the *demo* growth stages – the technical *walking skeleton* – we saw in that exercise. You may be surprised at how often you can actually use such a small system.

For a *walking skeleton* or slice 1 of the candy machine, we need:

- Some way to select a candy. We can get away with just one candy. "Selecting" is nothing more than pushing a button.
- The candy is free. We can add pricing and coin handling later.
- The machine drops the candy on the button push.

That's clearly not a commercial version of the system, since the candy is free. However, we now have a functioning machine, we've reduced risk and opened feedback on all our decisions.

For a small commercial version (slice 2), we add some simple coin handling. Notice how we are adding decisions and checking them out one or a small number at a time:

- The machine accepts and counts the money put in, but doesn't give change. This gets us the calculating of coins and prices.
- The candy only gets dropped when there is sufficient money.
- If there is a coin slot that needs to be opened, this also forces testing that the coin slot opens when the selection is made and closes when the candy is dropped.

For slice 3, we might add more products and buttons, still all at the same price, still needing exact change. This might be a viable deployment version, if slice 2 wasn't sufficient.

For slice 4, we add different prices, and so on, until we have the entire use case.

Here is the fraction of the use case implemented in the first delivery:

> **"Buy Candy" delivery 1**: one price, exact change only
> **Main success scenario**:
> 1. Customer selects candy *(only one possible)*; machine shows the price (*only one price supported*) and allows money to be put in.
> 2. Customer puts in the money.
> 3. Machine drops the candy ~~and the change~~ when the price of the candy is reached.
>
> **Extensions**:
> ~~1a. No more of that candy:~~
> ~~Machine shows "Empty" and doesn't accept money.~~
> 1b. No change available in the machine:
> Machine puts up "Exact change required."
> 3a. No change available in the machine:
> Machine drops the candy, but no change.

There you go, our baby elephant, built in four growth stages, with one technical *walking skeleton*, one business *walking skeleton* or MVP, and two more growth stages where the business can vary its strategy quite a bit.

Now let's work through at a more complicated example to see the full set of strategies available to us for slicing and growing in a fine-grained manner.

A Richer Example, in Detail.

In what follows, I present six ideas for finding thin slices in your use cases. The use case *Register for Courses* illustrates them nicely.

To make it easier to follow the development sequence, I copy the use case out each time to show each increment of the growing system, with the new part in *underlined italics*.

Here is the use case:

Register for Courses
Student using Course Enrollment System, User-goal level
Main success scenario:
1. Student requests to construct a schedule.
2. The system prepares a blank schedule form.
3. The system gets available courses from Course Catalog System.
4. Student selects up to four primary and two alternate course offerings.
5. For each course, the system verifies that the Student has the necessary prerequisites and adds the Student to the course, marking Student as "enrolled" for that course in the schedule.
6. The Student indicates the schedule is complete, and the system saves it.

Extensions:
1a. Student already has a schedule:
System brings up the current version of the Student's schedule for editing instead of creating a new one.
1b. Current semester is closed and next semester is not yet open:
System lets Student look at existing schedules but not create any.
3a. Course Catalog System does not respond:
The system notifies the Student and the use case ends.
5a. Course full or Student has not fulfilled all prerequisites:
System disables selection of that course and notifies the Student.

That's actually a really rich use case. We'll end up with over a dozen growth stages. Let's walk through the ideas you might use:

Idea 1. Find and develop the use case's *Walking Skeleton.*

The first and last lines of the main success scenario often make a *Walking Skeleton* of the business process and a great first development slice.

Main success scenario:

1. Student requests to construct a schedule. CES prepares a blank schedule form.
2. CES gets available courses from the Course Catalog System.
3. Student selects up to four primary and two alternate course offerings.
4. For each course, CES verifies that the Student has the necessary prerequisites and adds the Student to the course, marking the Student as "enrolled" for that course in the schedule.
5. The Student indicates the schedule is complete. CES saves it.

Let's pick out the first and the last steps:

Main success scenario:

1. Student requests to construct a schedule. CES prepares a blank schedule form.

5. The Student indicates the schedule is complete. CES saves it.

That is the *Walking Skeleton* of the use case: the system constructs an empty schedule and saves it. It makes a great first slice.

Notice how we did this with the candy machine:

Main success scenario:

1. Customer selects candy.

3. Machine drops the candy and the change.

Look for this pattern in your writing.

Idea 2: Separate out each sentence and each extension.

Let's continue with that same use case. It is a hefty one and benefits from being sliced and programmed, even deployed, in stages.

Slice 1: The Walking Skeleton (as we have seen)

1. Student requests to construct a schedule. CES prepares a blank schedule form.
5. The Student indicates the schedule is complete. CES saves it.

Slice 2: But the Student already has a schedule

1. Student requests to construct a schedule. CES prepares a blank schedule form.
5. The Student indicates the schedule is complete. CES saves it.

Extensions:

1a. Student already has a schedule: CES brings up the current version of the Student's schedule for editing instead of creating a new one.

Slice 3: Connect to the Course Catalog System (this one for risk reduction)

1. Student requests to construct a schedule. CES prepares a blank schedule form.
2. *CES gets available courses from the Course Catalog System.*
5. The Student indicates the schedule is complete. CES saves it.

Extensions:

1a. Student already has a schedule: CES brings up the current version of the Student's schedule for editing instead of creating a new one.

Slice 4: Course Catalog System doesn't respond

1. Student requests to construct a schedule. CES prepares a blank schedule form.
2. CES gets available courses from the Course Catalog System.
5. The Student indicates the schedule is complete. CES saves it.

Extensions:

1a. Student already has a schedule: CES brings up the current version of the Student's schedule for editing instead of creating a new one.

2a. Course Catalog System does not respond:
CES notifies the Student and the use case ends.

To implement step 3, we'll want several slices. This is explained in detail in Idea 3, "Implement just part of a step as its own slice".

Slices 5, 6 & 7: Student selects courses

1. Student requests to construct a schedule. CES prepares a blank schedule form.
2. CES gets available courses from the Course Catalog System.
3. *Student selects up to four primary and two alternate course offerings.*
5. The Student indicates the schedule is complete. CES saves it.

Extensions:

1a. Student already has a schedule: CES brings up the current version of the Student's schedule for editing instead of creating a new one.
2a. Course Catalog System does not respond:
CES notifies the Student and the use case ends.

Step 4 also suggests several development slices. Since the original extension 4a covered both full course and missing prerequisites, we have to separate those into different extensions, 4a and 4b:

Slices 8 & 9: CES enrolls the Student in the courses, checking prerequisites

1. Student requests to construct a schedule. CES prepares a blank schedule form.
2. CES gets available courses from the Course Catalog System.
3. Student selects up to four primary and two alternate course offerings.
4. *For each course, CES verifies that the Student has the necessary prerequisites and adds the Student to the course, marking the Student as "enrolled" for that course in the schedule.*
5. The Student indicates the schedule is complete. CES saves it.

Extensions:

1a. Student already has a schedule: CES brings up the current version of the Student's schedule for editing instead of creating a new one.
2a. Course Catalog System does not respond:
CES notifies the Student and the use case ends.
4a. Student has not fulfilled all prerequisites:
CES disables selection of that course and notifies the Student.
~~(4b. Course full: CES disables selection of that course and notifies the Student.)~~

Slice 10: Course full

1. Student requests to construct a schedule. CES prepares a blank schedule form.
2. CES gets available courses from the Course Catalog System.
3. Student selects up to four primary and two alternate course offerings.
4. For each course, CES verifies that the Student has the necessary prerequisites and adds the Student to the course, marking the Student as "enrolled" for that course in the schedule.
5. The Student indicates the schedule is complete. CES saves it.

Extensions:

1a. Student already has a schedule: CES brings up the current version of the Student's schedule for editing instead of creating a new one.

2a. Course Catalog System does not respond:
CES notifies the Student and the use case ends.

4a. Student has not fulfilled all prerequisites:
CES disables selection of that course and notifies the Student.

4b. Course full: CES disables selection of that course and notifies the Student.

Slice 11: Semester not in session (completing the use case)

1. Student requests to construct a schedule. CES prepares a blank schedule form.
2. CES gets available courses from the Course Catalog System.
3. Student selects up to four primary and two alternate course offerings.
4. For each course, CES verifies that the Student has the necessary prerequisites and adds the Student to the course, marking the Student as "enrolled" for that course in the schedule.
5. The Student indicates the schedule is complete. CES saves it.

Extensions:

1a. Student already has a schedule: CES brings up the current version of the Student's schedule for editing instead of creating a new one.

*1b. Current semester is closed and next semester is not yet open:
CES lets Student look at existing schedules, but not create new ones.*

2a. Course Catalog System does not respond:
CES notifies the Student and the use case ends.

4a. Student has not fulfilled all prerequisites:
CES disables selection of that course and notifies the Student.

4b. Course full: CES disables selection of that course and notifies the Student.

This may look preposterously fine-grained to you. However, my purpose in this section is to show you *how* to slice a use case for fine-grained incremental development. You are, of course, welcome to choose fatter slices on your own project. I am showing you my favorite slicing choices to give you a good example to copy.

Fine-grained slicing is valuable because it allows you to develop and test incrementally, to find errors and trouble spots early. Your system will be a lot more complicated than this example. In fact, even part of a step may require a lot of programming – which takes us to **Idea 3**.

Idea 3. Implement just part of a step as its own slice.

Steps 3 and 4 in Register for Courses are good candidates for slicing within a step. They are connected, so we have to take them together. There are several ways to slice, depending on what you like to defer.

If you defer prerequisites validation, you get the following sequence. We start with the *Walking Skeleton* of the business rule:

> Slice 5: Add one primary course, without checking prerequisites.
> Slice 6: Add up to four primary courses.
> Slice 7: Add the two alternatives.
> Slice 8: Check prerequisites and handle failure.

Let's look at those in detail.

Slice 5: Student selects 1 course, CES adds to the schedule, no prerequisites check

3. <u>Student selects just one course offering.</u>
4. <u>CES adds the Student to the course, marking the Student as "enrolled" for that course in the schedule.</u>

Slice 6: Student adds up to 4 primary courses, still no prerequisites check

3. Student selects <u>*up to four primary course offerings*</u>.
4. CES adds the Student to <u>*each course*</u>, marking the Student as "enrolled" for that course in the schedule.

Slice 7: Student also selects the alternate courses, still no prerequisites check

3. Student selects up to four primary and <u>*two alternate*</u> course offerings.
4. CES adds the Student to each course, marking the Student as "enrolled" for that course in the schedule.

Slice 8: Check prerequisites and handle failure

3. Student selects up to four primary and two alternate course offerings.
4. CES <u>*verifies that the Student has the necessary prerequisites for that course,*</u> adds the Student to each course, marking the Student as "enrolled" for that course in the schedule.

Extensions:

4a. Student has not fulfilled all prerequisites:
CES disables selection of that course and notifies the Student.

Personally, I prefer to check the prerequisites earlier, because it's "more different," that is, produces more learning, than just adding another course. This alternative strategy produces the slices (starting from the *Walking Skeleton*):

Slice 5: Add one primary course, without checking prerequisites.
Slice 6: Just one course, but check prerequisites. *(Notice we have to handle prerequisites failure right away!)*
Slice 7: Allow up to four primary courses.
Slice 8: Allow the two alternatives.

Slice 5: (Same as before, the Walking Skeleton of the business rule)

3. Student selects just one course offering.
4. CES adds the Student to the course, marking the Student as "enrolled" for that course in the schedule.

Slice 6: Just one course, but check prerequisites, handle prerequisites failure

3. Student selects just one course offering.
4. CES *verifies that the Student has the necessary prerequisites for that course,* adds the Student to *that* course, marking the Student as "enrolled" for that course in the schedule.

Extensions:

4a. Course full or Student has not fulfilled all prerequisites:
CES disables selection of that course and notifies the Student.

Slice 7: Add up to 4 primary courses

3. Student selects *up to four primary course offerings*.
4. CES verifies that the Student has the necessary prerequisites for the courses, adds the Student to that course, marking the Student as "enrolled" for that course in the schedule.

Slice 8: Finally, add the alternate courses

3. Student selects up to four primary and *two alternate* course offerings.
4. CES verifies that the Student has the necessary prerequisites for the courses, adds the Student to that course, marking the Student as "enrolled" for that course in the schedule.

Choose the sequence that suits where you see risks and opportunities.

Idea 4. Some sentences can be done *in* different *ways*.

This idea is, as far as I know, not generally mentioned in the use case literature. I taught it, but never wrote it up explicitly until *Unifying User Stories, Use Cases, Story Maps.*

Let's look at login. The user might log in via email, Google, Facebook or other apps, biometrics, or using a stored cookie.

1. User logs in (email, Google, Facebook, biometric, cookie).

When the teams are experienced enough, they might not need more than that – they know what to do. Others will want to be explicit. Also, that one step might be delivered in separate deliveries. So we need to find a way to break them out in detail.

My general preference is to list the variations at the end of the use case. That make tracking development easier. Like this:

1. User logs in.
2. ....

Step Variations:

1. Log in using:
    Email/password
    Google/Facebook/other app
    Biometric
    Stored cookie

Paying for goods is similar:

... 7. User pays for items in cart ....

Step Variations:

7. Ways to pay:
    Credit card,
    PayPal,
    bank transfer,
    reward points,
    in installments

The following is an example from a real project. (A 'muffin' was the project's name for a web resource.) Here is just one fragment:

VIEW-RATE-COMMENT A MUFFIN !

1. I, a casual viewer, go to Alistair's site and ***identify a muffin***.
2. The ***server serves up that muffin*** (with frostings).
3. I view / scroll / follow links, etc as usual in browsers.
4. I *rate the muffin*.
5. I ***add a comment to the discussion about the muffin***.

---

(1) identify a muffin:

(Work Token)	
name its direct URL	11/6/07
name its glossy URL	
name an archaic URL	
via whole-word fragment of the title/body	
via partial-word fragment of the title	
via a major category	12/14
see partial matches in real time as I type	

Seven ways to accomplish the same step! The next page shows more of that same use case.

VIEW-RATE-COMMENT A MUFFIN !

1. I, a casual viewer, go to Alistair's site and ***identify a muffin***.
2. The ***server serves up that muffin*** (with frostings).
3. I view / scroll / follow links, etc as usual in browsers.
4. I *rate the muffin*.
5. I ***add a comment to the discussion about the muffin***.

---

(1) identify a muffin:

(Work Token)	
name its direct URL	11/6/07
name its glossy URL	
name an archaic URL	
via whole-word fragment of the title/body	
via partial-word fragment of the title	
via a major category	12/14
see partial matches in real time as I type	

(2) serve up a muffin:

(Work Token)	
html	11/9/07
image (gif)	11/9/07
doc	11/12/07
YouTube	11/12/07
pdf	11/13/07
~~media-wiki~~	
textile wiki	11/13/07
xml	
voice	
PPT	2/2/07

(2) frostings:

(Work Token)	
comments on the muffin	11/6/07
number of visits to that muffin,	12/14
viewer ratings,	11/14/07
refs to next /prev chronological item,	
refs to next/prev item in top category,	
refs to a couple of purely randomly selected items	
refs to random items within the item's categories	
del.icio.us	
digg.	

As you can see, each step has its own list of variations. The complexity in the system wasn't the use case flow – the whole system consisted of only five or six simple use cases. The complexity lay in all the different ways that each step could be done.

It turned out that we never developed the complete set of any of the steps. You can see that in the dates and the check marks we applied as we went. As we deployed, we saw that many of the things we had thought would be valuable were never actually needed.

In practice, it is quick, fun, and easy to list all the possibilities. You then can decide which to implement now and which to defer. This is particularly important for startups and agile teams.

Idea 5. Slice your data, business rules, etc. similarly.

As with variations of a step, you will also slice your data, your technology variations, complex business rules, performance, and other things.

Here is a short list of the things you might slice up for incremental development;

1. A use case.
2. A subset of a sequence of actions.
3. Various ways to accomplish a single step.
4. Business rules.
5. Data.
6. Technology variations.
7. Interfaces.
8. Performance needs.
9. Risk: Learning *how* to do it versus actually *doing* it (**Idea 6**).

Idea 6. Split knowledge-acquisition from implementation.

This is pure project risk management. Imagine you have never connected to a credit card gateway before and are worried that it may be difficult. You have the team program just enough to learn how to do it, and then, knowing that you *can* do it, defer the actual doing until later.

I did that once when converting the data on a site to a new format. I learned that the programmer wasn't comfortable with the assignment and didn't know how to do it. So we split that work into two parts:

- Learn how to convert the data (early in the project).
- Actually convert the data (at the end of the project).

You may find yourself in a similar situation where it is useful to split the learning part from the accomplishing part.

Construct fine-grained growth stages while developing and deploying.

Idea 1. Find and develop the use case's *Walking Skeleton.*

Idea 2. Slice out each sentence and each extension.

Idea 3. Implement just part of a step as its own slice.

Idea 4. Some sentences can be done *in different ways.*

Idea 5. Slice your data, business rules, etc. similarly.

Idea 6. Split knowledge-acquisition from implementation.

Reflections and Key Points

Reflections

I recognize that you are probably not working with use cases. You might like to try them out a bit after reading this chapter – it doesn't really matter if you do them well or badly, just writing out the little stories is likely to give you a handy view of your system.

In all cases, whether you use numbered requirements, informal prose or sticky notes on a virtual wall, this line of thinking will help you with this key idea:

> *"The least writing, the fewest unvalidated decisions, the easiest to scan, that allows you to find value and risk. Spy trouble spots early without going into too many details too soon."*

Did you catch these key points?

Use cases "capture all the usage pathways your development team will need to consider; They are easily read, understood, and passed around the organization."

"spy trouble spots early without going into too many details too soon"

"what we are after: the least writing, the fewest unvalidated decisions, the easiest to scan, that allows us to find value and risk."

"if you write them all at once, you have spent a huge amount of time creating a terrible stack of unvalidated decisions, blocking early delivery of value and filling your organization with internal inventory."

"A Walking Skeleton is a tiny implementation of a process or system that supports a small end-to-end function."

"take the thinnest path through the most important sea-level use cases you will develop. That will make the *walking skeleton* of the use case."

"what is the *least* we can develop that will produce a functioning machine? … we now have a functioning machine, we've reduced risk and opened feedback on all our decisions"

"Idea 1. Find and develop the use case's Walking Skeleton.
Idea 2: Separate out each sentence and each extension.
Idea 3: Implement just part of a step as its own slice.
Idea 4. Some sentences can be done in different ways.
Idea 5. Slice your data, business rules, etc. similarly.
Idea 6. Split knowledge-acquisition from implementation."

"it is quick, fun, and easy to list all the possibilities. You then can decide which to implement now and which to defer."

Construct fine-grained growth stages from use cases while developing and deploying

---

9. The Programmer Version

Slice even more finely while programming to implement the Hexagonal Architecture in test-driven nano-increments.

Nano-incremental programming, "growing" your program, has been around since the 1960s. It hid in the background until Fred Brooks brought it into the mainstream with his 1986 article "No Silver Bullet".

First described by Harlan Mills as *growing* in 1971, it was published in 1975 by Vic Basili as *iterative enhancement* and finally declared a best practice by Fred Brooks in his "No Siver Bullet" article.

Here is Fred Brooks:

> *"Some years ago Harlan Mills proposed that any software system should be grown by incremental development. That is, the system should first be made to run, even though it does nothing useful except call the proper set of dummy subprograms. Then, bit by bit it is fleshed out, with the subprograms in tum being developed into actions or calls to empty stubs in the level below.*
>
> *I have seen most dramatic results since I began urging this technique on the project builders in my Software Engineering Laboratory class. Nothing in the past decade has so radically changed my own practice, or its effectiveness. The approach necessitates top-down design, for it is a top-down growing of the software. It allows easy backtracking. It lends itself to early prototypes. Each added function and new provision for more complex data or circumstances grows organically out of what is already there.*
>
> *The morale effects are startling. Enthusiasm jumps when there is a running system, even a simple one. Efforts redouble when the first picture from a new graphics software system appears on the screen, even if it is only a rectangle. One always has, at every stage in the process, a working system. I find that teams can grow much more complex entities in four months than they can build.*
>
> *The same benefits can be realized on large projects as on my small ones.*

Let's take a look at just how to do this, using the *Hexagonal Architecture* example.

This rest of this chapter is adapted from the book "*Hexagonal Architecture Explained.*" It shows the use of micro-increments to implement the Ports & Adapters ("Hexagonal") architecture.

We start with an introduction to the architecture so that you can follow the implementation. Then the nano-increments to implement it.

Preamble: What is Hexagonal Architecture?

The Ports & Adapters architecture, first documented in 2005 as the "Hexagonal Architecture" pattern, demands the following:

> *Create your application to work without either a UI or a database so you can run automated regression-tests against it, change connected technologies, protect it from leaks between business logic and technologies, work when the database becomes unavailable, and link applications together without any user involvement.*

The most surprising part of implementing it is this requirement:

> *"Never explicitly name any external object or technology. Always take a parameter for any external object or technology you wish to access."*

That requirement has a weak and a strong implementation.

In the "weak" implementation, the programmer knows that the database will use SQL (for example), and without tying to a particular database, still expresses the interface in SQL. While technically meeting the rules of the Ports & Adapters architecture, that still handcuffs the system to SQL, which is not what we are after.

To get a full, or "strong" implementation of the Ports & Adapters architecture,

> *"The app cannot know anything about the external technology."*

That is, whatever the application (the inside of the hexagon) needs must be expressed *purely* in terms of concepts that make sense in the language of the domain. The application can't even know that there is a database, let alone SQL.

Here is an example:

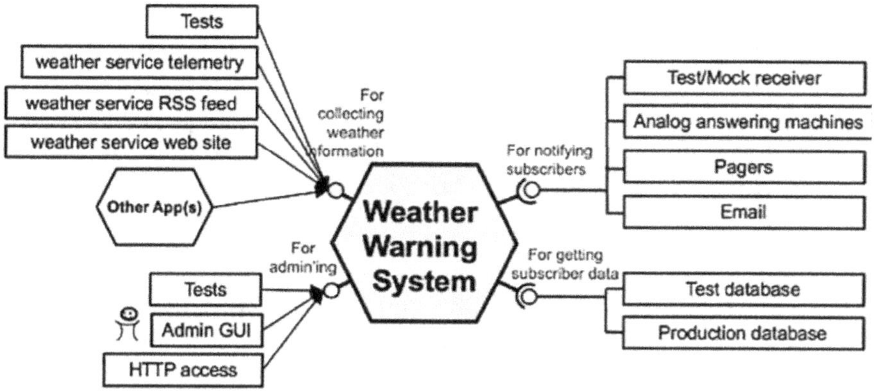

Figure 29, Chapter 9. An example showing both test and production connections

The original article [https://alistair.cockburn.us/hexagonal-architecture] phrases it this way:

> *Allow an application to equally be driven by users, programs, automated test or batch scripts, and to be developed and tested in isolation from its eventual run-time devices and databases.*
>
> *As events arrive from the outside world at a port, a technology-specific adapter converts it into a usable procedure call or message and passes it to the application. The application is blissfully ignorant of the nature of the input device. When the application has something to send out, it sends it out through a port to an adapter, which creates the appropriate signals needed by the receiving technology (human or automated). The application has a semantically sound interaction with the adapters on all sides of it, without actually knowing the nature of the things on the other side of the adapters.*

Why go to all this trouble?

So that:

- You can test the system's functions completely with test drivers and test doubles.
- You can catch programming leaks—either business logic leaking into the technologies, or technology dependencies leaking into the business core—immediately.
- You can change secondary actors easily, even dynamically.
- App developers can continue to develop using test doubles when production repositories are unavailable.

Short history of the pattern

This pattern has not only been growing for over 30 years, I'm still learning how to explain it. 😊 Here is the short history:

1988: Alistair unknowingly implemented Model-View-Controller in his Smalltalk prototype, but his C programmer didn't. When the need arose to change the input source, the C program had to be torn apart and rewritten.

1994: On a fixed-price, fixed-time project involving an object-relational mapper, the infrastructure designers found they had to change their design to the SQL database to improve performance. They shut down the project for several weeks because they had no way to allow the application programmers to use a mock test database.

2000: Alistair visited a friend who was having trouble with all the variants and versions of his application, with different input sources and notification methods. The Hexagonal Architecture pattern solved his problem. This was the first deliberate use of the pattern.

2005: Alistair finally implemented the pattern on a project, using Spring and gave it its correct name, *Ports & Adapters.*

2015: The terms *driving* and *driven* adapters were added, along with the naming convention for interfaces as "*for_doing_something.*"

2022: The pattern was seen as a special case of "Component + Strategy", along with the *required interfaces* concept.

2023: The pattern *Configurable Receiver* pattern replaced the earlier, slightly incorrect pattern *Configurable Dependency.*

2024: Alistair and Juan Manuel Garrido de Paz published the Preview Edition of *Hexagonal Architecture Explained.*

Why the name "Hexagonal" Architecture?

The name "Hexagonal Architecture" was a placeholder I came up with years before I understood what the sides of the hexagon stood for. I knew they had to be there, but I didn't really understand them.

The number 6 has no particular meaning. The purpose of the shape was to get rid of the rectangle with its left-to-right and top-to-bottom association. In practice you might have three, five, or any number of ports, not six. Hexagons don't show up anywhere in your software.

With the lollipop for the *provided* interface and the hook-and-ball for the *required* interface, we learned how to make the architectures expressive and easy to read even with rectangles.

The name became *Ports & Adapters* when I finally worked out what the facets meant. Here is what I wrote in the RSS feed from 2005,

> *Somewhere in the mid-90s I started drawing a symmetric architecture in which the database is considered not at the "bottom of the stack", but fully outside the application, just as we recommend doing with the user interface.*
>
> *To break up perceptions about top and bottom and left and right, I drew it with a hexagonal shape, and came up with the rather lame name Hexagonal Architecture --- simply because I could not identify think of what the "hexagon" meant, but knew it had to have facets, and no number smaller than 5 made visual sense (and pentagons are harder to draw than hexagons).*

Finally just worked out what the drawing meant and realized this picture or architecture should be called Ports and Adapters (think operating system or hi-fi ports, and Design Pattern "adapters").
https://web.archive.org/web/20060318201137/http:/alistair.cockburn.us/rss.rdf
(time stamp: 2005 07 15 13:01 MST)

The costs and benefits of this pattern

Here are the benefits to using the Ports & Adapters Architecture:

1. Testing: You can write and run system-level tests without production connections, making them purer and faster.
2. More on testing: You can swap out the production connections for test connections, and vice versa—for any of the connections, input or output—without having to recompile your system.
3. Leakage protection: The test wall around your application will detect whenever someone leaks UI details or technology details into the business section, or business logic into the UI or external technology sections.
4. Large system separations: Different teams can develop their sections of code independently, test them separately, and connect them according to defined and tested interfaces.
5. Long-running systems: You can replace one external connection with another as technology and business needs change over a period of years.
6. Domain-Driven Design: Once the technology elements are safely outside the application boundary, you are free to focus on the domain design without distraction.

There is also a complexity cost:

1. You will add an instance variable for each driven actor, or else get that information every time you need it.
2. You will add a constructor parameter or a setter function for each driven actor, or else a call to the configurator to get that information.
3. You must design and add a configurator.
4. In type-declared languages, you must declare the required interfaces (see Chapter 2.2. The Pattern Elements: Apps, Ports, Actors, Adapters.

5. In type-declared languages, you will add additional folder structure for the port declarations.

People who have never been hurt by changing technology, shifting interfaces, business logic leaking out, external technology details leaking in, or having to recompile the system to switch between testing and production, say that the costs look too high to be worth implementing the pattern.

It seems to take people suffering on a project for them to decide that adding a few interfaces and instance variables is worth the trouble. However, for those who once start using this architecture, it becomes their default way of building applications or systems.

What is the development sequence?

The brief description of the development sequence is as follows:

1. Test-to-test: Create the test as the first driver of the app, and connect it to a test double (in memory, mock, stub, fake, etc).
2. Real-to-test: Put the production driver in place, connected to the test double.
3. Test-to-real: Connect tests to the production database, or a test database that uses the same technology as the production database.
4. Real-to-real: Finally, when everything else works, connect the production driver and the production database.

Once you've completed step 1, the architecture is in place. After that, you can do the rest in any order. In particular, steps 2 and 3 might be swapped.

Figure 30 shows this sequence.

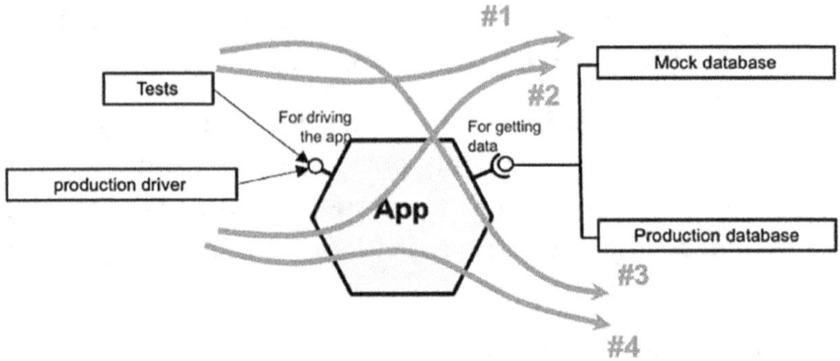

Figure 30, Chapter 9. The development sequence with tests first.

The long explanation is different for different languages, particularly different for type-declaring languages like Java and non-type-declaring languages like Ruby. As such, it will be easier to follow if they are written out separately.

In both cases, we show the most common configurator, in which you pass the driven actor to the app via the app's constructor. Other configurators are described in the book *Hexagonal Architecture Explained.*

For the folder setup, my teaching changed the moment I asked people to create the folders before touching any code. Things that had once been confusing to people became straightforward. With the folders in place, it was clear where to put everything. Hence step 0 in both sequences is to set up the folder structure.

We use the *Walking Skeleton* pattern as the baseline from which to grow the code. According to this pattern:

- Define the smallest behavior in the app needed to construct and connect the architecture. Specifically, the first step introduces driving but no driven ports, and has the app only return a constant.
- The second step introduces one of the driven ports with a test double as the driven actor.

Amazingly, at this point the Ports & Adapters architecture has been constructed. After that, you are free to grow the app, ports, adapters and external actors in any sequence you like.

The point I wish to make in this book is that we are looking to program the fewest decisions at any time and to validate (or break and fix) them as soon as possible.

Having the app return a constant means that the only two decisions in play are making a running app and implementing the driving port. We test that those two work before moving on.

We then tackle the next few decisions:

- taking an argument for the driven actor,
- storing and using it,
- defining and implementing the driven port.

Phreaks may separate those out into separate nano-increments for validation independently, but in our work, we consider that a small enough set of decisions to add at one time.

A Simple Example: the Tax Calculator

We chose a tax calculator because tax calculators can be as simple or complex as you need. We will start simple, with just one driving and one driven port. The driving port offers just the function *tax_on(amount).*

We present this example in four parts:

1. First, we grow just the *tax_on()* function. We use the simplest rate repository, which returns a fixed rate. This is the first step in creating architecture with as little code as possible.

   From this point forward, the drivers, port interfaces, business logic contained within the app and repositories can all change and grow, without any need to change the fundamental architecture.

   We use Java for this first part, because it helps show the ports being defined and used.

2. Second, the same code in Ruby. This illustrates how the code looks when it's not necessary to declare the ports or interfaces.

3. Third, using setter injection instead of dependency injection. The driven actor is not set in the constructor, but in a setter method. This allows the driven actor to be changed at any time.

4. Fourth, a different configurator, one that uses dependency lookup instead of dependency injection for the configurator.

   The tax calculator is augmented to hook to different rate repositories for different countries. The configurator is now a "rate repository broker" that says what rate repository to use for any country requested. This permits different tax tables for different countries, or for adapters to connect to the official tax authority for different countries.

Of course, we need a second port for this broker, and therefore a test double for it, as well as a configurator for the broker.

The simplest tax calculator (Java)

In this simple example of the tax calculator, the configurator main() passes the receiver to the sender at object creation time. It creates the FixedTaxRateRepository, the receiver, and sends it to the TaxCalculator as part of its constructor.

For early development, I use an in-code tax rate repository with just one fixed tax rate. We chose to begin with Java, to show the interfaces.

```
interface ForCalculatingTaxes {
  double taxOn(double amount);
}

interface ForGettingTaxRates {
  double taxRate(double amount);
}

class TaxCalculator implements ForCalculatingTaxes {
  private ForGettingTaxRates taxRateRepository;

  public TaxCalculator(ForGettingTaxRates taxRateRepository) {
    this.taxRateRepository = taxRateRepository;
  }

  public double taxOn(double amount) {
    return amount *  taxRateRepository. taxRate( amount );
  }
}

class FixedTaxRateRepository implements ForGettingTaxRates {
  public double taxRate(double amount) {
      return 0.15;
  }
}

class Main {
  public static void main(String[] args) {
    ForGettingTaxRates taxRateRepository = new
      FixedTaxRateRepository();
```

```
    ForCalculatingTaxes myCalculator = new TaxCalculator(
      taxRateRepository );
    System.out.println( myCalculator.taxOn( 100 ) );
  }
```

Notes:

- "ForCalculatingTaxes" is the driving port, with, just for the moment, only one function offered: "taxOn(amount)."
- "ForGettingTaxRates" is the driven port. It requires every repository to support the function "taxRate(amount)."
- The TaxCalculator implements the driving port, and uses the driven port.
- The FixedRateRepository implements the driven port, as every rate repository would do.
- Main acts as both the configurator and, in this tiny case, also the driving actor. The first two lines act as the configurator, creating the FixedRateRepository and feeding it to the TaxCalculator at creation time. The last line is using the driving port as any user might.

The simplest tax calculator (Ruby)

This code accomplishes the same work as the prior Java example, but in Ruby. The ports and interfaces don't have to be declared in Ruby, which makes it difficult to see where they are.

```
class TaxCalculator

  def initialize( tax_rate_repository )
    @tax_rate_repository = tax_rate_repository
  end

  def tax_on( amount )
    amount * @tax_rate_repository.tax_rate( amount )
  end
end
```

```
class FixedTaxRateRepository
  def tax_rate( amount )
    0.15
  end
end

tax_rate_repository = FixedTaxRateRepository.new
my_calculator = TaxCalculator.new( tax_rate_repository )
puts my_calculator.tax_rate( 100 )
```

Using a setter instead of constructor argument (Java)

In this example, we build upon previous examples to show that one doesn't have to set the driven actors in the constructor arguments (constructor injection). It is just as valid to use a setter method (setter injection). This allows the driven actors to be changed at any time.

Using setter injection instead of constructor injection comes with one hazard, namely that it is possible to construct the app and never actually set the driven actors, which leaves the app in an inconsistent state.

For long-running systems, setter injection is necessary, so the tests have to mitigate that hazard. Neither Juan nor I have experience with these systems, so we can't comment further.

Here is the example of using setter injection:

```
interface ForGettingTaxRates {
  double taxRate(double amount);
}

class TaxCalculator {
  private ForGettingTaxRates taxRateRepository;

  public void setTaxRateRepository(ForGettingTaxRates
       taxRateRepository) {
    this.taxRateRepository = taxRateRepository;
  }
  public double taxOn(double amount) {
    return amount * taxRateRepository.taxRate( amount );
  }
```

```
}

class FixedTaxRateRepository implements ForGettingTaxRates {
  public double taxRate(double amount) {
    return 0.15;
  }
}

class Main {
  public static void main(String[] args) {
    ForGettingTaxRates taxRateRepository = new
      FixedTaxRateRepository();
    TaxCalculator myCalculator = new TaxCalculator();
    myCalculator.setTaxRateRepository( taxRateRepository );
    System.out.println(myCalculator.taxOn( 2000 ));
  }
}
```

Using a broker instead of a fixed rate repository (Ruby)

The fourth adjustment shows the use of *dependency lookup* instead of *configurable receiver* to configure the driven actor.

We introduce a rate repository broker, which will tell the calculator what rate repository to use for any given country. This allows different rate repositories to handle the different tax rate tables in various countries, or to have an adapter that connects directly to a country's official tax authority.

To do this, we introduce another driven port, "ForGettingCountryBasedTaxRateRepository." This port requires one function, RepositoryForCountry(country).

Now that we have a second port, we need to be able to test it. There needs to be a test double as well as a production rate repository broker. This in turn means we need a configurator for the broker port. Here we use constructor injection to set the broker to use at the time the tax calculator is created.

We show this code in Ruby because it's easier to see the intention.

```
class RateRepositoryBroker

  def initialize
    @tax_rate_repository_FR = TaxRateRepositoryFR.new
    @tax_rate_repository_US = TaxRateRepositoryUS.new
  end

  def repository_for( country )
    if country == "US"      return @tax_rate_repository_US
    elsif country == "FR"  return @tax_rate_repository_FR
    else  return nil
    end
  end
end


class TaxCalculator
  def initialize( repository_broker )
    @my_rate_repository_broker = repository_broker
  end


  def tax_on( country, amount )
    tax_rate_repository = @my_rate_repository_broker.repository_for(
country )
    amount * tax_rate_repository.tax_rate( amount )
  end
end


class TaxRateRepositoryFR
  def tax_rate( amount )
    0.30
  end
end


class TaxRateRepositoryUS
  def tax_rate( amount )
    0.15
  end
```

```
end


my_tax_rate_broker = RateRepositoryBroker.new
my_calculator = TaxCalculator.new( my_tax_rate_broker )
puts my_calculator.tax_rate( "FR", 2000 )
puts my_calculator.tax_rate( "US", 2000 )
puts my_calculator.tax_rate( 100 )
```

4.9. What is the development sequence?

The brief description of the development sequence is as follows:

1. Test-to-test: Create the test as the first driver of the app, and connect it to a test double (in memory, mock, stub, fake, etc).
2. Real-to-test: Put the production driver in place, connected to the test double.
3. Test-to-real: Connect tests to the production database, or a test database that uses the same technology as the production database.
4. Real-to-real: Finally, when everything else works, connect the production driver and the production database.

Once you've completed step 1, the architecture is in place. After that, you can do the rest in any order. In particular, steps 2 and 3 might be swapped. *Figure 31* shows this sequence.

The long explanation is not only long, it is different for different languages. The detailed instructions for type-declaring languages like Java are different from non-type-declaring languages like Ruby. As such, we decided it will be easier to follow if they are written out separately.

Here are some notes common to both sequences:

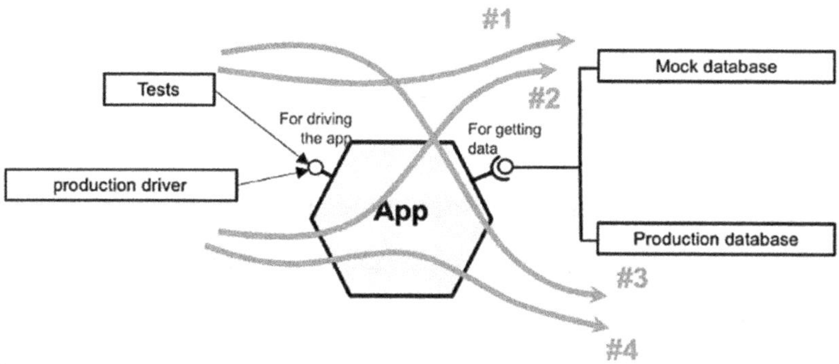

Figure 31, Chapter 9. The development sequence: Tests and mocks first.

1. We show the most common configurator, in which you pass the driven actor to the app via the app's constructor. Other configurators are described in detail in section 3 of the article Configurable Receiver (Chapter 6.5).

2. For the folder setup, Alistair's teaching changed the moment he asked people to create the folders before touching any code. Things that had once been confusing to people became straightforward. With the folders in place, it was clear where to put everything. Hence step 0 in both sequences is to set up the folder structure.

3. We recommend using the *Walking Skeleton* pattern (Chapter 6.2) to grow the code. According to this pattern:

    - We first set up the smallest behavior in the app needed to construct and connect the architecture. That is, the first step introduces driving but no driven ports, and has the app only return a constant.
    - The second step introduces one of the driven ports with a test double as the driven actor. At this point the Ports & Adapters architecture has been constructed.
    - After that, you are free to evolve and grow the app, the ports, the adapters and the external actors in any sequence you like.

Development Sequence for Type-Declared Languages

This sequence is for languages such as Java in which you declare types and interfaces.

[0: Preparation] Set up the folder structure

- Create the folders or projects where you will put the app code and the port declarations.
- Create three subfolders there: one for the app business logic, one for "Driving Ports", and one for "Driven Ports." Alternatively, make the Ports folder separate and at the same level as the App folder or project.
- Outside the app space, in a place that suits your coding conventions, create two folders: "Driving Adapters" and "Driven Adapters."
- Create the folder where you will write your driving tests.

[1: Driving Side] Test the app returning a constant

- Establish the first driving port. Since our purpose here is only to establish the architecture for the driving side, have the app only return a constant: 0, "Hi", or something equally simple. Here's how that goes:
- In "Driving Ports" add a file for your first port/interface declaration. Give the interface a name of the form "ForAccomplishingSomething", for whatever service you intend the app to provide.
- Declare the function signature for a function with no parameters, expecting only a simple value back.
- In the app folder, create the simplest app to service the driving interface. In this first step, it takes no arguments and just returns a constant. It should declare that the app "implements" the driving interface you declared (in whatever language form you need).

- In the test folder, write a test that calls that function and expects that answer. That test code may need to declare that it uses the interface definition, depending on your language and coding conventions.
- Run the test. Hopefully it passes. If not, see what you have to clean up to get the connection to work properly.

Congratulations! At this point, you have already implemented the first driving port in the Ports & Adapters architecture.

Note that this test will end up being thrown away, because all future tests, and the production system, will make use of the driven actors. We have not yet found a way to keep this test running without creating waste code in the final system. With tears in our eyes and chills on our skin, we prepare to comment it out later. It served its purpose.

[2: Driven Side] Test a driven actor returning a constant

Now add a driven port:

- In the "Driven Ports" folder, define just one interface with one function signature for the driven actor. Use the simplest interface possible, ideally with no parameters. Give the interface a name of the sort "ForAccomplishingXYZ", for some service the app needs from its driven actor. This will be the *type* of the arguments and variables holding the driven actor.
- In the "Driven Adapters" folder, add a class that implements the required interface and returns a simple value. You now have your first driven actor. Make sure the code says that it "implements" the required interface.

  Note: This class is a test double. It is actually an actor, not an adapter. To escape ongoing difficulties with terminology here, we use the word 'interactor', to mean "adapter, or actor that doesn't need an adapter." This test double is an example of an actor that doesn't need an adapter.

- Now change the app to use the driven interactor (the test double):

  (1) Add an instance variable to hold the driven interactor. The type of the instance variable is the driven interface you just defined: "ForAccomplishingXYZ."

  (2) Add a constructor that accepts a driven interactor as an argument and stores it in the instance variable. The *type* of the argument is the driven interface "ForAccomplishingXYZ", not the driven interactor's class.

  (3) Change the code so that, instead of returning a constant, it asks the driven interactor for the result to use and then returns that.

- Comment out, delete or change the first test case:

  (1) Create an instance of the new driven interactor (the test double). Declare the type of the driven interactor as the driven interface and not its class.

  (2) Create the app, passing the driven interactor into the app constructor.

- Test that the app now returns the simple value expected from the test double. We like to use a different value from the first test, to be sure we really made all the correct changes.

Congratulations! You have now implemented the Ports & Adapters architecture! Your system has its first configurator, driving port, driving actor, driven port, driven actor, and the app itself correctly interacts with all of them. From here on, you can evolve the system in any direction you like.

Your next steps will be to put a real UI on the driving side (or connect it to the web or wherever the real driving actor will come from), and to put a real repository or receiver on the driven side, in whichever sequence you prefer.

[3: Driving Side] Add a real driving actor

At this point you are in your own technology. This may be a human interface, a web interface, a microservice, or whatever you choose.

- Add an adapter, if that is needed, in the "Driving Adapters" folder. You may need an adapter for a web interface, and you might not need an adapter to use your app as a microservice. You will have your own preferred place to put a UI to a human. At this point, it's up to you how you work.
- You may need to declare that your adapter, or driving actor, "uses" the driving port definition.

At the end of step 3, you have two drivers for the system which is still only connected to your test double.

[4: Driven Side] Add a real repository or receiver

- Choose a technology for your driven actor. This may be a file with data, a database interface, access to the web, or whatever you deem appropriate.
- Add an adapter to the "Driven Adapters" folder that declares and implements the same driven interface. Add the repository or receiver wherever appropriate for you.

At this point, you have multiple driving and driven actors. The architecture is in play.

- Add more driving and driven ports and actors on each side as you need.

Development Sequence for Non-Type-Declared Languages

The following is for languages such as Ruby in which you don't have to declare types and interfaces. As before, we chose the most common configurator, in which you pass in the driven actor via the app's constructor, we set up the folder structure first, and we use the Walking Skeleton pattern.

[0: Preparation] Set up the folder structure

- Create the folder where you will put the app code.
- Outside the app space, in a place that suits your coding conventions, create two folders: "driving_adapters" and "driven_adapters."
- Create the folder where you will write your driving tests.

[1: Driving Side] Just test the app returning a constant

- Establish the first driving actor. Since our purpose here is only to establish the architecture for the driving side, have the app only return a constant: 0, "Hi", or something equally simple. Here's how that goes:
- In the app folder, create the simplest app to service the driving interface. In this first step, it takes no arguments and just returns a constant.
- In the test folder, write a test that calls that function and expects that constant.
- Run the test. Hopefully it passes. If not, see what you have to clean up to get the connection to work properly.

Congratulations! At this point, you have already implemented the first driving port in the Ports & Adapters architecture.

Note that this test will end up being thrown away, because all future tests, and the production system, will make use of the driven actors. We have not yet found a way to keep this test running without creating waste code in the final system. With tears in our eyes and chills on our skin, we prepare to comment it out later. It served its purpose.

[2: Driven Side] Test a driven actor returning a constant

Now add a driven actor:

- In the "driven_adapters" folder, add a class that implements the required interface and returns a simple value. You now have your first driven actor.

  Note: This class is a test double. It is actually an actor, not an adapter. To escape ongoing difficulties with terminology here, we use the word 'interactor', to mean "adapter, or actor that doesn't need an adapter." This test double is an example of an actor that doesn't need an adapter

- Next, change the app to use the driven interactor:

  (1) Add an instance variable to hold the driven interactor.

  (2) Add a constructor that accepts a driven interactor as an argument and stores it in the instance variable.

  (3) Change the code so that, instead of returning a constant, it asks the driven interactor for the result to use and then returns that.

- Comment out, delete or change the first test case:

  (1) Create an instance of the new driven interactor (the test double).

  (2) Create the app, passing the driven interactor into the app constructor.

- Test that the app now returns the simple value expected from the driven actor. We like to use a different value from the first test, to be sure we really made all the correct changes.

Congratulations! You have now implemented the Ports & Adapters architecture. Your baby system has its first configurator, driving port, driving actor, driven port, driven actor, and the app itself correctly interacts with all of them. From here on, you can evolve the system in any direction you like.

Your next steps will be to put a real UI on the driving side (or connect it to the web or wherever the real driving actor will come from), and to put a real repository or receiver on the driven side, in whichever sequence you prefer.

Shortening the descriptions, they look like this:

[3: Driving Side] Add a real driving actor

At this point you are in your own technology. This may be a human interface, a web interface, a microservice, or whatever you choose.

- Add an adapter, if that is needed, in the "driving_adapters" folder. You may need an adapter for a web interface, and you might not need an adapter to use your app as a microservice. You will have your own preferred place to put a UI to a human. At this point it's up to you how you work.

At the end of step 3, you have two drivers for the system. Both should be connected to your test double.

[4: Driven Side] Add a real repository or receiver

- Choose a technology for your driven actor. This may be a file with data, a database interface, access to the web, or whatever you deem appropriate.
- Add an adapter to the "driven_adapters" folder. Add the repository or receiver wherever appropriate for you.

At this point, you have two driving and two driven actors. The architecture is in play. Add more driving and driven ports and actors on each side as you need.

Reflections and Key Points

Reflections

The theme of this book is

> *Unvalidated decisions* are your internal inventory. They slow your organization and make it more expensive to fix mistakes. Learn to move and validate them in small quantities.

Thus, even if you don't use the Hexagonal or Ports & Adapters pattern, I hope you saw the use of nano-increments:

- Only have the app return a constant to test that the port definition is done correctly and the driving connection work.
- Only have the mock database return a constant to test that the constructor works correctly, as do the use of the internal variable, the driven port definition and the connection to an unknown external repository.

Looking to validate (or break) the fewest number of decisions at a time, you have two in the first nano-increment and four in the second nano-increment. Any mistakes you make in either of these should be easy to find, and once you have them in place, they are solid for the future.

Hence, even though they may look "too small to be interesting," they fit the idea of validating (or breaking) the smallest number of decisions at a time. Additionally, you will almost never have to open your debugger, because you will only ever have typed a few lines of code since your previous test. This saves cognitive load and time.

Did you catch these key points?

Hexagonal ("Ports & Adapters") Architecture is briefly stated as:

> "The app cannot know anything about the external technology," so it can "equally be driven by users, programs, automated test or batch scripts, and to be developed and tested in isolation from its eventual run-time devices and databases."

The development sequence is:

Test-to-test: Test cases driving, test doubles as driven actors.

Real-to-test: Real UI driving, test doubles as driven actors.

Test-to-real: Test cases driving, real systems on the driven side.

Real-to-real: All real external systems, driving and driven.

"program the fewest decisions at any time and to validate (or break and fix) them as soon as possible."

After two nano-increments: "*Congratulations! You have now implemented the Ports & Adapters architecture!* Your system has its first configurator, driving port, driving actor, driven port, driven actor, and the app itself correctly interacts with all of them. From here on, you can evolve the system in any direction you like."

Slice even more finely while programming to implement the Hexagonal Architecture in test-driven nano-increments.

---

10. The Project Manager Version

Visualize what is happening on the project with burn charts. Show status on complex projects with fox-and-rabbit charts.

The two articles in this chapter show the project manager how to track and show the project's trajectory while using incremental development. Teaser: *Figure 32* :).

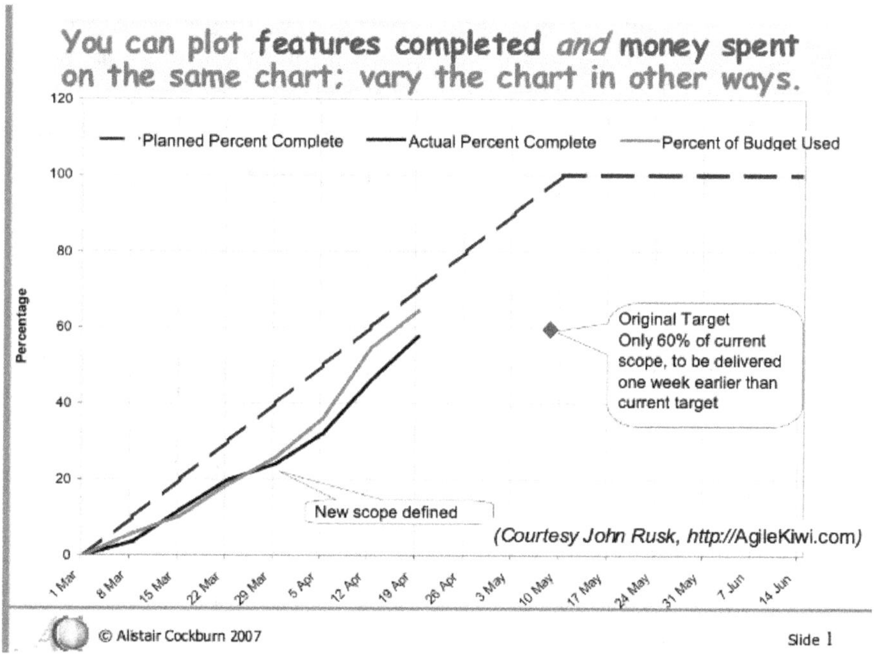

Figure 32, Chapter 10. Preview: Burn- and earned-value charts are great at showing what's happening on a project.

Earned-Value and Burn Charts

Extracted from Chapter 3 of "Crystal Clear,"
©Alistair Cockburn, Addison-Wesley, 2004

Burn charts have become a favorite way to give visibility into a project's progress. They are extremely simple and astonishingly powerful. They reveal the strategy being used, show the progress made against predictions, and open the door to discussions about how best to proceed, including the difficult discussions about whether to cut scope or extend the schedule. They have a natural mapping to the earned-value charts used in military/government projects. They should part of your standard bag of tricks for project planning and reporting.

It turns out that packing a house has striking similarities to software development as far as planning and tracking go. I use the following exercise to illustrate the use of burn charts:

> *Imagine you have 30 days to pack up a house you are living in (with a couple of kids, just to make it more painful). Assume there are 14 rooms or room equivalents on 3 floors. Chart your plan so that you always know what is done, what is left, and how well you are doing.*

Most people plan to pack the house as shown in *Figure 33*. They plan to first throw out all the junk, then pack the non-critical items, and pack the essential living items in the last few days. This is, of course, the technique I used the first two times I was in this situation, and I can speak with first-hand pain in saying that it is terrible.

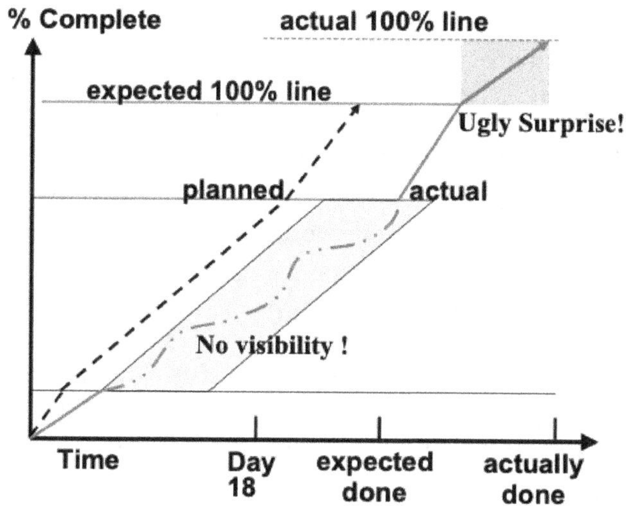

Figure 33, Chapter 10. Scheduling with no definitive milestones.

The big flaw in it is the absence of clear intermediate milestones.

It is practically impossible to tell whether one is 60% or 70% done (speaking to both software and room-packing). For most of the project, one sees neither the true size of the task at hand, nor the (slower than expected) rate of progress. Missing both of those, it is impossible to tell when one will get done. In both cases, an ugly surprise awaits at the end, when a myriad little unexpected items suddenly become visible (think about when you loaded all the boxes into a moving truck and walked back into the house, only to discover all sorts of things that suddenly "appeared" when everything else was taken out). The classical result on software projects is that programmers keep reporting that things are 80% complete, or "We'll be done when we're done."

The repair is to find "interesting" and clear intermediate milestones.

In packing, those milestones are rooms completely packed and empty, containing "not even a sock" (and possibly with police tape across the doorway to keep people from dumping stuff back into them!). The thinking is that if there is so much as a sock left, then there is possibly something else besides the sock, and the reporting is flawed. We will see an application of this "sock" idea in just a few pages.

In software, those milestones are the delivery of running, tested code, as **Frequent Delivery**.

This new strategy has implications that make life a little awkward (again, both for software and house packing). In house packing, people have to move out of their rooms, and eventually the kitchen becomes unusable. In software, tests have to be re-run and designs and documentation must be altered on each delivery. These are not free – cost and discomfort both come with the strategy.

The payback for the cost and the discomfort is improved visibility, improved tracking, and less likelihood of an unexpected project overrun. In most cases, this benefit is well worth the cost.

Let's look at this strategy on a software project.

- Make a list of all the items to be delivered. You might work from the *Project Map*, *Blitz Planning* or XP's planning game. Associate with each delivery item a *relative cost.* Try to associate with each item also a relative *business benefit*, so that you can discuss with the *Executive Sponsor* the value being delivered to the business over time (*Figure 34* shows a fragment of such a list). The reason for using relative estimates instead of absolute ones is that if you are, for example, 10% over on your first set of items, all the remaining items will scale accordingly. The burn charts will show this automatically.
- Sort and sequence the work items by development dependency, cost and value, and cluster them into a sequence, as shown in *Figure 35* (you may recognize the similarity of what we are doing here and what happens in a *Blitz Planning* session).
- Estimate how much can be accomplished in each iteration or delivery period. Draw a line under the last item that fits in each. Number the releases.

	Feature	Feature Description	Value	Est ideal days	Est. Elapsed Days
1	User Interface			8	
1.1	Configuration generates order line item comments	Allow the configuration to populate order line item comments with detailed configuration information along with configuration comments. Stop change of line item notes other than from within the appropriate configurator.	M	2	5
1.2	Configurator UI Rework: Verbose wizard style	Rework user-interface to match the prototype discussed in collaborative review session. Fast, simple data entry. No unnecessary frills.	H	6	15
1.3	Configuration generates customer specific pricing	Configuration is passed current order customer for use in determining customer specific pricing.	H	5	12.5
1.4	Allow adding a configuration and continue	Currently a configured blind may be added to an order. To add a subsequent similar blind you'd need to go back into configurator and reenter all the information. This feature would allow the user to accept a finished configuration and immediately allow adding an additional configuration using the data from the previous configuration.	L	2	5
2	Special Order PO Generation			5	
2.1	PO generated correctly for configuration	Currently POs are generated for regular order line items. Change to allow configuration components to generate 1 or more purchase orders at a cost furnished by the component.	H	5	12.5
2.2	Create/Confirm vendor items exist for skus	confirm that a vendor item exists for each sku used for base window treatments and options. Where no vendor item exists for an assigned vendor, dynamically create the vendor item.	H	1.5	3.75
2.3	PO generation is automatic	Currently Pos can be generated after a special order is saved and a deposit is made. Allow automatic PO generation immediately after deposit is tendered, or immediately if no deposit is required.	L	4	10
3	Advanced Order			9	
3.1	Advanced Order form shows more details	Alter Advanced Order form to show an "overflow" are for each line item where additional information such as comments, Po number, PO order date etc.. Can be shown.	M	4	10

Figure 34, Chapter 10. Extract of feature list with estimates of size and business value (Thanks to Jeff Patton)

Module	Feature Name	Value	Raw Dev. Time (ideal days)	Estimated Elapsed Days	release #
1.1	Configuration generates order line item comments	M	2	5	1
1.2	Configurator UI Rework: Verbose wizard style	H	6	15	1
2.1	PO generated correctly for configuration	H	5	12.5	1
2.2	Create/Confirm vendor items exist for skus	H	1.5	3.75	1
3.1	Advanced Order form shows more details	M	4	10	1
3.2	Order fulfilled at PO cost	H	2	5	1
3.3	Repeat orders works with blind configurations	M	3	7.5	1
3.4	Configuration comments are viewable, not editable	L	1	2.5	1
4.1	Base hierarchy change	H	1.5	3.75	1
4.2	Style can locate price charts based on color selection	H	2	5	1
4.3	Assign specific color group colors to price charts	H	2	5	1
4.4	Separate messages from options	H	2	5	1
4.5	Separate questions from options	H	2	5	1
1.3	Configuration generates customer specific pricing	H	5	12.5	2
1.4	Allow adding a configuration and continue	L	2	5	2
2.3	PO generation is automatic	L	4	10	2
3.5	Order shows sq. footage & running length	L	2	5	2
3.6	Vendor orderable items show additional detail	L	2	5	2
3.7	Printed window treatments show disclaimers	M	6	15	2
3.8	Allow order line item copying	H	2	5	2
4.1	Associate style with Retail.net DCL	L	1	2.5	2
4.11	Grid validation	L	1	2.5	2
4.6	Assign customer specific selling discounts	H	3	7.5	2
4.7	Customer lookup	H	1	2.5	2
4.8	Customer account type lookup	M	1	2.5	2
4.9	Options may have required questions	L	3	7.5	2

Figure 35, Chapter 10. The Iceberg List with Product Backlog.
(thanks to Jeff Patton)

I have come to call this the *Iceberg List.* The "above water" part lists all the items that can be delivered in the current delivery cycle. The "below water" part lists every that will be delivered in later delivery cycles. The name reflects that when you add a new item to the above water part, it pushes everything else down, and something that was above water falls below water (will not be delivered in the current delivery cycle). The *Iceberg List* is particularly useful on projects where the requirements change frequently. In Scrum terminology, the below water part is referred to the *Product Backlog* and the above water part is the *Sprint Backlog.* (Scrum's backlog: [http://wiki.scrums.org/index.cgi])

The primary difference between this list and the standard systems engineering work-breakdown structure is that *you get no credits for any item that does not result in running, tested code.* OK, you also get credit for *final deliverables* such as training materials and delivery documentation.

At this point you can make a *Burn-up* or a *Burn-down* chart, both fabulous ways to communicate what is happening. The following sequence of figures show all the variations I've encountered for these charts with the advantages, disadvantages and caveats for each.

Figure 36 shows a *Burn-up* chart from a real project. Each item listed is a software package that had to get updated. The packages would take different lengths of time to update, so the line is not straight, but taken straight from the work estimates.

Here is how to construct such a chart:

- Mark either relative work units or % complete on the vertical axis, and calendar time on the horizontal. Draw a line from the origin to the completion point, either by estimating the rate at which work can be accomplished, or as often happens, the "drop dead" delivery deadline. That shows the "planned" progress.
- After each iteration, mark how much relative work got completed. You will find that with just two marks on the chart you can see how far slower you are moving than you expected! Yes, that may be bad news, but at least it is *bad news detected early*, as opposed to *bad news detected too late to do anything about it!*

The burn-up chart resembles the classical earned-value chart (Lett 98, Fleming 88). The essential difference is only that people traditionally include on the earned-value chart *tasks completed*, whether or not they resulted in code getting integrated. On agile projects, credit is only given when code is integrated and tested (the "no leftover sock" rule). The agile strategy yields more reliable information about the project's actual state than the general one.

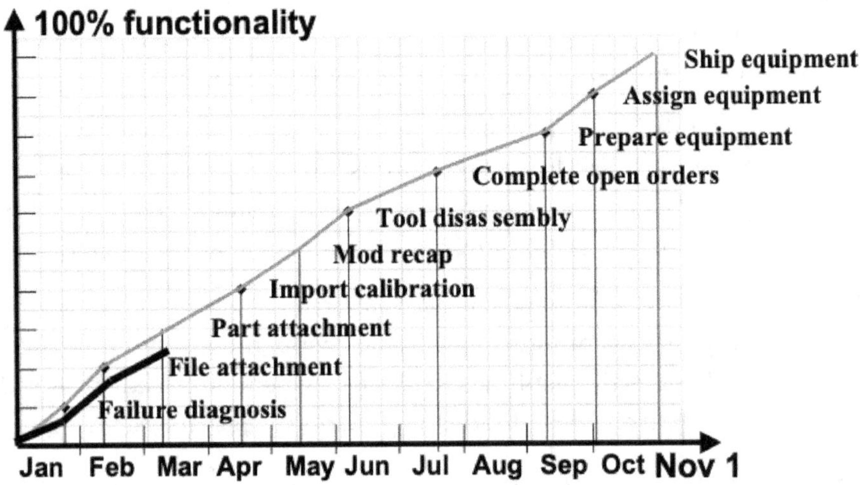

Figure 36, Chapter 10. The Burn-up chart shows progress and earned-value quickly.

The long thin line shows the planned functionality & schedule; the thick line shows progress to date.

The *burn-up* chart has many nice features.

- It shows both the status and rate of progress ("velocity") in a way that is both clear and easy to discuss.
- If you plot business value on the vertical axis instead of development effort, you get a chart that properly shows how much value you have delivered over time. Plotting both on the same chart may help remind the team about where the real business value lies in their work. If you sequence the Iceberg List to float the greatest business value items to the top, and track business value delivered, then no matter when the project

gets terminated, it will be clear to everyone that they got the most business value in the time spent.

- Finally, the burn-up chart is a key part of a good one-page project status report (examples of status reports are shown in the Word Products chapter). Such one-page status sheets simplify the work of executives looking at reports from many projects.

Even though the burn-up chart is very nice, there is a nasty surprise if you are not careful in choosing the units you use for the vertical axis.

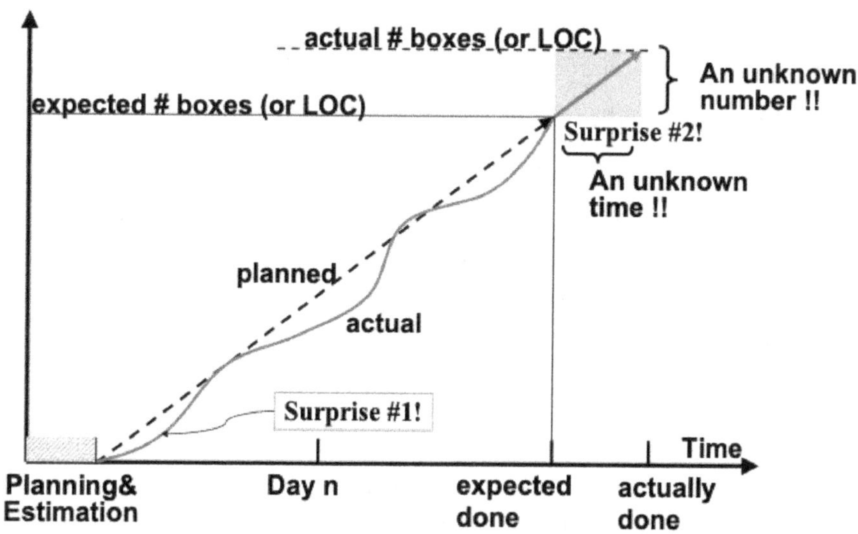

Figure 37, Chapter 10. Burn-up chart when the wrong units are measured.2

In house packing, the obvious unit of estimation and tracking is the packing box. In programming, the obvious unit is the line of code (LOC). These are convenient and give wonderful detail.

The problem is that you won't know the actual number of boxes or lines of code needed until the very end (shades of "We'll be done when we're done."). The graph tracks *rate* wonderfully, but *progress* poorly. Not only will you not discover bad news early, but you will not know how many boxes or LOC you need until the last item is packed or programmed. That is too late. See *Figure 37*.

The ideal repair is to choose a unit of measure that can't possibly expand. In house packing, the replacement measure is easy: use rooms instead of boxes (it would be quite a surprise to discover a new room after you have packed all the rest). The answer is not generally obvious on a software project. You may be lucky and have a relatively stable number of use cases, or a fixed number of modules to replace, but there is no generally applicable answer.

I met several project teams that had found similar answer for this. Each project was a system replacement project where the subsystems communicated in a work-flow pattern.

- Their non-expanding unit was the work-flow component.
- They colored each subsystem yellow as they started work on it.
- The colored it green as it was completed.
- They were able to use "components replaced" as their non-expanding unit (see the sample status sheet in the Work Products chapter of *Crystal Clear: A Human-Powered Methodology for Small Teams*).

In the more usual situation, project scope does in fact change over time.

Phil Goodwin and Russ Rufer introduced the idea of marking the raising and lowering of the ceiling, or 100% mark, as the project progresses. This charting allows the team to show the original plan and actual accomplishments even in the face of scope changes.

Figure 38 shows the Goodwin-Rufer style burn-up chart in a situation where the team actually performed better than their estimates but scope kept increasing. (The project actually used the standard Scrum burn-down chart shown in *Figure 41*. I think you will agree that their conversations with the sponsors would have been easier had they used either *Figure 38* or *Figure 43*.)

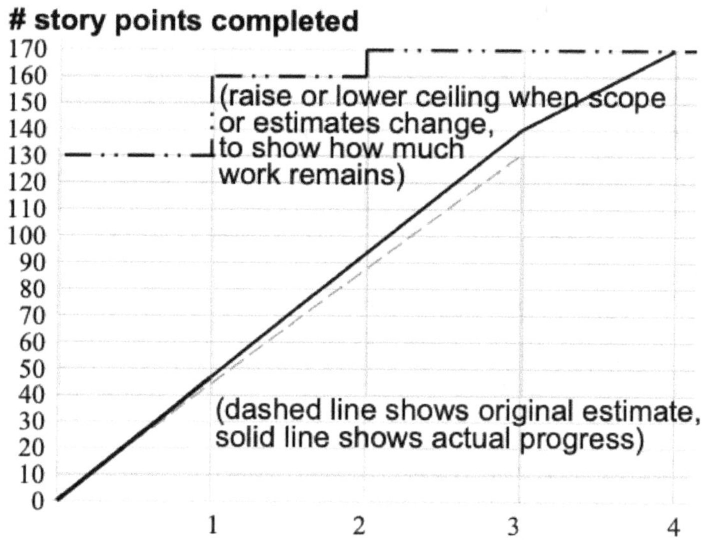

Figure 38, Chapter 10. A *burn-up* chart with predicteds & actuals, a changing 100% line using the Goodwin-Rufer style.

If you are lucky enough to have a good non-expanding unit of measure, then you can use the *Burn-down* chart, which some people find emotionally more powerful (see *Figure 39*).

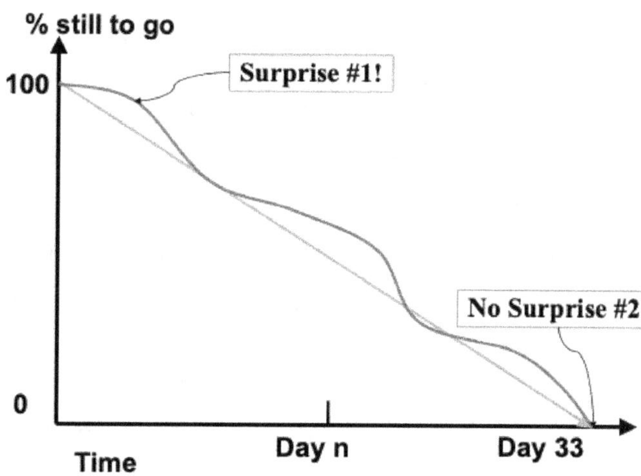

Figure 39, Chapter 10. A basic Burn-down chart.

The *burn-down* chart is emotionally powerful because there is a special feeling about hitting the number zero that helps people get excited about completing their work and pressing forward. I can speak first hand in saying that as soon as we shifted our house packing chart to using to rooms as the unit of measure and put the rooms on a *burn-down* chart, our confidence that we would actually meet our schedule increased dramatically. I have seen the same apply to a software project team.

It is easy to say, "We can't use the burn-down chart, because nothing is fixed on a software project." Oddly, the first people to say this were those working on the system replacement project just mentioned. After a bit of examination, we discovered that they had exactly the house-packing problem in front of them. They were able to convert immediately to the burn-down chart, using replaced subsystems as their non-expanding unit of measure.

There are three wrinkles left to discuss that direct the way we draw these charts.

The first is the little white lie I just told in the last paragraph about non-expanding unit of work. The team discovered after a short while that their *Executive Sponsor* kept adding demands for new functionality in both the old system and the replacement. In other words, although they were promised that the scope would be fixed (since the time and budget was), that wasn't really true. As if that were not bad enough, he was actually opposed to the project itself, and was obliged to support it only because of pressure from the user community (see how powerful user community support can be!).

This put the team in a damned-if-you-do-and-damned-if-you-don't position. They couldn't report a subsystem complete (not even a sock left in it) if he was going to keep throwing more socks back into the room, and they couldn't stop him from throwing more socks in.

Their eventual strategy has some bearing on burn charts, but also some bearing on the positive role of intermediate managers. The intermediate manager decided that they would take their project mission as originally stated, to replace the existing system. They would deliver that successfully, and track all increased scope as growing "post-replacement" activity.

They charted this as shown in *Figure 40.* With this strategy and chart, they were able to keep their **Focus** on the critical issue of replacing the existing system, show they were tracking the new functions being added, and keep the *Executive Sponsor* from derailing their project.

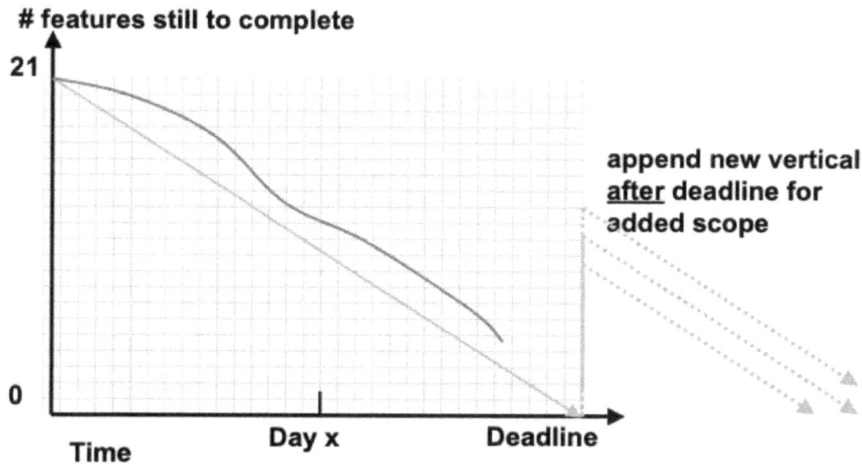

Figure 40, Chapter 10. The *Burn-down* chart for a hard-deadline project with scope increase added at the end.

Mike Cohn reports a similar situation in his book *User Stories*, although in friendly circumstances. The team was given 130 story points (a relative unit of size for XP user stories) to deliver in three iterations. After each iteration, the sponsors added new stories and the team revised the relative sizes of the remaining stories. Both increased the estimate of the amount of work remaining. Mike and I discussed how they should chart the team's progress against changing scope, assuming they like the emotional power of the burn-down chart.

Figure 41 shows what the team showed the sponsors at their meetings (Cohn 2003).

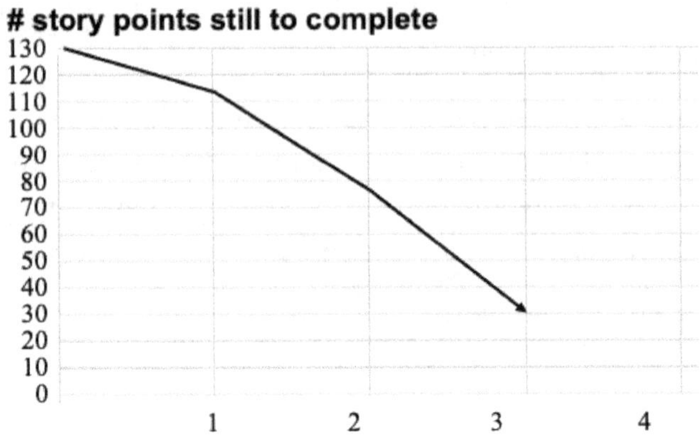

Figure 41, Chapter 10. Scrum-style *burn-down* chart as shown to the project sponsors (after Cohn 2004).

Mike and I felt that this chart conceals very important information about the changing scope.

Figure 42 shows how I thought to modify the chart to illustrate the actual accomplishments against the changing scope.

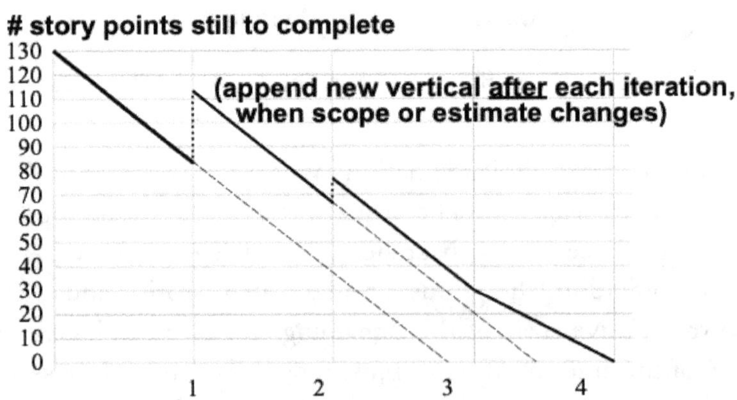

Figure 42, Chapter 10. Burn-down chart for the same project showing scope increase after each iteration.

Figure 43 shows how Mike proposed to modify the chart to show the changing situation. You may notice that it is the downward version of the Goodwin-Rufer burn-up chart.

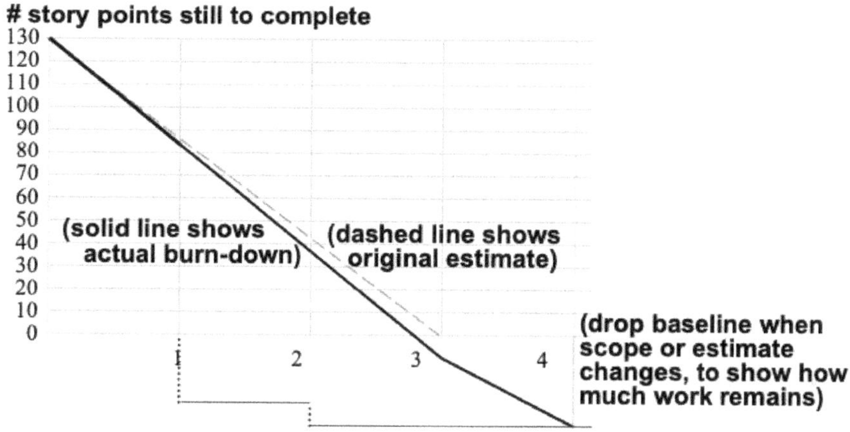

Figure 43, Chapter 10. Burn-down chart for the same project using the 'down' version of the Goodwin-Rufer chart.

We offer these examples of charts to show different ways in which you can show predicted and actual accomplishments with simplicity and expressive power. There are probably more variations to discover, but these should get you started.

The second wrinkle to be discussed is the size of the selected unit of measure. This is very relevant at the start of a project because the team will almost always move more slowly at the beginning than expected, and just *how* much more slowly is a valuable piece of information.

Let us return to the house packing example to see this clearly. The graphs in Figure 32 show that the coarser the unit of measure, the longer the blackout period during which no information is available. Having already rejected "boxes packed" as a good unit of measure, we can choose "rooms packed" or "floors packed" as non-expanding units.

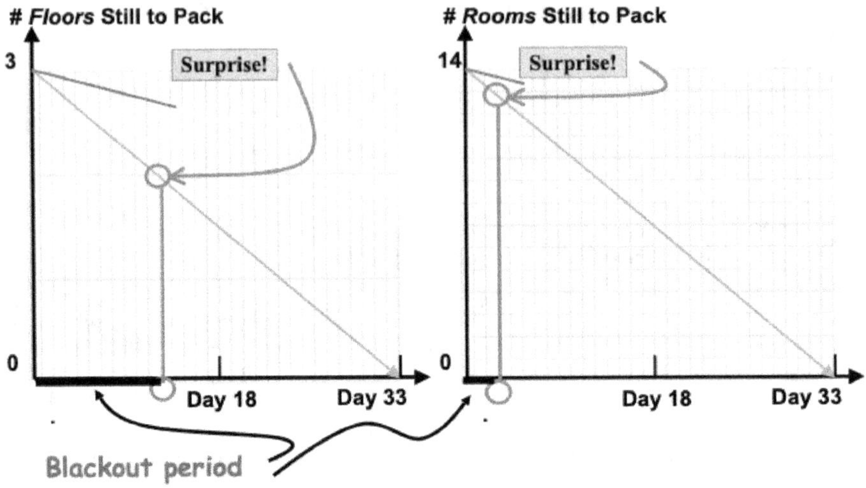

Figure 44, Chapter 10. Burn-down charts for different base units. The smaller the unit, the shorter the initial black-out period.

Figure 44 shows burn-down charts for both of those choices. In each case, the people fall behind at the same rate. However, with floors as units, they don't discover how bad the news is until a third of the way through the project, which is a relatively long time. Using rooms as units, they discover how bad the news is after only a few days. The moral of the story is to choose the smaller non-expandable unit of measure.

The final item to discuss is handling items that change priorities. This gets us back to the *Iceberg List*, which has shown great utility on projects in which the priorities change frequently and violently.

> *A large project was delivering value to a customer on a regular basis. The customer would change work assignments and priorities so often and so late that no project plan was meaningful. The customer was, however, happy with the software being delivered, so they kept requesting more work done.*
>
> *In desperation, the project manager just put all requested features into a single prioritized list with estimated sizes. He announced that whatever was above the "water line," as calculated from the size estimates and team's velocity, would get delivered in the next release, and everything else would be*

> ***delivered "later." The customer could insert, remove, modify or reprioritize features at any time, even affecting the current release. Without resorting to argument, all parties could calculate what would reach delivery during this cycle and what was pushed back.***

The name *Iceberg List* comes from the rising and sinking effect the list shows: adding high-priority items to the top of the list causes some above-water items to sink below the water line; removing above-water items may cause a new item rise above the water line). Just as with an iceberg, the above-water portion is only a fraction of the total size.

The *Iceberg List* is useful in hostile environments, where the sponsors change the requirements and priorities on a daily basis and without warning. In such an environment, post the current *Iceberg List* in a highly visible place, and make sure the contents of the next releases are *derived* rather than argued.

Figure 45 shows how this works, starting from the example in *Figure 35.*

- The size estimates changed.
- "Automated PO generation" got moved above the water line.
- As a result, "separate messages/questions from options" fell below the water line and got deferred to a later release (I kept the original release number in those moved lines so you can see them more easily).

Item	Feature Name	Value	Dev. Time (ideal days)	Revised estimate	release #
1.1	Configuration generates order line item comments	M	2	2.6	1
1.2	Configrator UI Rework: Verbose wizard style	H	6	7.8	1
2.1	PO generated correctly for configuration	H	5	6.5	1
2.2	Create/Confirm vendor items exist for skus	H	1.5	2	1
2.3	**PO generation is automatic**	**H**	**4**	5.2	**2**
3.1	Advanced Order form shows more details	M	4	5.2	1
3.2	Order fulfilled at PO cost	H	2	2.6	1
3.3	Repeat orders works with blind configurations	M	3	3.9	1
3.4	Configuration comments are viewable, not editable	L	1	1.3	1
4.1	Base hierarchy change	H	1.5	2	1
4.2	Style can locate price charts based on color selection	H	2	2.6	1
4.3	Assign specific color group colors to price charts	H	2	2.6	1
4.4	Separate messages from options	H	2	2.6	1
4.5	Separate questions from options	H	2	2.6	1
1.3	Configuration generates customer specific pricing	H	5	6.5	2
1.4	Allow adding a configuration and continue	L	2	2.6	2
3.5	Order shows sq. footage & running length	L	2	2.6	2
3.6	Vendor orderable items show additional detail	L	2	2.6	2
3.7	Printed window treatments show disclaimers	M	6	7.8	2

3.8	Allow order line item copying	H	2	2.6	2
4.1	Associate style with Retail.net DCL	L	1	1.3	2
4.11	Grid validation	L	1	1.3	2
4.6	Assign customer specific selling discounts	H	3	3.9	2
4.7	Customer lookup	H	1	1.3	2
4.8	Customer account type lookup	M	1	1.3	2
4.9	Options may have required questions	L	3	3.9	2

Figure 45, Chapter 10. The Iceberg List from *Figure 35* revised on the second iteration.

A Governance Model for Incremental, Concurrent or Agile Projects

This article was originally published as Humans and Technology Technical Report HaT TR 2005.03, Sept. 07, 2005.
[https://web.archive.org/web/20140329202800/http://alistair.cockburn.us/A+governance+model+for+agile+projects]

> *Regain oversight of a complex multi-project that uses concurrent and incremental development strategies in differing amounts on different subprojects, by estimating and then tracking intended versus actual functionality integrated each month or quarter.*

This article discusses a graphic that shows the status of larger projects, how to gather the information needed, read the status chart, and when needed, show more detailed breakdown for each subproject.

Motivation

Imagine a steering committee opening a large binder for a fairly large project, hoping to see its status. They are met by Gantt charts, cost expenditure tables, and if they are lucky, earned-value graphs. None of these show them quickly and accurately what is going on with the project, which components are in trouble, and where they stand with respect to delivery. Worse, many projects these days use incremental, concurrent, or agile approaches, which don't fit into the standard governance milestones of "requirements complete, design complete, code complete, integration complete."

This is not the article to review all the problems with that standard project governance model. The problems may, however, be briefly summarized as follows:

- The standard governance model is a single-pass waterfall model that has been roundly criticized over the years.
- It does not support incremental or concurrent approaches, both of which are being recommended more frequently these days.

- The Gantt chart does not show "percentage complete" very well, nor expected versus actual progress.
- The standard earned-value graph shows "tasks complete" well, but "tasks complete" does not reflect true progress on the project; true value in software development accrues suddenly (or fails suddenly) only at the moment at which the new features are integrated into the code base.

What we are looking for is a way that more accurately shows true value, more readily shows expected versus actual progress, and allows teams using different combinations of waterfall, incremental, concurrent, and agile approaches to show their varied strategies.

This article describes a proposed graphic that meets those constraints. We are starting to use it on a program that is fairly large for the private sector: about a dozen applications and two dozen supporting components and databases to be installed in various configurations in two dozen receiving sites. The graphic appears to work in our situation and has let us update a waterfall governance model to permit agile-, concurrent-, and incremental development.

The figures in this article are simplifications of the more complicated version we are using on our project, so we have a sense that it scales reasonably. We see ways to update the graphic either manually or automatically each month for the steering committee meeting. While not fully tested, it shows promise.

Here are the details.

(Note: the figures in the article are printed in black and white; the digital versions use colors.)

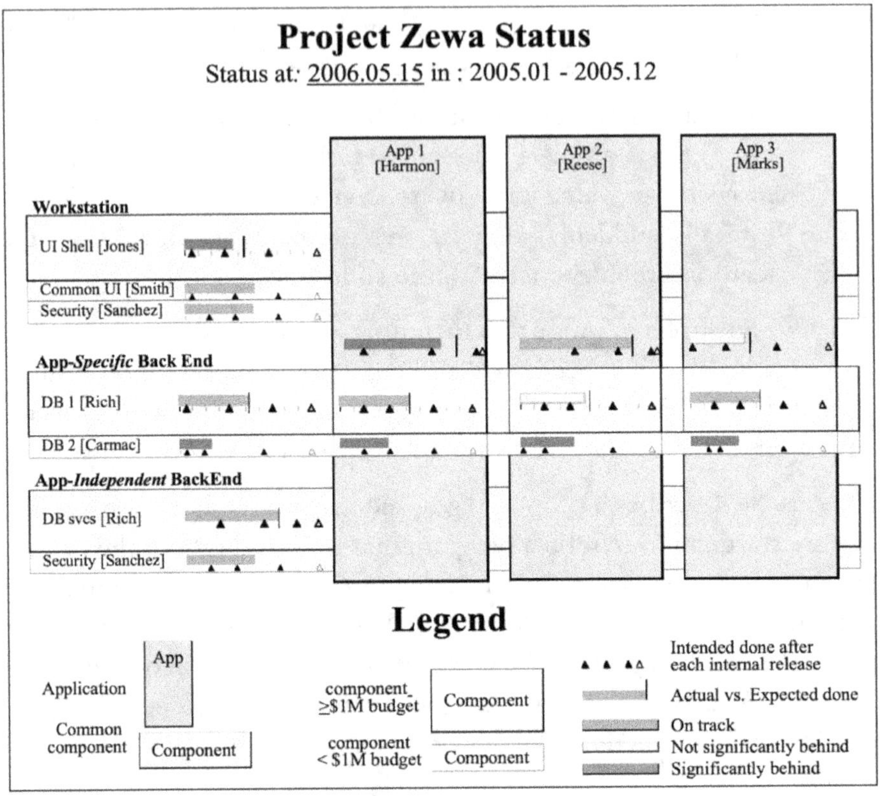

Figure 46, Chapter 10. Composite graphic for a complex project.

The Graphic

The graphic contains the following elements:

- The components being built, how each fits into the system architecture, the person responsible for each.
- Codependency relations between horizontal and vertical components.
- The incremental growth strategy for each component over the project life.
- The expected versus actual amount of work completed to date.
- A color or shading to mark the alarm level for each component.

Here follows a discussion of those topics in three categories: the system structure, the declaration of strategies, and expected versus ideal progress.

System structure

In *Figure 46*,

- The three vertical rectangles indicate *applications*, items bought separately for end-user functionality.
- The seven horizontal rectangles indicate service components needed across applications, on the user's desktop or the back end.
- Two of the horizontal components cross *in front of* the applications to indicate that the horizontal component contains specific, different functionality or data for each application.
- Domain databases that get extended for each new application are likely to be among these application-specific back-end components (more on this later).

The system shown in *Figure 46* is fairly simple. The first project for which I drew this graphic had 17 horizontal and 15 vertical components, and additional coloring to show legacy components that were to be removed over time. We were still able to draw it legibly on legal-sized paper.

Intended strategies

Although incremental development has been around much longer than the agile movement, the question of how to show different incremental strategies for governance purposes, preferably in a small space, is still open.

Agile project teams measure progress not according to how many requirements have been gathered, but by how much running functionality has been designed, programmed and integrated (Ron Jeffries neatly calls these Running, Tested, Features, or RTF [2]). A common way to show the growth of RTF is through burn-up charts, as in *Figure 47*, which shows the expected versus actual integration of a set of work-flow components by month.

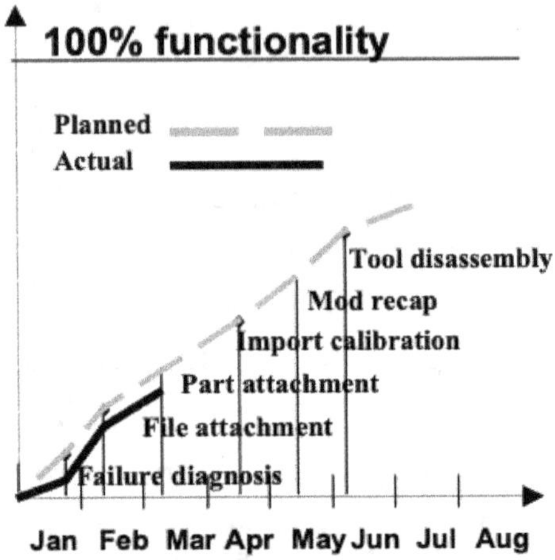

Figure 47, Chapter 10. Burn-up chart with expected versus actual integration of work-flow components by month.

Agile burn-up charts are very similar to traditional earned-value charts, with one crucial exception: the team only gets credit when the features are integrated into the full code base and the result passes testing [3]. This single shift in charting makes a big difference in the reliability of the progress data presented.

Burn charts show more than we need and take too much space for governance oversight purposes. To reduce their size and information, we use the idea of an "internal release" (IR).

A team that can't deploy its system to live users every few months can *pretend* to deploy the system. It can test, integrate and deploy the system to the computer of one or two "friendly" but real users. The team thus exercises the end of their development process, and gets true user feedback. Putting the system in front of real users (as opposed to a test machine in the basement) motivates the development team to take their work seriously.

Such an internal release should happen every one, two or three months. There are many reasons not to deploy fully every three months, but there is almost no reason not to carry out an internal release. These internal releases fit very neatly into a monthly or quarterly reporting mechanism.

With RTFs and internal releases, we are ready to capture various development strategy or strategies that might show up on an incremental-development project.

Figure 48, Chapter 10. Target progress markers.

In Figure 48:

- The vertical tick-marks show 10% units of completed RTF from left to right (100% complete at the right).
- The triangle milestone markers show the amount of RTF the team targets to have completed and integrated at each internal release milestone.

The figure shows three teams' strategies:

- The top team plans to get less than 10% of its functionality in place in the first internal release, and to add functionality in roughly equal thirds after that.
- The middle team intends to get 25% done in the first quarter, 60% by the end of the second quarter, and almost 85% by through the third quarter (possibly so they have time to fix mistakes in the fourth quarter).
- The bottom team expects to get almost 20% completed and integrated in each of the first two quarters, and then to speed up and get 30% done in each of the last two quarters.

Alert readers will notice that these tick-mark drawings capture the vertical axis of the burn-up charts at the internal-release times.

These small diagrams let different teams work in different ways and report on their intentions. This is our goal.

Intention-completion bars

Figure 49 adds the work actually completed compared to the work targeted for any point in time.

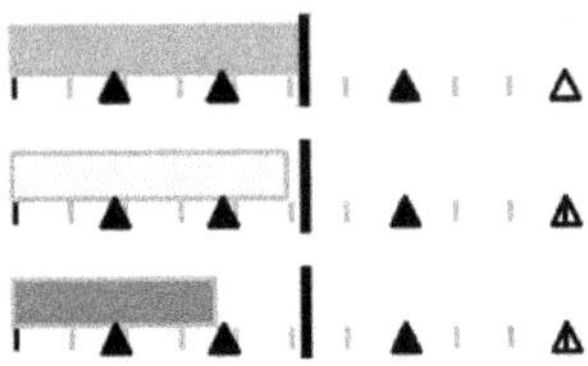

Figure 49, Chapter 10. Intention-completion bars (green, yellow, red).

In colors:

- The top bar is green, to indicate it is up to date.
- The middle bar is yellow, to indicate it is only a little behind.
- The bottom bar is red, to indicate it is far behind.

In *Figure 49*, the taller vertical bar moves from left to right within each internal release period to show the current targeted accomplishment. It can run at a constant rate within each period according to the calendar, or it can be synchronized with the team's iteration plans (2- to 6-week planning and tracking time windows). The shaded rectangles show the functionality (RTF) completed and integrated to date.

We see that the top team is delivering according to schedule, the middle team is a little behind, and the bottom team still has not finished the work scheduled for the second internal release.

Two comments must be made at this point about RTF. The first is that not all final deliverables consist of "features" that "run". Content databases and end-user documentation are examples. Teams can create intention-completion bars for whatever their final deliverables are, since those bars show growth of accomplishment over time.

The second comment is that measures not tied to RTF are naturally hazardous, since it is so easy to start tracking completion of artifacts that don't directly get bought by customers. Linking accomplishments to RTF makes the reporting of actual *value* both easier and more accurate.

Application-specific components

Horizontal components such as application databases require new work and new content for each new application. Progress on these application-specific horizontal components is typically difficult to report on, since "where they are" varies from application to application.

To show the status of such a component, we use intention-completion bars for the independent portion of the component, and for each application it must serve. This lets the teams move at different speeds as suits their particular situations, and the steering committee to see each team's status.

Summarizing the graphic

Let us review the elements of the graphic briefly:

1. The rectangles represent components, subsystems or applications.

    Vertical rectangles show applications;

    Horizontal ones show components that get used across multiple applications

    (This could be reversed for better layout if, for example, there are many applications and only a few cross-application components).

2. Each rectangle shows the place of the component in the overall architecture:

    -- The top set of horizontal components reside on the desktop.

    -- The middle and bottom sets of horizontal components reside as back-end services.

-- The horizontal rectangles running *behind* the applications get created independently of the applications.

-- The horizontal rectangles running *in front of* the applications require application-specific work or content.

3. Intention-completion markers are created for each component.

   -- They show the percentage of RTF intended for completion at each internal release milestone, the expected and the actual current accomplishment, and the alarm level.

   -- Intention-completion bars are created for each component and for each intersection of application-dependent components.

Collecting the information

The information rendered graphically in *Figure 47* also fits into a spreadsheet, a more useful place to keep it while gathering and updating the information. We can use automated tools to gather information about each component every week or two and roll up each team's accomplishments into reports at various levels. The highest level is the one that gets "painted" onto the graphic either by hand or automatically. (The graphic can be generated automatically using graphic markup languages, but that programming effort may take longer than simply coloring the bars each month).

Gathering the estimates

Figure 50 shows a spreadsheet that can be used to capture the estimates. Note that the confidence rating is accompanied by a smiling, neutral or frowning face to visually tag this important information.

It is one thing to say, "We intend to be 20% done after the first internal release", but the governance board needs to know, "20% of what?" Being behind on 20% of two use cases is very different than being behind on 20% of 80 use cases.

Project/ Component	Sub-component	Owner	% done in IR1				Total size	Units	Confidence in Estimate (L, M, H)
			IR 1	IR 2	IR 3	IR 4			
Desktop	frame	Mr. A	0	20	80	100	30	UI widgets	Med :-|
Desktop	APIs	Mr. A	20	50	80	100	60	API calls	Lo :-(
App 1	UI	Mr. B	5	60	90	100	450	UC steps	Lo :-(
App 1	app	Mr. B	10	60	90	100	450	UC steps	Hi :-)
App 1	bus svcs	Mr. B	5	50	80	100	450	UC steps	Lo :-(
DB 1	setup	Ms. C						??	Lo :-(
DB 1	App 1	Ms. C					60	codes	Lo :-(
DB 1	App 2	Ms. C					10	codes	Lo :-(
DB 2	setup	Ms. C						??	Lo :-(
DB 2	App 1	Ms. C					2000	entity attributes	Lo :-(
DB 2	App 2	Ms. C					1500	entity attributes	Lo :-(

Figure 50, Chapter 10. Spreadsheet to capture the data.

To capture the "of what" for tracking, we need three pieces of information. The first is "what is the unit of accomplishment?" This will often consist of use cases, or more likely, individual steps in use cases. Sometimes, something quite different is appropriate. A desktop component might have as units of accomplishment user interface (UI) widgets (frames, pull-down lists, buttons) and interface calls used by the applications. A database might have entities and attributes; a web site might have articles and images; a medical database might have medical codes as a unit of accomplishment.

The second piece of information is obviously "about how many units do you expect to create?"

The third piece of information is the confidence level on the estimate. At the beginning of the project, it is appropriate to have low confidence ratings in the estimates: "We expect somewhere between 15 and 50 UI widgets, call it 30, plus or minus 50%", with the caution, "You called me into this room and made me give you numbers, but it's not like I have a really good basis for those numbers!" The initially rough size estimate is still useful for getting an early handle on the size and shape of the thing to be built. That is why the information is collected even when the confidence rating is low. Marking a low confidence rating is useful to the project leaders, because they can then raise the priority of getting enough information to improve the estimation confidence.

Needless to say, the estimate should be updated at the start of each successive iteration, with raised expectations about its accuracy and confidence levels.

Gathering the status

To tag the timeline, we need to give each iteration or planning window a milestone number, such as internal release completed followed by iteration completed. Thus, milestone 0.3 means before the first internal release, at the end of the third iteration, and milestone 2.1 means after the second internal release, the end of the first iteration after that.

Project/ Component	Sub-component	Owner	% done in				Total size	Units	Expected at IR 2.3 (%)	Expected at IR 2.3 (units)	Actual at IR 2.3 (units)
			IR 1	IR 2	IR 3	IR 4					
Desktop	frame	Mr. A	0	20	80	100	30	UI widg-ets	50%	15	15
Desktop	APIs	Mr. A	20	50	80	100	60	API calls	65%	39	36
App 1	UI	Mr. B	5	60	90	100	450	UC steps	75%	337	310
App 1	app	Mr. B	10	60	90	100	450	UC steps	75%	337	320
App 1	bus svcs	Mr. B	5	50	80	100	450	UC steps	65%	292	280

Figure 51, Chapter 10. Spreadsheet updated after two iterations.

After each iteration, the teams send in their RTF numbers, which get rolled up into a summary spreadsheet at any level of granularity desired. The nice thing here is that this roll-up can be produced automatically with simple tools.

Figure 51 shows how the first few rows of such a spreadsheet might look after iteration 2.3.

The Status Report Packet

The graphic in *Figure 46* serves as a good *summary page* of the package put in front of the steering committee. That package also needs detail pages for the separate subprojects.

Detail Sheet for UI Shell

Product Manager: Jones

status at: *2006.05.15*

	Targeted accomplishment	**Work being deferred**	**Dominant problem/risk**
Composite	<What the accomplishment was to be in this period for this subproject?>	<What got moved out of this period into the next period?>	<The dominant risk for this subproject>
Requirements	<The amount of requirements intended to be completed in this period>	<What requirements got moved out of this period into the next period?>	<The dominant risk for the requirements gathering effort >
UI Design	<The amount of user interface design intended to be completed in this period>	<What user interface design got moved out of this period into the next period?>	<The dominant risk for the UI designers>
Program	<The amount of RTF intended to be integrated in this period>	<What programming got moved out of this period into the next period?>	<The dominant risk for the programmers>
User Doc.	<The amount of end-user documentation intended to be completed in this period>	<What end-user documentation got moved out into the next period?>	<The dominant risk for user documentation>

Surprises this period:

<Surprises the manager or the team discovered. (i.e. The productivity of the programmers wasn't as high as expected.)>

Lessons learned this period:

<The lessons to be taken out of the period's work. (i.e. In the future, multiply developer estimates by a factor of 1.5 before committing to them.) >

Items needing special attention:

<Anything the team wishes to report out. It may expand on risks, or highlight some particular worry.>

Cost / budget

	This Period	Total to date
Expected	$	$
Actual	$	$

Figure 52, Chapter 10. Detail page for the project status.

Figure 52 shows a fragment from a sample detail page. This detail page has three sections after the header:

- a status / targeted / deferred / and risk snapshot for each section of work within the component,
- a commentary, including surprises and lessons learned during the previous period, and
- cost rollup information

The most unusual part of this status page is the way in which the intention-completion bars are constructed to describe the strategy and accomplishments of non-RTF work

Intention-Completion Bars for non-RTF work

When someone sees a component marked with a high-alarm status bar on the summary page, they will naturally want to read more detail. They will need to understand what is happening with respect to requirements gathering, UI design, design and programming, and user documentation.

The good news is that we can use the intention-completion bars to show progress within each specialty, whether the team is using a sequential (waterfall) strategy or a concurrent strategy. Figures 8 and 9 illustrate the two.

Figure 53, Chapter 10. A sequential development strategy.

Figure 53 shows a team planning to work in sequential fashion.

- The plan to finish all their requirements in the first period.
- They don't plan on starting either the UI design or the programming in that period.
- They expect to get the UI design fully complete in the second quarter.
- Tey plan to get perhaps 10% of the programming done in the second quarter and the rest done equally in the third and fourth quarters.

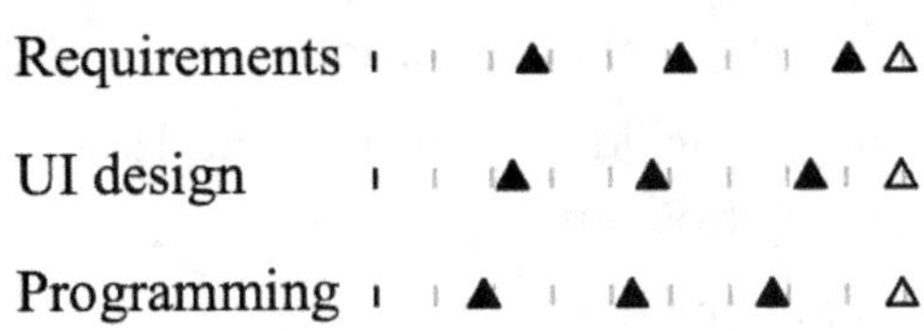

Figure 54, Chapter 10. A concurrent development strategy.

Figure 54 shows a strongly concurrent strategy.

- This team plans to get not quite a third of their requirements settled in the first period
- They plan to have nearly as much UI design and programming done as requirements gathered.
- The requirements people will lead the UI design people by a small amount, and the UI design people will lead the programmers by a small amount, but otherwise these groups will run alongside each other and in parallel.
- They intend to continue in this fashion throughout the entire project.

In this article I don't wish to indicate that either approach is superior to the other. What is important here is that both sequential and concurrent strategies (and many combinations) can be shown using the intention-completion bars.

Status, targeted, deferred, risks

For any component, the steering committee members will want to see at the top of the detail page:

- The intention-completion bars for the whole component from the summary sheet, and for the work efforts within the component, including non-RTF work as just described;
- What was targeted for accomplishment during this reporting period;
- What work is being deferred from this period into the next;
- Wat dominant problems each subteam is facing, or the risks they expect.

The risks and problems column lets the team signal for help, whether that means more people, more equipment, more time with customers, or whatever.

Surprises, lessons learned, items needing special attention

The middle of the page allows the team to reflect and report on what happened during the reporting period.

The first section describes the surprises discovered. On projects I've visited, these have included the programmers not getting as much done as expected, a piece of technology not working as expected, or a new practice, such as daily stand-up meetings, being effective and to be kept.

The second section describes the lessons to be taken out of the period's work. These might include multiplying developer estimates by a factor before committing to them, doing technology spikes before committing to technology, or choosing to keep new practices such as daily stand-up meetings. These must be truly lessons *learned* within the period, not speculations on what might work in the future.

The third section is for anything the team wishes to report out. It may expand on risks, or highlight some particular worry they will be paying close attention to.

Cost Rollup

Finally, the steering group needs to see how fast the money is being used. This section may be presented in tabular or burn-up form, and include staffing sizes as well as budget information, as desired.

Summary

The first contribution of this article is the description of the intention-completion graphic, showing

- the strategy that the team has in mind for their work, whether sequential or concurrent,
- how much they had expected to have done at this reporting point, and
- how much they actually have done at this point.

The intention-completion graphic is so important because it allows different teams to choose different strategies and report on them, all in the same format. The absence of a common reporting format has been a pain point for incremental, concurrent and agile projects for a long time.

The second contribution is the project summary graphic and its spreadsheet counterpart. The spreadsheet allows the leadership team to collect estimates and plans at a very early point in the project, and update them easily using automated tools. The graphic provides a way to show at a glance the entirety of a quite complex project. This addresses the question of "What are we building? and How are we doing?"

The third contribution is the description of a sample one-page detail sheet for each component or subproject. This page shows at a glance the strategies and status within the sub-project, along with key information the steering committee needs to understand and respond to.

The resulting packet of information allows people who meet only once a month or quarter to assess the intentions and status of projects that use various mixtures of waterfall, incremental, concurrent, and agile strategies.

If you use this model and find ways of improving it, please let me know at alistair.cockburn@acm.org

Related Reading

[1] The online version of this article online: www.crosstalk. / ... / ...

[2] Jeffries, R., "A Metric Leading to Agility", 2004.06.16, online at http://www.xprogramming.com/xpmag/jatRtsMetric.htm

[3] Cockburn, A., "Earned-value and Burn Charts", Humans and Technology Technical Report 2004.04, online at http://alistair.cockburn.us/crystal/articles/evabc/earnedvalueandburncharts.htm

Using Burn Charts in Practice

Burn charts are so powerful because our eyes pick up the trend and slope of the line. With no conscious effort, the viewer immediately sees the trend and where the lines are heading.

Burn charts and earned-value charts

The burn charts that originated in the agile world are very much the same as the earned-value charts that originated in traditional project management. The main difference is that standard earned-value charts give credit for tasks.

The agile manifesto is very clear that tasks are not the interesting unit of completions: Chapter 3, *Why decisions matter* describes why.

Tasks such as writing a spec, writing a design document, writing tests, writing code only *add decisions* to your internal inventory. Those belong on the negative side of the ledger – they are debt.

The only way to cancel that debt is to validate or break and fix those errors. Until the code is tested and integrated, it is all speculation. (This is the origin and mean of the 2nd value in the Agile Manifesto.). The agile world only credits code that has been at least tested and integrated, if not yet deployed and used.

Replace tasks with completed functionality, and burn- and earned-value charts become identical. This is good news, since there are already a lot of practice and tooling around earned-value charts.

Additionally, show both work completed and cost burned on the same chart for a good snapshot view of the project.

Burn-down versus burn-up charts

Burn-*down* charts are good for when the list of things to finish is stable and won't change. The number of rooms in a house and the number of items a team promises to complete in a sprint both make good vertical axis in a burn-down chart.

The power of a burn-*down* chart is the emotional motivation it gives the team. Driving a graph to zero is a powerful emotion force.

In timeboxed iterations such as Scrum's sprints, the burn-down chart is great *within a sprint and within the team*, but is generally not interesting outside of the team.

Burn-*up* charts show progress at the organizational level, how teams are doing over time. The sprints are the tick marks on the graph. What happens inside a sprint is not so interesting, because the sponsors are interested in how the work of the sprints add up over time.

Where burn charts are not so powerful is when there is no concept of 100% completion. In this case, there is no baseline or top bar to measure against. This can be for projects that are funded to go as far as possible in a given time, without a specific quantity. Companies using continuous development techniques might fall into this category, if there is no quarterly product goal.

Using one-dimensional charts for compound projects

Burn charts are easy to read, but take a lot of space. To get a compact view, project the burn-up chart onto the vertical axis, as described in the preceding article and shown in *Figure 55*.

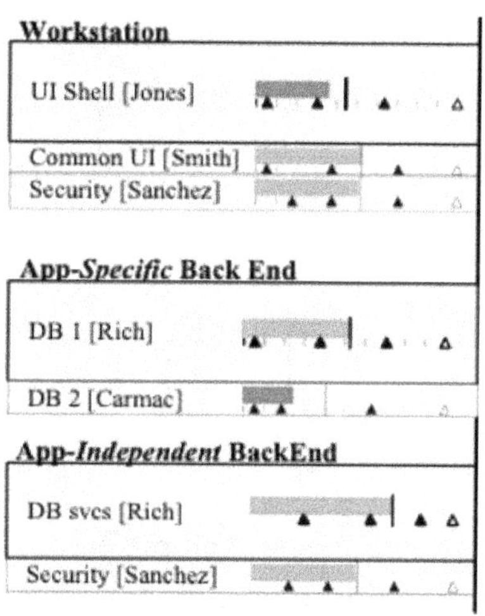

Figure 55, Chapter 10. One-line charts for a multi-team project.

This gives us a visualization that is useful when there are a lot of projects or project sub-parts to look at. One executive put all the one-line charts on the wall in front of his office and held the weekly status meeting for each at that wall.

Figure 55 shows part of a detail page from a complex project, with the status of the sub-system teams, as described in the preceding article.

You can liven up the chart with animals (I'm not even joking). At one company, one manager had little post-its with just a feature number on each moving from left to the right, going from start to shipped. Although accurate and informative, it was boring to look at.

Another manager simply replaced the post-its with pictures of race horses, the story number on the saddle. I was fascinated by how much more compelling and interesting the same chart was just changing the square post-its to horses. Try it.

Both of those people only showed % done. Better is to use two animals, one for where the project *should* be, the other for where it *is*. Since most projects are always behind schedule, I like to use a fox or greyhound as the *actual* and a rabbit as the *predicted*, so that the fox or greyhound appears to be chasing the rabbit. *Figure 56* illustrates.

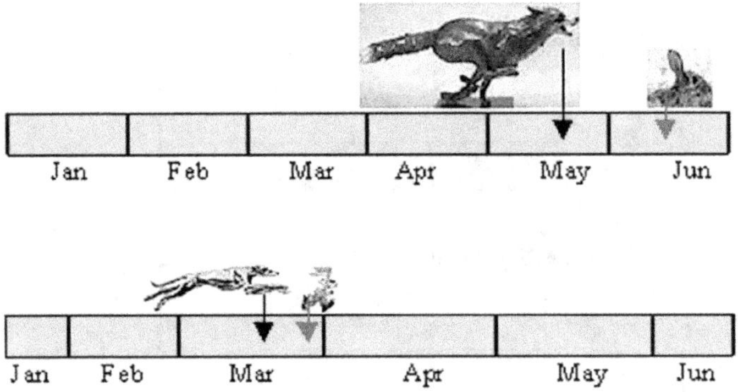

Figure 56, Chapter 10. The fox-and-rabbit chart.

These variations allow you to show all the same information as the one-line chart, just a little bit more fun.

Reflections and Key Points

Reflections

Reading that article 20 years later, I find my favorite thoughts are:

> *"Burn-up charts have a natural mapping to earned-value charts."*
>
> *"They reveal the strategy being used, show the progress made against predictions, and open the door to discussions about how best to proceed."*

Did you catch these key points?

From: *Earned-Value and Burn Charts*

"They have a natural mapping to earned-value charts."

"They reveal the strategy being used, show the progress made against predictions, and open discussions about how best to proceed."

"Find "interesting" and clear intermediate milestones. … In software, those milestones are the delivery of running, tested code."

"The *Iceberg List.* The "above water" part lists all the items that can be delivered in the current delivery cycle. The "below water" part lists every that will be delivered in later delivery cycles. / The *Iceberg List* is useful in hostile environments, where the sponsors change the requirements and priorities on a daily basis and without warning"

"*you get no credits for any item that does not result in running, tested code." p142*

"it is *bad news detected early*, as opposed to *bad news detected too late to do anything about it!*"

"It shows both the status and rate of progress ("velocity") in a way that is both clear and easy to discuss."

"Burn-down charts provide emotional motivation."

"project scope does in fact change over time. / raising and lowering of the ceiling, or 100% mark, as the project progresses."

A Governance Model For Incremental, Concurrent or Agile Projects

"Ron Jeffries neatly calls these Running, Tested, Features, or RTF."

"A team that can't deploy its system to live users every few months can *pretend* to deploy the system / test, integrate and deploy the system to the computer of one or two "friendly" but real users."

"Intention-completion markers show the expected and the actual current accomplishment, and the alarm level."

"Intention-completion bars are created for each component and for each intersection of application-dependent components."

"use the intention-completion bars to show progress within each specialty, whether the team is using a sequential (waterfall) strategy or a concurrent strategy."

"it allows different teams to choose different strategies and report on them, all in the same format."

Using burn charts in practice

"The intention-completion graphic is so important because it allows different teams to choose different strategies and report on them, all in the same format."

"tasks are not the interesting unit of completions."

"Tasks such as writing a spec, writing a design document, writing tests, writing code only *add decisions* to your internal inventory. / The only way to cancel that debt is to validate or break and fix those errors. Until the code is tested and integrated, it is all speculation."

"puts all the 1D charts on the wall in front of their office."

"it shows a fox or a greyhound chasing a rabbit."

Visualize what is happening on the project with burn charts. Show status on complex projects with fox-and-rabbit charts.

---

11. The Product Manager version

Slice your product features according to Kano's subjective quality elements. Fit those into the Learning-Value-Tail curve.

This chapter contains the blog posts and articles I wrote from 2007 to 2011 while working out how to slice and grow product features both with and without considering Kano's subjective quality article.

Jeff Patton and the ABCs of Quality (May 27,2007)

It's a rare pleasure to get two small epiphanies in one week. For the first one I am indebted to Volkmar Nitz of the O.C. Tanner company here in Salt Lake City and, who is writing what I expect will be a great book on design from the outside in (whenever he finally gets it done).

Volkmar opened the critical doors in my brain by introducing me to "Kano's Theory of Attractive Quality and Packaging" (1984) (which I have seen on paper but not on the web). Jeff then hammered me about the head with his idea of iterative growth until, finally, using my slight reinterpretation of Kano's work, his idea finally made wonderful sense to me. This blog entry is about how it makes sense, and uses words that I think may be easier to understand than either Kano's or Jeff's. (No doubt you will let me know if that is not true.)

Kano uses two dimensions of quality, things that must be there and things that are wonderful if they are there. He calls them "must-be" quality and "attractive" quality. His paper is quite lovely, but ends up overly complicated. Just for starters, he really has **three** buckets of qualities that he jams onto his two dimensions, which is fine for his graph, but too much to 'grok' as is needed in daily work.

Here's my simplification of Kano's quality statement, suitably abridged to suit my needs. If you think I've missed something critical, write to me:

There are three buckets of things we might include in products or services. For simplicity, I will simply call the buckets **A**, **B**, **C**.

- Bucket **A** holds things that you would be unhappy without. Brakes on your car are an example. No brakes, bad car. Not going to buy that car (unless I have some other thing up my sleeve). There also needs to be a spare tire, and so on.
- Bucket **B** holds things that you are happier the more of, less happy the less of. Mileage, power, trunk space, leg room, price (inverted). You'll not get no mileage, no power, no leg room,

etc., so it's not binary. Buying a car, you presuppose there will be brakes, so now you fidget endlessly over how much extra you have to pay for the extra horsepower, leg room, mileage, etc.

(Jeff calls these 'scalable' features because their qualities live on a continuous scale, but people think of other things with the word "scale", so we're looking for other words. I'll use "on a gradient", but that's not wholly satisfactory either).

- Bucket **C** holds things you won't be unhappy if you don't get, maybe rather are surprised if you do get. The first sun-roof on a car would have been in this category; the first gas station where you could pay by credit card at the pump, MP3 player input jacks on cars right this year (2007). These are often binary – putting 10 sunroofs on my car doesn't give me more 'wow' than just one.

Kano does 2-dimensional graph things with those buckets that we don't need to look at. He usefully observes that over time, items get introduced at **C**, then move to **B** then to **A**. This drives innovation to create more **C** items. Gas stations these days "had better" have credit-card payment at the pump, or drivers will simply drive off – credit-card payment at the pump has moved from **C** to **A**.

That's Kano. Now for Jeff.

Jeff gets upset with the agile crowd for treating features as binary things that are either "in" or "out". Most agilists "cut" features from the backlog when they can't get them all done in the targeted time period. Jeff prefers to "thin" the features, so he can optimize how much business value he delivers. Two features thinned down to a barely-usable quality level may deliver more business value than a full one at a "gorgeous" level and the other not at all. Jeff has been going nuts trying to teach people how to thin features.

My little epiphany was seeing another way to describe his idea. See if this works for you:

Convert as many features as possible from bucket **A** to bucket **B**, reworking their description so they aren't binary (in/out) but gradient-based (better/worse).

Now shift from a discussion of "how many are present?" to "will I be happier if this feature is higher on the quality gradient, or would I be "more" happier if something else gets to move from absent to present at a lower quality rating on the gradient?"

'Example':

- Of course you need a brake and a spare tire … we've installed a hand-brake and a deflated mini-spare with an air can.
- Now we have some free time to install the barely-acceptable version of something else you want.
- Now you can upgrade the brake on a category **B** basis to caliper brakes, disc, anti-lock braking, and so on, in competition with getting an inflated mini-spare or a full-size spare tire, or going from /just/ lights to fog lights, halogens, etc, and in competition with 2 doors, or 4 doors, or gull-wing doors, etc etc.

In a sense, using Kano's terms, unhappiness is minimized, because you can have "a little bit" of everything, or at least a little bit of a lot more things than you otherwise were going to get, and you get to choose the amount of each, because everything is in the **B** bucket instead of the **A** or **C** buckets.

* * * * *

That was the good news. Now for the bad news (isn't there always some?). Putting everything into the **B** bucket means steering the project feature list on a very complicated gradient. When is any one feature "sufficient" compared to any other? What is the business value of improving this / these over that / those? On the technical side, what is the technical cost of revisiting intermediate-quality features and improving them a notch or two?

I know people who "can" steer projects this way; I know people who do. It's Jeff's challenge to teach more people how to do it.

That was the first little epiphany of this week. The second one is outlined in , with full exposition in the article

[https://web.archive.org/web/20140329201744/http://alistair.cockburn.us/Collaboration:+the+dance+of+contribution]

See the original blog post at:

[https://web.archive.org/web/20140329205655/http://alistair.cockburn.us/Jeff+Patton+and+the+ABCs+of+Quality]

Agile in Tables (June 25, 2011)

I'm not much of one for running a project in tables, but other people are, and we are now at a point where some of the tables are looking interesting and useful. Here are a few I would consider using:

1. Learning-Value-Tail (LVT) table

Figure 57 and *Figure 58* show the LVT table, mapping a list of projects, features, or user stories against their risk or knowledge-acquisition aspect, their value aspect and their tail or gloss aspect (see Trim the tail).

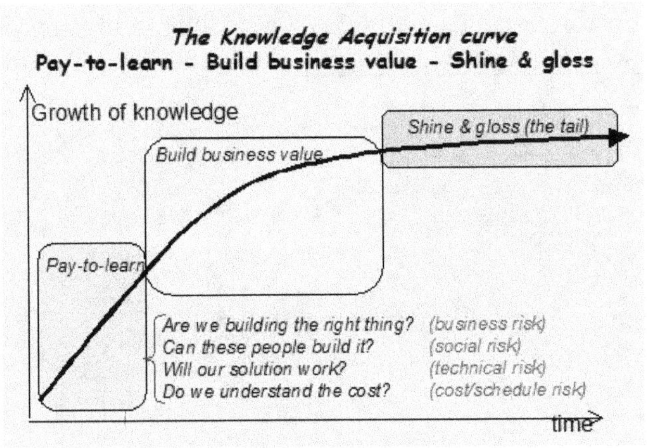

Figure 57, Chapter 11. LVT: Learn, grow Value, Trim the tail.

Project/feature/story	Risk (knowledge)	Value	Tail (gloss)
P1	Whatever it might be	Whatever it might be	Whatever it might be
P2	Etc.	Etc.	Etc.
P3			

Figure 58, Chapter 11. LVT table: Learn, grow Value, Trim the tail.

The purpose of the LVT table is to expose the 3 schedule aspects of each project, feature or story, thus allowing the team to tackle them in any order they might prefer – column-first, row-first, or some funny diagonal.

The good thing about this table is that it permits all possible implementation schemes, and maps to the trim the tail curve.

2. Knowledge acquisition table

As I've been exploring the front section of the knowledge-acquisition or Trim the tail curve, four risk or knowledge acquisition areas keep showing up:

- Business risk: Are we building the right thing?
- Social risk: Can these people build it?
- Technical risk: Will all the parts of our idea work together?
- Cost/schedule risk: Do we understand the size and difficulty?

These can be gathered and framed as a single question: *"What are we trying to learn right now?"*, which is quickly followed by, *"What is the cheapest, fastest way to get that information?"*

We can put these into an extension of the LVT table just for the risk/knowledge question, the Knowledge Acquisition table:

Project /feature /story	How do we know we're building the right thing?	How do we know these people can build it?	How do we know the solution will work as imagined?	How do we know the size and difficulty is as we imagine it?
F1	experiment	experiment	experiment	experiment
F2	etc	etc	etc	etc
F3				
F4				

Figure 59, Chapter 11. Tracking certainty in a table.

3. Feature Grade table

This table is due to Jeff Patton and his grades of quality idea, turned into a table by Gery Derbier.

Grade each feature or story separately as F (not acceptable), D (minimally acceptable but not something you would want to ship), C (minimally usable), B (quite nice), and A (top quality).

One strategy for using this idea is to get every mandatory feature to a C level first, before trying to get any of them to a B or A level. Then use the time available to get the important features up to B or A as desired. In principle, this delivers the highest "perceived" quality of the final product.

Feature	Grade
F1	D
F2	C
F3	F
F4	C

Figure 60, Chapter 11. Feature-graded table, after Patton and Derbier.

4. Hexagonal architecture micro-increment table

This table comes from the [Hexagonal Architecture] description, particularly the "barn door" image. See *Figure 61*.

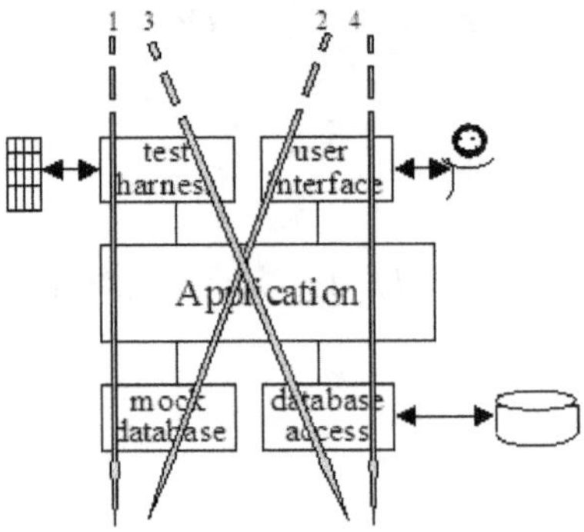

Figure 61, Chapter 11. Hexagonal architecture's "barn door" sequence.

This picture suggests developing features in three stages:

1. Test harness functionality loopback in lieu of database
2. Real UI functionality loopback in lieu of database
3. Real UI functionality real database

(where the UI and the real database can be added in either order)

I first came up with this table when contemplating a serious piece of multi-site development on a large portfolio of projects, being shipped to multiple countries, where we were not sure what the quality of the programmers might be.

In order to regulate the development and keep track of the quality, we proposed setting into place the following rules:

1. Every developer **must** first check in **A [test harness to mock database]**, with tests. The build manager or iteration manager or customer or product owner would reject any feature checked in without it being (a) free from the UI and (b) with automated tests
2. Then the UI and the database are added in any order at any time, with the caveat that the **A** version must still run at all times.

This yields, as with the Risk-Value-Tail table, a rich set of possibilities for sequences in which the feature set might be implemented: all **A** sections, then **B**, then **C**, or some of each, as long as the two rules are followed. It also allows the UI and database work to proceed somewhat disconnected from the feature set, allowing them to go slower or faster, as needed.

Figure 63 shows the resulting HA table:

Feature	Test-app-loopback	+UI	+database
F1	Due/done date	Due/done date	Due/done date
F2	Due/done date	Due/done date	Etc
F3	Etc	etc	etc

Figure 62, Chapter 11. Micro-incremental development with Hexagonal Architecture.

Four tables is a lot of tables – I'm not sure how to use them together… However, one of them might do your project some good, perhaps even a couple of them. Write me and tell me if you use them.

Alistair (June 25, 2011)

See the original blog post at:
[https://web.archive.org/web/20140329203043/http://alistair.cockburn.us/Agile+in+tables]

Reflection on the Use of Tables

Tables give your project a useful "parts inventory" of sorts. It doesn't dictate the path you follow; that is entirely up to you. Once you decide, you can use various status visualization techniques, coloring the items done or putting them on the burn-up chart.

One idea I wish to highlight, which might have escaped your attention, as the blog post only described it briefly, is the brilliant adjustment Géry Derbier made to Jeff Patton's idea of grading features.

Jeff taught us that features are fractal: features contain sub-features. By *thinning* the sub-features and adding them in competition with adding new features at a basic level, you can balance quality or feature-richness against quality at a very fine-grained level. This allows you to get the maximum net value for the time and money spent.

Kano and Quality (Aug 28, 2007)

In Jeff Patton and the ABCs of Quality I tried setting out Kano's 2D map of how features fit into a perceived-quality landscape. Have been trying this out on a couple of my own projects and something hasn't been working very well (actually, other people tried it on me for my projects, and it didn't work very well).

I start off by saying something like, "Where I'm hurting is; what I really want is." Then my friends start pushing back on me and saying "Why don't you just do xyz?" And I say, "Because my "minimum" requirement is xyz." And then they say, "Well, you can buy system xyz which will help you do that." And I go, "But I don't care about of that system." And so on.

Before I drew this grid, they'd alternate between inadequate and gold-plated solutions, not seeing that they weren't providing the minimum requirements, or were handing me a bunch of stuff I didn't care about.

They keep alternating between two poles, neither of which suited me, and we all got frustrated. Analyzing again what I was asking for or rejecting, I found Kano's grid was missing all the negatives —-stuff I don't want to see or even talk about.

In the end I came up with 7 feature categories. The first three are Kano:

1. What I require to be present or we're not in the game.
2. What I'd like more of, makes me happier, generally on a gradient
3. What I'm not expecting, has a positive WoW factor

Here's what's missing in Kano:

4. What I consider irrelevant, don't especially want, won't go out of my way for. Some people call this "gold plating"
5. What I hate, don't put this in (e.g., you give a free sample of my competitor's product with every purchase)
6. What I'd like less of, makes me unhappier, on a gradient.
7. What I'm not expecting and has a negative (YucK) factor.

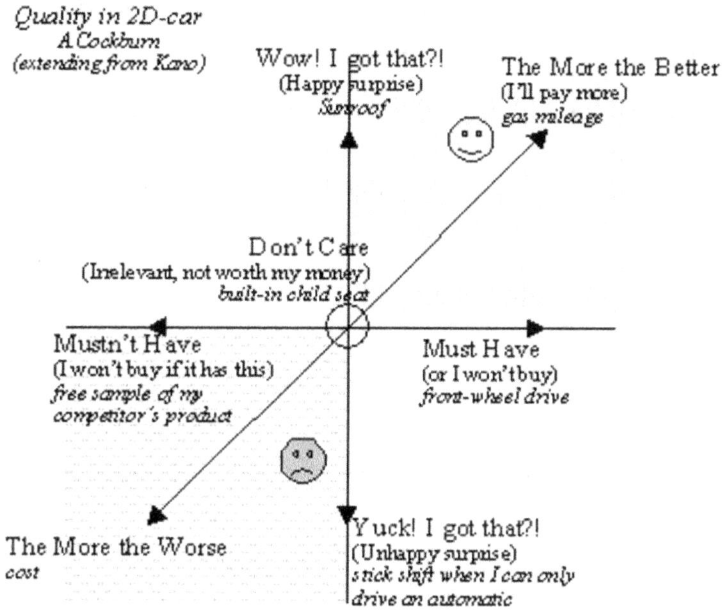

Figure 63, Chapter 11. Extending Kano's qualities for a car.

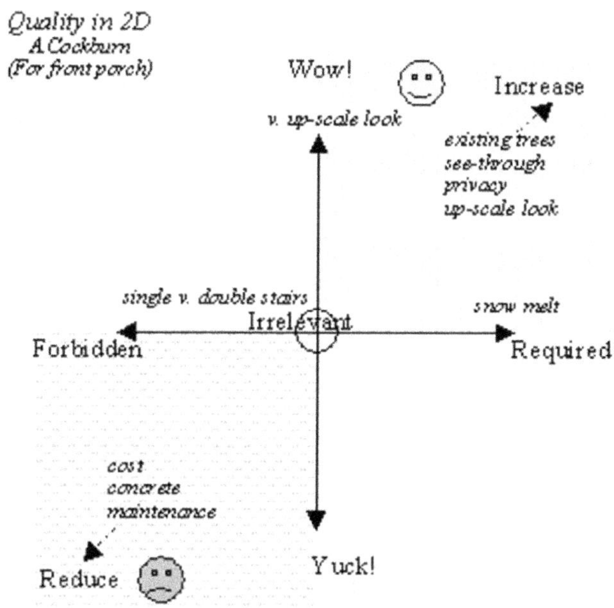

Figure 64, Chapter 11. Kano's extended qualities for my front porch.

Figure 63 and *Figure 64* show these on Kano's grid for buying a car and putting new steps on our front porch.

I don't think we're done with this topic, but this is a new direction. (By the time we get done, I'm sure we'll have rediscovered something totally well known. ... the reason this is worth pursuing is that Kano's 2D quality grid has gained quite a bit of acceptance in certain circles).

... more later …

* * * * *

OK, it's later (2 days later)... and already two people have commented that it's too complicated and making distinctions that may not be necessary. So let's go back to "the ABCs of Quality (discussion: Re: Jeff Patton and the ABCs of Quality)", where I was trying "simplify" things instead of making them complicated (side note: I've noticed that although we have this great 2D visual system, using two dimensions is actually already too complicated. So let's map it back to the ABC list as in "that post (discussion: Re: Jeff Patton and the ABCs of Quality)".

... question to self … do I add 'D' or 'Z' for the negative stuff? what is the "negative" letter? ... let's pick Z and see what happens (no doubt someone will write in with a comment) ...

OK, so from before:

- **A** holds things that you would be unhappy without (Mike Cohn calls them **baseline**).
- **B** holds positive things on the sliding scale (Mike Cohn calls them **linear**).
- **C** holds things you won't be unhappy without, maybe rather surprised to get (Mike Cohn calls them **exciters**).
- **Z** holds things you don't care about or don't want for whatever reason (the origin and all lower-left quadrant in the examples above) (Mike Cohn doesn't mention these, maybe I'll just wait until he coins a usable term ;-).

Figure 65 shows how the car and porch examples now look.

Level	Car	Porch
A (baseline)	front-wheel drive	snow-melt system
B (linear)	gas mileage trunk room power	up-scale look keeping existing trees see-through railings privacy
C (exciters)	sun roof backing-up video camera	very up-scale look
Z (irrelevant, avoid, or reduce)	built-in child seat free sample of my competitor's product cost	single or double stairs concrete maintenance cost

Figure 65, Chapter 11. The extended Kano table for car and porch.

Is that better? Have we made progress?

End note: Exciters fade over time. That was one thing that Kano's original papers did describe and discuss. The first gas station chain that allowed payment by credit card after hours had a competitive advantage for a while – people would expressly drive to those stations for gas after hours. Once the competition copied that technology, it moved from a pleasant surprise / competitive advantage to a minimum requirement. Bummer, but that's what happens. Currently, one might put in this category the backing-up video cameras in cars. Perhaps in 10 years it might even be mandated by government.

Also, note that things move from the must-have to the sliding scale dimension. That was the entire point of the "Jeff Patton and the ABCs of Quality" posting, describing how he does this deliberately … first provide the minimally acceptable version of the feature, covering any 'must-have' dimension, thus moving it to the 'pay-as-you-go' or sliding scale dimension.

— Alistair (Aug 28, 2007)

See the original article at : [https://web.archive.org/web/20140329205631/http://alistair.cockburn.us/Kano+and+quality]

Fitting Kano into the Knowledge Acquisition Curve (2026)

There appears to be a contradiction between the knowledge acquisition curve presented in Chapter 5, *Disciplined Learning*, and the three Kano categories *mandatory, linear* and *delighter.*

For a refresher, *Figure 66* shows the knowledge acquisition curve, which I will call the *Learning-Value-Tail* curve from here out:

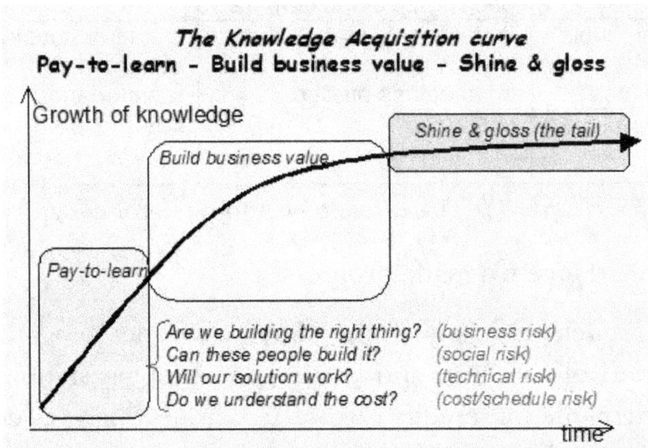

Figure 66, Chapter 11. The Learning-Value-Tail curve.

The learning-value-tail curve suggests three categories, to be done in this sequence (more or less):

1. Pay-to-learn (risk reduction items)
2. Early high-value items
3. Later low-value items

Traditional project management suggests the MoSCoW sequence to choose what might constitute high- versus low-value items:

1. Must have
2. Should have
3. Could have
4. Would like to have

But Kano suggests something different:

1. Mandatory

2. Linear
3. Delighters

How do we reconcile these different approaches?

As usual, the best insights come from live situations:

> *It was a small, private company with very sensible leaders. They were kicking off a large-for-them initiative for a new product. The first version needed to be delivered in exactly 8 months. The meeting was to work out the shape of the project to deliver that product. I was the facilitator.*
>
> *We worked in the following steps, which I would be happy to repeat under similar circumstances:*
>
> *1 – Using a Motivation Map, list all the people who cared about the product at any level: students, professors, providers, sales people, etc. We had maybe 6-8 stakeholders listed.*
>
> [https://web.archive.org/web/20140329205931/http://alistair.cockburn.us/Games+stakeholders+play]
>
> *2 – Using an "in/out" list, list every aspect of any topic that would be considered in-scope for the first-delivery project, and out of scope for that project. Anything was fair game for this list, from features to architecture to advertising to hiring to ... anything. This list guided the conversation for the rest of the session. (Side note: Constructing this list took a long time; however, it paid for itself as people started to raise an issue, then looked at the list and said, "Oh, that's out of scope*

3- Write down the Kano elements for each stakeholder in a 4-column table: Stakeholder / Mandatory / Linear / Delighter as shown in *Figure* 68.

It was at this point that something interesting happened. Someone asked, "Can we give a delighter to any of the stakeholders in the first delivery?"

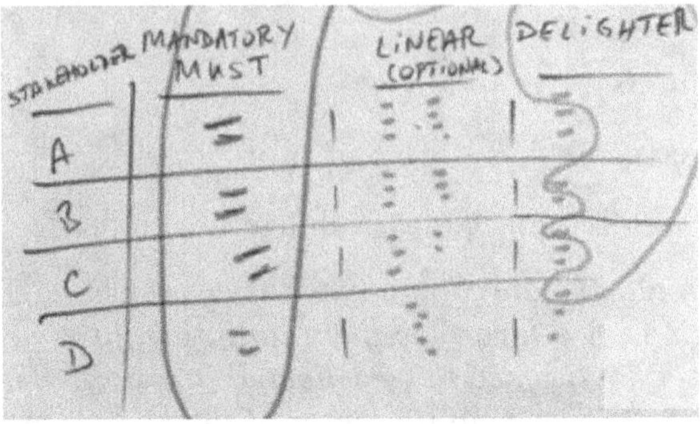

Figure 67, Chapter 11. Listing Kano elements by stakeholder.

It was obvious that we had to give the mandatory elements to each stakeholder in the first delivery. Knowing that, the room reduced the mandatory set to truly the minimum – not just features, but using Jeff Patton's *feature-thinning* idea, the thinnest implementation of each mandatory element that each user would accept.

It was also obvious that the team would work to put in whatever parts of the linear elements in that they could – but this would naturally fit the "trim the tail" strategy: Put them in as time permitted, to the extent that the product manager would decide on the fly.

What was not obvious was that it could be worthwhile to put in any of the delighters. In normal MoSCoW thinking, these live in the Could or Would-like category, for sure not the Must-have category.

However, once we got started, we saw that we could indeed find a small delighter for each stakeholder and deliver the absolute minimum set of mandatory items plus one delighter for each stakeholder.

The energy in the room changed immediately.

> ***After a long, quiet, thoughtful pause in the room, one of the two company owners said: "I think we can run the project from here. We don't need anything more."***

I had other exercises to go through: Key business use cases, the actor-goal list, a few sea-level use cases to identify main usage and secondary actors, feature prioritization, enough for the planned two-day session.

But looking at items we had on the table, it was obvious that this team could do all of those things on their own over the next months.

The meeting was declared a success and adjourned.

The company developed and delivered that first delivery as planned.

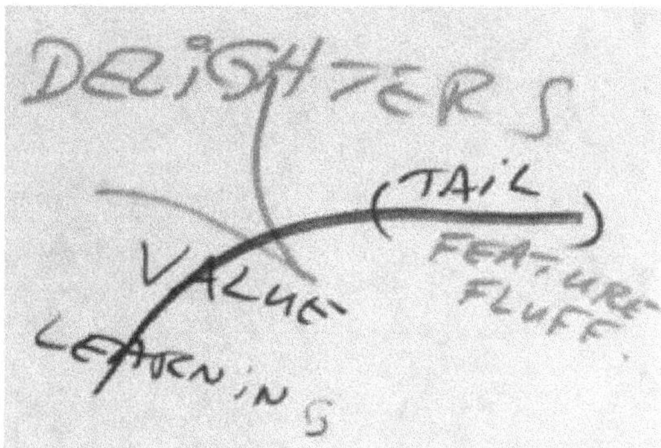

Figure 68, Chapter *11*. Injecting Kano's delighters.

Figure 68 shows how we put Kano quality elements into the knowledge acquisition curve.

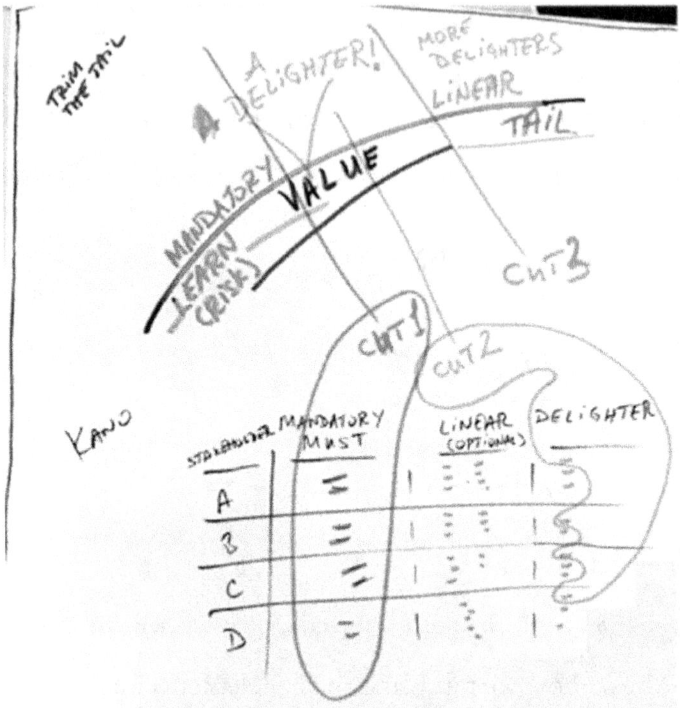

Figure 69, Chapter *11*. Inserting Kano into Learning-Value-Tail.

Figure 69 shows how we overlaid a Kano sequence of

> *Mandatory* → *One Delighter* → *Linear* → *More Delighters*

on top of the

> *Learning–Value–Tail*

curve.

The table part in *Figure 69* shows including all mandatory items, but just *one* delighter for each stakeholder.

Reflection on Kano and Fine-Grained Incremental Work

To recap the last few sections on product features and fine-grained incremental development:

1. Organize your project around Learning-Value-Tail.

   The experiments you run are your learning. Your key minimal features are the initial value elements. Refine and add in a fine-graine manner until you run out of time or money, then deliver.

2. Learn from Patton and Kano how to *thin down* your features to the minimum mandatory elements to form your minimal first delivery.

   Add the idea of one delighter per key stakeholder to make your first delivery pop. Your buyers and users naturally expect you to expand your feature set over time, so you can stage the linear and other delighters over time.

2. Use the Patton–Derbier grading method ABCEF to grow feature and system quality to fit schedule and budget.

   In every sprint or timebox, get the most critical features up to level C (usable). Then decide whether to take any of them to B (nice) or you prefer to include a new feature to level C. Then decide whether to take any B-quality feature to A (fabulous) or upgrade a C to a B, or add another feature to quality level C. Do this until time runs out.

While that might not seem easy, it's the first time I've seen a written-down approach for fine-grained incremental growth of features, paying attention to risk, learning, Kano qualities and feature quality.

Reflections and Key Points

Reflections

Reading that article 20 years later, I find my favorite thoughts are:

> *"Use the Patton–Derbier grading method ABCEF to grow feature and system quality to fit schedule and budget. You can have a little bit of a lot more things than you otherwise were going to get, and you get to choose the amount of each.*
>
> *"one delighter per stakeholder to make your first delivery pop"*

Did you catch these key points?

Jeff Patton and the ABCs of Quality

"you can have 'a little bit of a lot more things than you otherwise were going to get, and you get to choose the amount of each."

Agile in tables

"The Learning-Value-Tail table shows a set of features against their risk or knowledge-acquisition aspect, their value aspect and their tail or gloss aspect."

"allowing the team to tackle them in any order they might prefer – column-first, row-first, or some funny diagonal. / and maps to the trim the tail."

"four knowledge acquisition areas: Business risk, Social risk, Technical risk, Cost/schedule risk."

" 'What are we trying to learn right now?', which is quickly followed by, 'What is the cheapest, fastest way to get that information?' "

"Feature Grade Table / use the time available to get the important features up to B or A as desired. / this delivers the highest "perceived" quality of the final product."

"Hexagonal architecture micro-increment table: developing features in three stages:

1. Test harness functionality loopback in lieu of database

2. Real UI functionality loopback in lieu of database
3. Real UI functionality real database"

"This yields, as with the Risk-Value-Tail table, a rich set of possibilities for sequences in which the feature set might be implemented."

Reflections on the use of tables

"Tables create a map of the project. They give it a parts inventory."

"*thinning* the feature elements and adding minor improvements in competition with new features/ balance time against quality at a fine-grained level to get the maximum net *value* for the time spent."

Kano and quality

"Baseline – Linear – Exciters – Avoid"

"Exciters fade over time."

"things move from the must-have to the sliding (linear) dimension."

Fitting Kano into the Knowledge Acquisition Curve

"the *Learning-Value-Tail* curve is a more appropriate name"

"The absolute minimum set of mandatory items plus one delighter for each stakeholder."

Reflections on Kano and fine-grained incremental work

"Organize your project around Learning-Value-Tail."

"add in a fine-graine manner until you run out of time or money, then deliver."

"one delighter per key stakeholder to make your first delivery pop."

"Use the Patton–Derbier grading method ABCEF to grow feature and system quality to fit schedule and budget."

Slice your product features according to Kano's subjective quality elements. Fit those into the Learning-Value-Tail curve.

---

12. How Big Should Your Slices Be?

Smaller is generally better, but your mileage may vary, so learn how to choose.

This book has shown why and how to make your slices or growth stages as small as possible. They punchline is this:

> *Unvalidated decisions form your internal inventory. Validate and break and fix them as soon as possible, in the smallest quantities possible.*

Having said that, let's look at different context that produce different recommendations:

Integration and deployment. In some organizations and with some systems, there are so many dependencies between teams and subsystems that it takes weeks to months just to integrate and deploy a system. This can also happen with security concerns in certain industries, where a full stream of people need to sign off on the deployment.

One thing to do, of course, is learn how to improve that sequence to shorten that time period. Unless you manage to automate it completely, though, it will still represent the minimum window for deployments.

Users won't accept frequent deployments. Sometimes it's the users who don't want frequent releases, because they don't want to have to re-learn how to use the system.

Some companies deal with this by having three tiers of end-user deployment: For eager users, happy to try out the new features as they get done; for standard users, perhaps at the quarterly level; for die-hards, this is when a new release is forced out and the previous version discontinued.

If you can manage to find some eager users, they will help validate or break your delivery, and can help you shrink your internal inventory of unvalidated decisions.

Technology stack. Some technologies naturally support smaller slices.

Interpreted languages or those that don't do compile-time type checking, such as Python and Ruby, make it much easier to work in nano-increments, as we did with the Elephant Carpaccio. Languages and large systems that require large compile-and-build times can make it more economical to work in slightly fatter slices (perhaps an hour instead of ten minutes).

I did the Elephant Carpaccio exercise with COBOL programmers once. It worked, but was a lesson in why certain languages really beg for fatter slices. Think sashimi instead of carpaccio.

Personal preference. Not everyone wants to work in ten-minute nano-increments.

This is a question of taste. This book has been aimed at developing the skill of slicing, but when you return to your desk, you will have your own personal philosophy, style, and habits. Simply pay attention to the slicing you are doing, and see if you can shrink it.

Here is a short summary for different people in the organization:

- The *executive sponsor* operates in quarterly and annual timeframes.

  Quarters make great units of delivery at the executive level. Every executive needs to be able to ask for meaningful deliveries at the 3-month level, using trim-the-tail to steer the quarterly delivery.

  If you can't actually deliver to users each quarter, for some reason, have a fire-drill practice deployment, where the running, tested feature set is deployed to any one workstation, friendly customer, or practice site, just in order to force closure on all the open issues. Every team, every quarter.

- Business in general should be able to slice requests into *one-month* slices, asking for a demo every month, if a delivery isn't practical.

  Business people managing or interacting with the development group should grow the skill of slicing down to what can fit into a month, using trim-the-tail to steer the monthly demo or delivery.

- Developers should look to completely close some unit of development (with demo or delivery) every 3 weeks or shorter.

  It is different to program and test locally and shout "I'm done!" than it is to test, integrate and demo a feature or backlog item ready for delivery (see *planning horizon*).

- I am a fan of having a 1-week "planning horizon," which might not close out any particular development item, but is used to track what is happening.

  At the start of the week, said out loud what each person and the team think they can get done by the end of the week. These may not be delivery-ready completion, but at least task completion.

  Use the Friday afternoon or next Monday to compare what did get finished (not *nearly finished*, but completely finished) with what was said at the start, to track actual progress and learn about how to make predictions for the following week.

- Programmers: 15 minutes to 2 days

  Practice the Elephant Carpaccio exercise until you can speed type that exercise and learn to program in the smallest slices that fit your personal style. For sure, you should not check out and hang onto a piece of code for more than two days. Most people can get it down to half a day. For those who like, make each micro-programming episode, with test and code, under half an hour. See what you can do with a 15-minute timebox.

Reflections and Key Points

Reflections

The most important sentence in there may be this one:

> *"Quarters make great units of delivery at the executive level."*

Did you catch these key points?

"If you can't actually deliver to users each quarter, for some reason, have a fire-drill practice deployment."

"1-week "planning horizon," which might not close out any particular development item, but is used to track what is happening."

"Programmers: 15 minutes to 2 days."

Smaller is generally better, but your mileage may vary, so learn how to choose.

Part 3. Learning Over Time

It took me all these years to get to:
Pay to learn/ Grow business value/ Shine & gloss or trim the tail.

The following are articles I've published on the subject of incremental versus iterative development between 1993 and 2014. The first one, published in the IBM Systems Journal in 1993, shows the state of our understanding at the time. These topics were not new – what I wrote was the consensus view at that time. You can see I elaborated on those views for over a decade, then made a slight shift after some agile projects had had some practice and people were speaking with different examples.

In 2008 I came up with the knowledge-acquisition or early-learning graph, and that changed my way of describing what is going on.

Early learning is the advanced form of risk reduction. In ordinary risk reduction, you ask: "Will we get there, going as we are going?", "Do we have adequate people on the team?", "Will we hit time and budget targets?" and "Will people use this?"

On the other hand, with early learning you ask those, but also: "What would be a better thing to build than what we originally thought of?" and "How can we help the people on the team learn to work better together?" Much more powerful questions.

Enjoy the time travel and watch the explanations shift, bit by bit.

1993: The Impact of Object-Orientation on Application Development.

My first attempt, in the IBM Systems Journal, 1993. I still use those definitions today. (Note: this is not the entire article – You can read that online. This excerpt contain only the section on incremental and iterative development

Staging and scheduling deliverables. Some methodologies address the scheduling of activities and passing on of deliverables. What has been called "Waterfall Development" carries the restriction that all requirements be defined, reviewed and approved before high-level design or analysis can begin; in turn, high-level design must be completed before component design can begin, and so on. Alternatives to this staging and scheduling strategy are the incremental and iterative strategies recommended by the OO community. As is discussed next, the incremental staging and scheduling policies of OO methodologies are basically the same as those of non-0o methodologies. They are, however, more vocally expressed and perhaps more uniformly practiced in the OO community.

In order to examine the assertion that incremental and iterative development are much the same with object-orientation as before, we must be careful about the terms incremental and iterative. They are used almost interchangeably by some people, possibly for historic reasons. At one time, just allowing a project to pass through requirements and high-level design twice was a major topic for discussion, so iterative was an apt term.

Today, numerous strategies involve repetition of phases and are all iterative in some sense. The meanings of iterative and incremental have evolved to refer to distinct, in fact, independent, development strategies. The definitions that follow do not match the way in which everyone in software development uses the terms incremental and iterative (none could, given the existing conflicts in terminology), and a succinct definition of the terms does not appear in the literature. With this apology, I provide definitions for the terms as used in this paper.

- **Incremental development** is a scheduling and staging strategy allowing portions of the system to be developed at different times or rates, and integrated as they are completed.
- **Iterative development** is a scheduling and staging strategy supporting predicted rework of portions of the system.

These definitions identify incremental and iterative as independent concepts to be used separately or together.

- The intent of an *incremental* strategy is to develop a system piece by piece and to permit additions to the requirements, improvements to the development process, or changes to the scheduling.
- The intent of an *iterative* strategy is to allow correction of mistakes and product improvements based upon user feed-back, performance tuning, or maintenance criteria, and to allow it in a controlled manner.

Speakers and authors of an incremental methodology sometimes apologize when showing the chain of activities governing the evolution of deliverables. They (accurately) fear in advance that the audience will interpret the diagram as endorsement of "Waterfall Development."

- In the context of this discussion, waterfall development (not capitalized or in quotes) is defined as a one-pass scheduling and staging strategy requiring a given set of deliverables to pass checkpoints together, with the exact set of deliverables left unspecified. Any set of deliverables that must pass checkpoints together follows a waterfall development.

This is only natural and needs no apology, since every line of code should have been preceded by design and that by some requirement. It should be unremarkable that a portion of a product undergoes waterfall development within any single iteration. From a project manager's view, waterfall development is simply the progression to completion of each component of the system. It is useful for tracking purposes.

The above definition may be contrasted with "Waterfall Development" (here capitalized and in quotes) referring to when *all* of the requirements must be approved before high-level design begins, etc. A single changed requirement would force all work to grind to a halt while all the deliverables get back into sync. Such a strict interpretation may be so difficult in practice that even groups claiming to use it may actually perform a form of incremental development, just to keep development of the product progressing.

In incremental development, the repetitions of activities address new parts of the system, adding either end function, robustness, error checking, or security facilities (see *Figure 70*).

Figure 2 Incremental development model

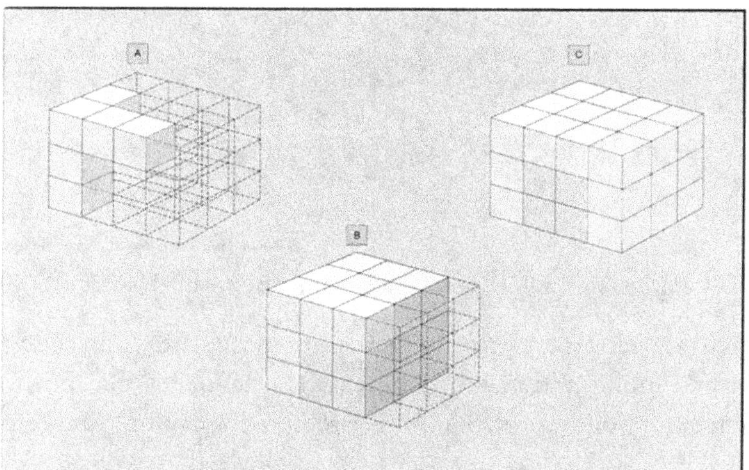

Courtesy Don Hough, IBM Consulting Group

Figure 70, Part 3. Incremental development means adding.

The essential characteristic of incremental development is that the system is developed in portions. As the portions are completed, they are added to the growing system. There may be a period of evaluation after the integration of one increment and before work on the next increment is begun to gather feedback and new requirements. Alternatively, the increments may be staged in parallel. In a noniterative but incremental project, the increments are developed to full production standards from the start. Further discussion of incremental development is given by Hough' and Pittman. 3

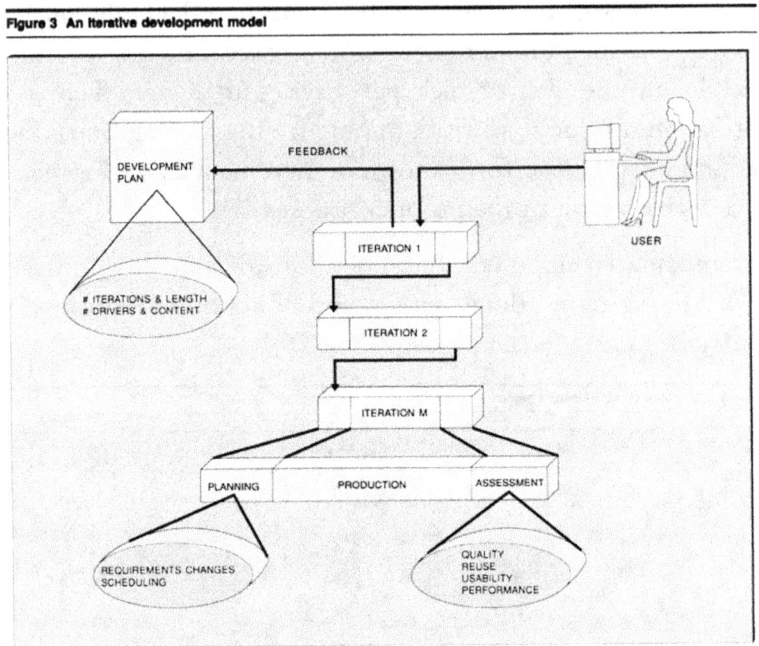

Courtesy Mark Lorenz, IBM OO Technology Council

Figure 71, Part 3. Iterative development means changing.

Iterative development no longer just means that an activity is performed multiple times in one project, it indicates that portions of the system undergo rework in a predicted manner. McMenamin* wrote:

> *Iterative refinement accommodates two widespread human traits:*
>
> *Misconception: We get things wrong before we get them right.*
>
> *Improvement: We make things badly before we make them well.*

and added, verbally,

> *When each iteration is considered "rework," that is your clue that iteration is not considered affordable. In truth, iteration is rework.*

McMenamin's description omits a key element of iterative development: the positive act of discovery. Iterative development allows one to discover new information and improve the design, both positive undertakings. This positive act may require creating a disposable prototype for requirements gathering, altering portions of the system following usability tests, or restructuring the system in preparation for evolution.

Iterative development may explicitly call for planning, execution, and evaluation phases within each iteration in order to control the scheduling of rework (*Figure 71*). In Boehm's "spiral" model, various risk management techniques are used to decide what parts of the system need schedule time for preliminary work and rework.

Most phrases describing iterative development give it a somewhat stately and ordered appearance (spiral, fountain, gestalt round trip, etc.). A more evocative and perhaps accurate term was coined by a leader recently reporting on an iterated OO project: "[The] "Tornado' model has resulted in the highest quality for the least amount of work." [7]

Incremental development may be used with or without iterative development. A project team may plan on an increment reaching shipping quality in a single pass, or it may, in pursuit of quality or because of known risk, plan on an increment being reworked one or more times (developed iteratively). *It is important to bear in mind that on a real project, the precise distinction between incremental and iterative is not critical, as long as the project team understands what they are to produce and when.*

Prototyping. Prototyping is linked with incremental and iterative development. Unfortunately, two very different meanings are associated with the word prototype. A **disposable prototype** is one not intended for production and thus possibly not meeting production quality standards. An **evolutionary prototype** is one incomplete in scope but intended for eventual production, hence meeting production quality standards.

A disposable prototype is useful for gathering requirements and is not intended to evolve to a product. The hazard with a disposable prototype, of course, is that in the pressure to meet dead-lines, it may be pressed into service as the final product (at which point it is neither disposable nor a prototype). An evolutionary prototype is one created according to full production standards so that it may evolve to be added to the final product.

It may be disposed of in the course of evolution, or it may become one increment of the final system. Evolutionary prototypes are becoming increasingly preferred as organizations suffer maintenance and evolution costs following instances in which disposable prototypes were turned into products.

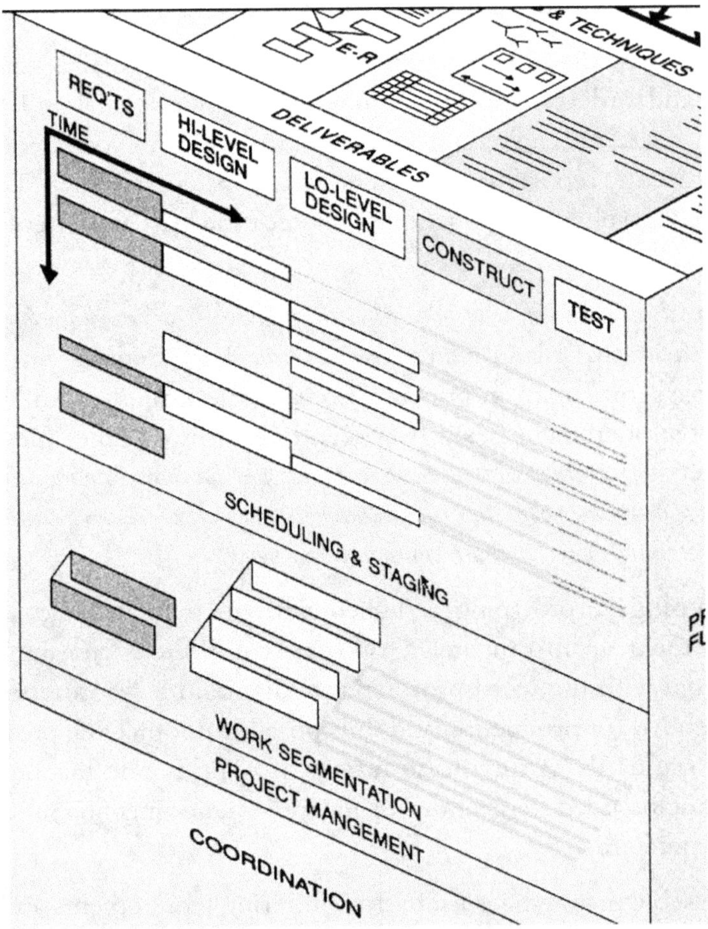

Figure 72, Part 3. Blending incremental and iterative in a project plan.

The referenced notes from the article:

1. Observation of Wayne Stevens, IBM Consulting Group, Southbury, CT.
2. D. Hough, "Rapid Delivery: An Evolutionary Approach for Application Development," IBM Systems Journal 32, No. 3, 397-419 (1993, this same issue).
3. M. Pittman, "Lessons Learned in Managing Object-Oriented Development," TEEE Software 10, No. 1, 43-34 (January 1993).
4. S. McMenamin, "The New Economics of Requirements Modeling and Prototyping," The First National Conferences on Software Methods, Orlando, FL, presented by Technology Transfer Institute, 741 Tenth Street, Santa Monica, CA 90402 (March 30, 1992), Section 9.362.
5. M. Lorenz, Object-Oriented Software Development: A Practical Guide, Prentice-Hall, Inc., Englewood Cliffs, NJ (1992).
6. B. Boehm, "A Spiral Model of Software Development," Computer 21, No. 5, 61-72 (May 1988).
7. McGehee, Corporate Infusion of Object Technology: The "Big-Bang" Approach, Texas Instruments Microelectronics Manufacturing Science and Technology, presented at Experience Session, OOPSLA '92.

See the full article online at:

[https://web.archive.org/web/20140329210102/http://alistair.cockburn.us/The+impact+of+object+orientation+on+application+development]

1994: In Search of Methodology

My first description of an Agile methodology, following several years of investigating successful and failing projects in order to construct the IBM Consulting Group's official methodology for object-technology projects.

In this article, I describe how I selected the only three elements needed for a small project: incremental development for the scheduling and staging strategy, use cases for requirements, and responsibility-driven design for the design of the software.

It generated some controversy for being so simple, some people saying it couldn't possibly work, others saying, well, actually it's about all you need. These days, of course, we recognize it as an early Agile methodology.

It got published in Object Magazine, July 1994. You can read it at https://web.archive.org/web/20140329210015/http://alistair.cockburn.us/In+search+of+methodology.

Over the last several years, the methodology department of the IBM Consulting Group conducted a series of studies of object-oriented projects, of both successful and unsuccessful uses of the technology. Originally, we were interested in the question, "Which of the dozens of OO methodologies should one use?" Over time, that changed to, "How would we know whether to recommend or reject any particular element of an OO methodology?" "What affects acceptance?" Finally, it became, "How does one integrate the desirable aspects of diverse methodologies?" This article presents a view of what we found in the case studies, with some conclusions and a view of the near future.

The study results are of most value to those about to undertake their first OO project and to those about to train new OO developers. There are many OO techniques on the market, and there are experts who can turn any tool or technique to effective use. At the same time, the field is growing so fast that the majority of practitioners are relatively new.

They have to learn or revise a considerable number of their work habits. It is for them that the study has most significance.

The study was conducted independently of any other survey, such as the Taligent study [1] or the projects described by Dr. Love in Object Lessons [2]. The Taligent study put several prerequisites on the companies to be surveyed, which we did not and collected different information. We noted selected aspects of OO projects as practiced by whatever group was able to practice them. We found remarkable similarity of experiences with Dr. Love, despite there being little overlap in the projects and organizations sampled.

In highly digested form, our study results may be summarized: <u>a methodology is more likely to be used as it is simple, clearly effective, and small in terms of required work products.</u> The acceptance and use of a methodology are limited by the group's ability to change its work habits and by its tolerance for seemingly bureaucratic content. Both quantities are typically small. (Note that this result is independent of object technology, as was pointed out to us repeatedly during the study.)

Design techniques do not have to be complicated to be useful. Quite the contrary, to be useful they must be used, and simpler techniques are more likely to be used than complicated ones. In particular, there were two design techniques found to be simple, small and effective as required: use cases and responsibilities. Not only do they meet the requirements, and are available and documented today, but they actually comprise a complete design methodology. They fit well with the use of incremental development, the most successful scheduling strategy found in the projects. They leave room for newer ideas such as design patterns.

The Cases Studied

We were able to get specific information from between one and two dozen organizations having a cross section of characteristics.

- OO projects within IBM, which could be investigated in great detail. These projects included networking, system software, and IS applications.
- Companies with large IS groups, primarily in insurance and utilities, that either had done OO projects or were trying them out.
- Some small companies that were already expert and highly productive in the technology.
- Companies in Canada, Hong Kong, New Zealand, Europe and the U.S.
- Organizations doing systems-level or business application programming, as opposed to engineering applications.
- We were able to find one or more expert OO developers as well as an easy majority of novices in each size, location, and type of software.
- We discussed the findings with people in similar situations in Australia and Europe, with people in engineering organizations, and with people who had experienced the move to structured techniques a decade ago.

The story we heard was very much the same (with one exception), independent of size, experience, country, decade, or even structured vs. object. What we found was:

- Development teams disliked spending time in design activities that did not directly lead to the final product.
- They did not like having to manually update design documents to keep them current with the product (typically, they just did not go back to update them).
- They were given very limited time and resources to learn new techniques and not much extra time to integrate those techniques into their daily work habits.
- Developers could often avoid aspects of the methodology they did not like.

The major exception appeared that engineering organizations seemed to be more comfortable with relatively complex methods than were the IS organizations and had somewhat more patience for redundant design documents than the others.

The developers' opinion of a method strongly influenced their success in using it, particularly regarding work products that did not directly and obviously contribute to the final product. In most organizations, developers could and did avoid aspects of the methodology they felt were bureaucratic. This was either because the organization gave them that level of empowerment, or because the organization did not track their use of the methodology. There were several cases in which the project manager did not even know that the methodology was being subverted.

None of this is unique to object orientation, as those who had watched the "structured" revolution were careful to tell us. The above results are just reality, a reality that has been chronically ignored by (and been the frustration of) methodologists and CASE tool vendors for two decades. The reason the results warrant attention again, now, is that OO methodologists are again ignoring this reality and producing book upon book of complex methods. CASE tool developers are producing tools that do not do what developers really need help with. Instead, they ask stressed developers to draw complicated pictures of relationships, function flows, and state machines, all time consuming and detailed work products requiring special training and special machines.

These work products are so expensive to produce that it would be reasonable to expect to find tools that generate the final data and code from them automatically. That expectation is not being fulfilled. The work products are not properly connected to the final code and data, so they get out of date quickly and have to be manually updated whenever the requirements change. Object-oriented methods recommend iterative development, so requirements are guaranteed to change. Seen in this context, it is understandable that such work products are regarded by busy developers as "bureaucratic" overhead.

Simple Methods

The above discussion notwithstanding, good developers continue to put out good systems, dragging novice designers along with them and developing useful tools as they go. Interviews with these designers revealed consistent strategies and techniques that are simple, effective and efficient. Some of these have even been written down, although they tend to get embellished in the writing.

Three techniques stand out for simplicity and effectiveness from among the published OO techniques: responsibilities [3,4], use cases [5], and incremental development [6,7]. What is remarkable about them is that they are at the same time simple enough for small (2-5 developer) systems and sufficient for fairly large (100 - 150 developer) systems.

In the two years of studying object-oriented projects, responsibility-based design showed itself to be the most commonly used design technique, and an effective one. By common agreement, responsibilities as currently documented need to be augmented with interaction diagrams (fortunately, also nicely described in [5]). Use cases had not been well published, and so were less known and less used. However, they clearly filled several difficult needs, such as capturing requirements, checking completeness of the design, and partitioning the system into meaningful increments. The projects that had used them spoke highly of them. Other projects had invented their own ways to describe the system's intended use, to good effect. The acceptance of use cases recently has become almost universal. Incremental development was the most successful scheduling and staging strategy encountered.

The best news about these techniques is that there is a book that describes "responsibility - driven design" clearly and in detail [4]. Medium news is that there is a book that introduces use cases [5], although it does not articulate how to find and document them, and misses exploiting the power of stating their *intent.* Bad news is that incremental and iterative development have been described many times and in many ways since 1988 [6], but are still not understood and practiced by many development managers. The worst news is that there are still methodology and tool producers who appear to think that these techniques are too simple to work and "enhance" them in complexity without enhancing their value.

Responsibilities

Responsibilities are a way to state the rationale of the system design. The identification and allocation of responsibilities across the system are the primary activity of design (followed closely and accompanied by reuse of existing components). Some experts in structured analysis look upon responsibilities as "old news", having long recommended that any system module or major component have a distinct and simply stated purpose in life. Such a simply stated purpose is not much different from a responsibility. The difference is that in OO design, responsibilities are defined and allocated at the same time, whereas in structured analysis, they are defined but not allocated.

People seem naturally well equipped to work with responsibilities and their allocation, perhaps just from the way our societies are built. Dr. J. Fisher, professor emeritus of Towson State University, wrote, "A rational society, be it a corporation or a country, can only maintain itself if personal responsibility and accountability are at its core; that is, from top to bottom, every agent or citizen must be empowered to conduct her or his role and to be fully accountable for its performance." [8] My suspicion is that people living in such societies develop a sensitivity to the ramifications of responsibility allocation. Whatever the reason, personal experiences in teaching object orientation in various countries were seconded by advanced designers in each of those places: not everyone is equally good at inventing and allocating responsibilities, but most people quickly relate to the following questions and can answer them,

- "Is it really the responsibility of this object to handle this request?"
- "Is it its responsibility to keep track of all that information?"

Even newcomers to object design give a quick sensation of comfort or discomfort with a proposed responsibility allocation. That sensation is closely in line with the evaluations of experienced object designers. We seem well prepared to state, "It is not my responsibility to track that information.", or, "Yes, it is that organization's responsibility to handle this request."

Although responsibility-driven design is well described in both the original article [3] and the book [4], the developers uniformly commented on the need to document the interactions between the objects to show the hand-off of responsibilities. Responsibility allocation is a design technique, and interaction diagrams document the resulting design. Fortunately, most OO methodologies support documenting interactions in some way, calling them alternately interaction diagrams, object diagrams, or event traces. Jacobson [5] provides a good introduction and discussion of interaction diagrams.

Responsibility-driven design is appropriate for more than designing classes. It can be applied equally well to the partitioning of a system into subsystems. A subsystem is just a one-of-a-kind object, perhaps the only instance of its class. Responsibility-driven design appropriately defers concern about the internal structure of the subsystem and focuses on its role and interaction with its colleagues.

Use cases

Responsibilities reveal which object or subsystem will carry out a part of the required function, interaction diagrams show how the function is carried, but neither say why it is required in the first place. That is what scenarios and use cases provide.

Jacobson defines a use case as, "a behaviorally related sequence of transactions in a dialogue with the system" [5, p.129]. The developers needed this plus one thing more: "What is the actor (user) trying to accomplish with this sequence of actions?" What is the intent of the use case? Capturing the intent is in line with Ivar Jacobson's more recent writings and discussions. He has commented that in practice, coarser-grained selections of transactions and scenarios seem to be more effective than finely grained selections. In the operation of a tape recorder, for example, one can make a use case of just pushing the Fast Forward button or of pushing some combination of Fast Forward, Rewind and Play. We may ask,

"Well, why are you pushing these buttons?", and answer,

"To find some particular place on the tape."

A good use case combines Fast Forward, Play and Rewind. The description of intent is, "Find a particular place on the tape."

Use case intents provide an envelope, a "use envelope", as it were. On the outside is written the intent. On the inside, how the intent is accomplished, in terms of use cases, scenarios and even other use envelopes. The intent is important to capture because it is concise and remains valid over a range of designs. In the case of the tape recorder, knowing that the intent is to find a particular place on the tape, the designers may alter the design without disturbing the intent, by adding a tape counter or even an index (with pull-down menus and all).

The sum of all use case intents comprises the functional requirements of the system. There is probably no shorter, more readable description of the requirements for the system than the collected use case intents. That the use cases and intents are written in plain text make them easier for all types of people to work with, although it complicates the life of tool vendors a little (it is not meaningful simply to make another graphics editor for them).

The intents of the use cases can be thought of as responsibilities at the system level. These responsibilities can be mapped to subsystem-level responsibilities using responsibility-driven design. The interactions between subsystems can be interpreted as use case descriptions of the subsystems, and the design process repeated to decompose the subsystem further, down to existing services, subsystems or classes. Thus, responsibilities and use cases complement each other recursively from system requirements down to the level of classes or existing subsystems or services.

Use cases address several critical needs of the development team. They provide a way for the system designers and project manager to sit together to plan a sensible division of the project into increments and teams, and for the project manager to track the development of the system. They then help the design answer several constant questions: "What am I really trying to do?", "How do I know when I am done?", "What do I work on next?"

All in all, design with responsibilities and use envelopes were found to be the common design thread among the most successful projects examined. These techniques demonstrated themselves to be very nearly unavoidable, and quite sufficient, even for fairly large systems. What was most surprising was how many different kinds of tools could be used effectively with them, including even spreadsheets and word processors. The tool requirements for profiting from these techniques is very low.

Incremental development

The third technique consistently encountered in successful projects was incremental development, used to manage the scheduling and staging of the system. Incremental development was key to the success of so many projects that I was able to use it as a predictor in the interviews (its absence was a good predictor of failure). Nonetheless, relatively few of the managers we encountered used or understood the mechanics of incremental development.

There appeared to be two reasons for this. The first is that incremental development affects the work habits of project managers just as new design techniques affect the work habits of system designers -- and project managers as a group did not demonstrate any greater ability to change. The other reason is that incremental and iterative development have been described using hard-to-follow multi-dimensional metaphors such as spirals [6] and cubes [7], or fashionable but fuzzy terms, such as "gestalt round trip" [10]. What project managers need is a simpler description, one that unwinds the spiral, unfolds the cube and demystifies the "gestalt round trip".

Incremental development is so important that it deserves an entire article to itself. I shall describe it in a following article in another issue. Between now and then, interested readers are invited to try straightening the time lines in references [6] and [7].

Conclusion

Substantial systems are being built and have been built using object technology. The hard and important aspect of design is in accurately stating:

- the intents of the requirements,
- the allocation of responsibilities across components, and
- the interactions between the components.

Responsibilities and use cases excel in an economic and natural way. They are simple and effective. They have low entry cost in tools. They integrate well with incremental development and with the proposed design patterns. Small wonder, then, that they are being rapidly integrated by most of the methodology authors and have become the bedrock of our OO methodology work.

It has been commented that object-oriented methodology mirrors human organizations. It is therefore apt that a recent article on making organizations more effective [11] summarizes our study results: "...reduce supervision, combine fragmented tasks, eliminate work that fails to add value, and cut the activities within each process to a minimum. Use as few teams as possible to perform an entire process." OO methodologists take note.

References

1. "Lessons learned from early adopters of object technology," Taligent Corp., 10725 N. De Anza Bvd, Cupertino, CA, 1993.
2. Love, T., *Object Lessons*, SIG Publications, NY, 1993.
3. Beck, K., Cunningham, W., "A Laboratory for Teaching Object-Oriented Thinking", ACM SIGPLAN , 24(10), OOPSLA Proceedings, October 1989, pp.1-7.

4. Wirfs-Brock, R., Wilkerson, B., Wiener, L., *Designing Object-Oriented Software*, Prentice Hall, 1990.

5. Jacobson, I., Christerson, M., Jonsson, P., Overgaard, G., *Object-Oriented Software Engineering*, Addison Wesley, 1992.

6. Boehm, "A Spiral Model of Software Development and Enhancement", COMPUTER, May 1988, pp.61-72.

7. Cockburn, A., "Object-Orientation and Application Development", IBM Systems Journal, 32(3), August 1993, pp.420-444.

8. Dr. J.L.Fisher, president emeritus of Towson State University, in the Salt Lake Tribune, Jan. 11, 1994, p.A6.

9. Gamma, E., Helm, R., Johnson, R., Vlissides, J., "Design Patterns: Abstraction and Reuse of Object-Oriented Design", ECOOP '93 Proceedings.

10. Booch, G., *Object-Oriented Analysis and Design with Applications*, Benjamin/Cummings, 1993.

11. "The Horizontal Corporation", Business Week, Dec. 20, 1993, pp. 76-80.

1994: Unraveling Incremental Development.

My second attempt, 1994. The "validation V" is a great way to unroll cyclic processes.

Staying with a design through coding, testing, and verification gives the team some feedback and insight into themselves, their group dynamics, their process, and their task.

Introduction

Incremental Development *is a scheduling and staging technique* nicely suited to projects using technology and techniques new to an organization.

During a two-year study of object-oriented projects, incremental development showed itself as a key ingredient in success. In fact, it was such a key item in the stories of the projects that I began to use it as a predictor in the interviews: *absence of an incremental process was a good predictor of failure.*

There were several projects that were turned from disasters to successes by taking advantage of the breathing spaces afforded by incremental development.

In the most dramatic of the turnarounds, the breathing spaces between the increments were used to completely replace the development team (first), change the management and team structure (second), and, finally, change the scheduling and estimation techniques. The project team rebuilt itself from a guaranteed disaster to a smoothly running team of over 150 people over several continents delivering system increments every four months.

Despite being well-publicized since 1988, incremental development and its relative, iterative development, still were not widely understood or used in the projects I encountered.

Two factors may account for this.

- One is the significant changes required in the way that project managers approach their work. During the study of projects, it became apparent that changing work habits is among the hardest thing you can ask people to do.
- The other is that the literature of incremental and iterative development does not portray their use in operation very clearly. Authors tend to use complex, multidimensional metaphors such as spirals [2], cubes [3], or fashionable but fuzzy metaphors such as "gestalt round-trip." [4]

People live and operate in linear time, not in spirals, cubes, or gestalt round trips. The project management team needs an image of development that shows how to coordinate teams and results day by day and week by week. They need to define what activities occur at specific points of the schedule, and how to measure progress toward completion. Time may appear in any picture in only one direction.

In this article, incremental development is **"a scheduling and staging strategy that allows pieces of the system to be developed at different times or rates and integrated as they are completed."** Specifically intended is that between increments, additions could be made to the requirements, process changes could be incorporated, or the schedule could be improved and revised. Incremental is distinguished from iterative development in that the latter sup- ports "predicted rework" of parts of the system. A good grasp of incremental development helps in applying iterative development.

The intent of this article is to unravel the spiral of incremental development to show how the project management team can get a straight-line view of multiple teams making progress toward completion, delivering in increments.

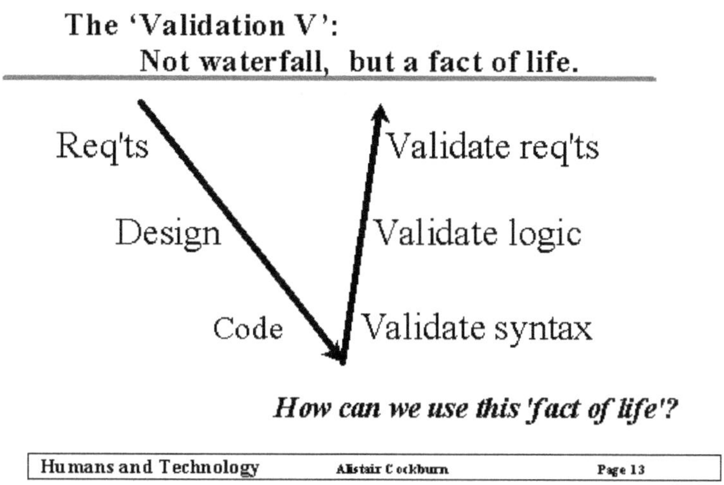

Figure 73, Part 3. The V model of project evolution.

The Validation "V"

An inescapable and unpleasant fact of system development is that the earlier and more crucial design decisions can be validated only after some later and less important decisions have been addressed and validated. This is the *validation V* (*Figure 73*). The idea of a "V" is not particularly new. The "Vee" model, a 3-dimensional V describing the evolution of an entire project, was described by Forsberg and Mooz in 1991s (and earlier references to the V shape can be found in the 1980s). Hodgson describes an "x" model, with one V inverted under another to take into account the feedback introduced by reuse. These and other authors are dealing with the fact that the validation V is unavoidable, and must be incorporated into the process model somehow.

The validation V reflects that a system can be validated only if it runs. Before it runs, it must be built and debugged. Each piece is based upon a design, which is based on requirements. In other words, regardless of any metaphor, the team must gather requirements before they design, design before they build, build before they test, and test before they validate the initial requirements. Some (and particularly object - oriented) developers claim that object orientation, with prototyping and rapid application development, has made the validation V obsolete. Some scorn any scheduling diagram reminiscent of "waterfall development." However, prototypes are themselves examples of the validation V. They must be designed and debugged before they can be measured against their requirements. The difference is that the prototype's V occurs early, and typically is short so as to validate a design decision as early as possible. However one tries, in the end one must deal with the validation v.

Incremental Development as a Series of Vs

If the V is inescapable, it has at least one surprising virtue:

a person's skill improves dramatically at the end of a development V.

This was mentioned by several of the teams using incremental development. Staying with a design from design through coding, testing, and verification gives the team some feedback and insight into themselves, their group dynamics, their process, and their task. The improvement is so dramatic that one organization said they put new members through a one-week development program just to let them gain the understanding that comes with completion.

Four months of design, they said, does not produce the same productivity and quality as four months placed in four separate Vs.

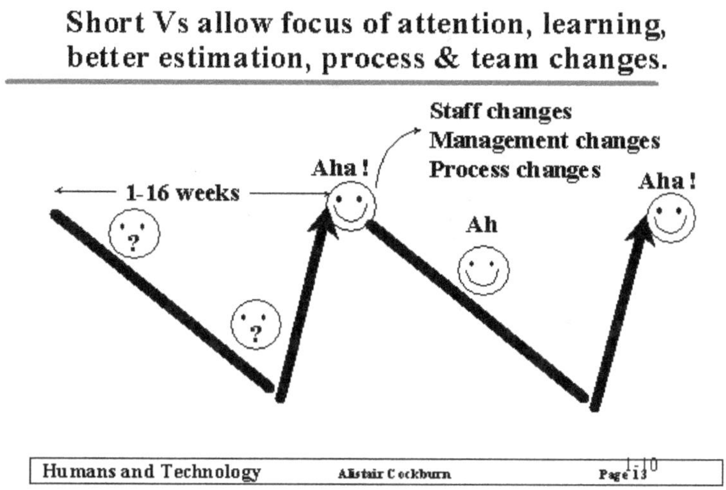

Figure 74, Part 3. Incremental development is Vs forming a W.

Incremental development is a matter of converting a single V into a series of shorter vs. The sequence of vs resembles a W (*Figure 74*), hence the management of a series of vs is called the *project management W* in this article.

The project management W turns the necessity of the Validation V to an advantage. It addresses these issues:

1. The validation V is unavoidable.
2. Developers get better at the end of each cycle.
3. The project needs a steady stream of results.
4. The project's process could stand improvement during the project itself.

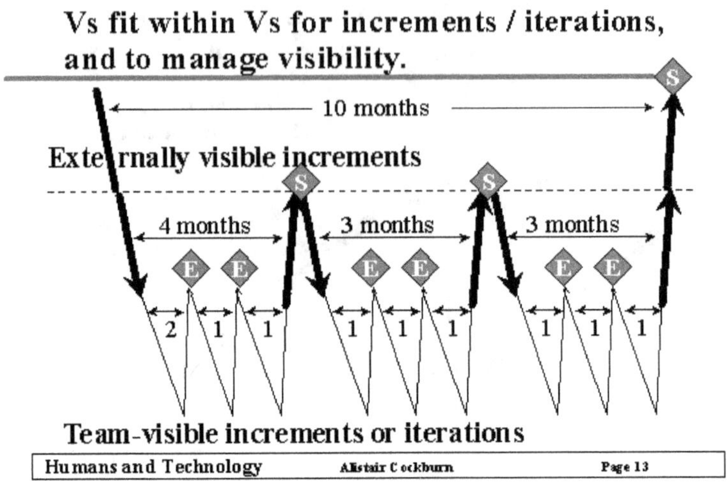

Figure 75, Part 3. Subproject Vs can be further broken down into a series of increments, each with its own V.

- The project is broken into a series of subprojects, each with its own V. Each of those maybe broken down further (*Figure 75*). One sub- project and its V may address a production increment, a proto- type, or, in fact, any decision that needs to be made and validated. Some vs may be short enough that they have no intermediate checkpoints, only "done and verified." The width of the Vs are set to give steady feedback to the management team as to how the project is progressing. The development process is examined and possibly revised after selected increments.
- The Vs should be short enough to keep the team motivated, give feedback on both the design and process in a timely way, and be fairly accurate to predict. There is some team disturbance in starting and ending a V, so the Vs need to be wide enough that the disturbance does not swamp progress. The teams that were comfortable with their increments suggested a range of 4-8 weeks.

If the increment period is set short enough, the project can be managed according to increment results, as opposed to "phase deliverables" (requirements, analysis, design, and code). Each increment is just delivered or not. Project scheduling is scheduling the completion points and the dependencies between the increments. The attraction in such an approach is that the number of inter- mediate deliverables can be reduced, to the extent that their purpose is either to hand documentation off to another team or just to demonstrate progress. In the case of managing by increments, the same team does analysis, design, code, and test, so there is no hand-off or retraining to prepare for (note, the team needs to include a qualified analyst, designer, coder, and tester!). The Vs are short and self-sufficient enough that their end results adequately indicate the rate of completion.

Use of the project management W brings with it a number of advantages. By far the greatest is that a natural breathing space can be provided between Vs. During this breathing space, the team constitution can be changed and the project's process can be changed. As mentioned earlier, one project changed everything about itself except its end goal by pausing for a period of self-examination at the end of each increment.

A second advantage of managing the W is that several Vs may be accumulated before results are shown (*Figure 75*). This is useful when a team is given a relatively large task to do, and wishes to break it down into smaller increments to manage their own development better. Or, it may happen that some higher level of management or the user community needs only quarterly reports, but a development increment is set for 6 weeks. The management or user group will see only the results of lower-level Ws.

A third advantage of working to the W is synchronization of teams. A team commits to a section of design, and delivers production code to other teams at predictable times. The other teams use the code, and provide feedback to be incorporated during sub- sequent increments, improving product quality. As it does take effort to prepare a delivery to another team, such preparation is one of the issues to be considered in selecting the width of the Vs.

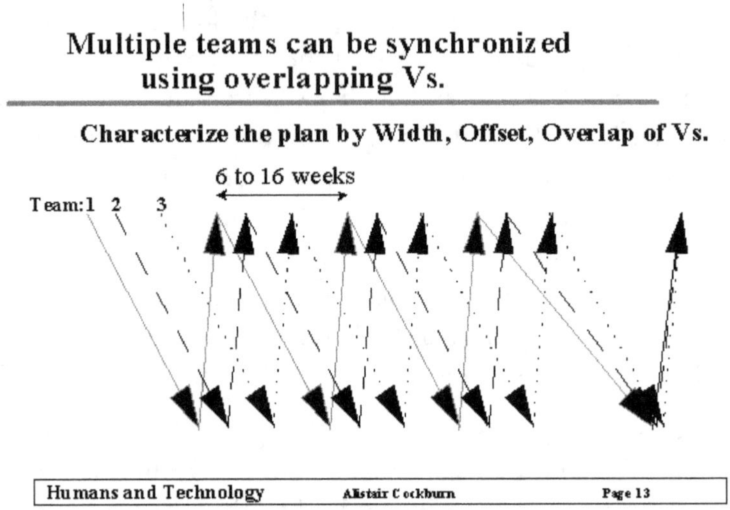

Figure 76, Part 3. Team schedules can be staggered to obtain more parallelism between teams.

Team schedules may even be staggered. This allows for a project management W with Vs of differing length, or to allow schedule checkpoints shorter than the V period. The parallelism that can be obtained is a function of the dependency characteristics of the project itself, and must be settled by the project managers and the lead architects.

Finally, the consecutive Vs making up a W help improve the accuracy of estimating project size and duration. It has been well established by now that the quality of an estimate depends on the project's similarity with previously documented projects. unfortunately, projects vary so fast that almost certainly the task, people, or tools are different. This makes it difficult to get accurate estimates. With the consecutive Vs, the project develops its own internal history, a history that is as similar and accurate as can be hoped for.

Although the estimates for the first V may be no better than before, the estimates for the subsequent Vs should be increasingly more accurate. Several of the projects interviewed did this sort of estimating:

> *They had to live with the inaccuracies of the first estimate, but only for one increment. Estimation accuracy improved during the project.*

It is well-documented that incremental development has a natural affinity to object orientation. One possible unit of increment is the "use case," which defines a unit of delivered service. Designers and project managers examine use cases for project dependencies, divide the project into teams and increments, and size the increments for the teams. The delivery of the system in terms of use cases gives the user community sections of the system to evaluate in manageable quantities.

Summary

Incremental development is a technique that recognizes and takes advantage of the fact that requirements analysis precedes design, design precedes coding, coding precedes testing, and code testing precedes final validation against the initial requirements. Using incremental development, a project is broken into smaller developments, which are integrated as they are completed. The project management team monitors the progress of the project by examining the end product and duration of each increment, building an increasingly accurate picture of the size of the project and the rate of progress. Each increment follows its own Validation V, so the project as a whole is the management of the series of Vs, the project management W.

Incremental development and the project management W can offer the following benefits:

1. The performance of the developers improves with each increment.
2. Process improvements can be made at the end of each increment.

3. Project estimation accuracy improves with each increment.
4. Phase deliverables can sometimes be eliminated.
5. There is a steady stream of results.
6. User, developers, and manager get early feedback, and morale is boosted as a result.

In setting up the component Vs of the project management W, the project team needs to consider and adjust the width of each V, the overlap of Vs between teams, and the number of Vs done between reports.

Finally, while incremental development has demonstrated itself to be successful, it is difficult to put into practice the first time. It requires a noticeable change of habits for the project managers.

References

1. A Cockburn. In search of methodology, *Object Magazine* 4(4):52-56,1994.
2. B Boehm. A spiral model of software development and enhancement, COMPUTER, May, 61-72,1988.
3. A Cockburn. The impact of object orientation on application development, *IBM Systems Journal*, August, 420-444, 1993.
4. G Booch. *Object-Oriented Design With Applications*, Benjamin Cummings, Menlo Park, CA, 1991.
5. K Forsberg and H Mooz. The Relationship of System Engineering to the Project Cycle, Joint Conference sponsored by the National Council of System Engineers and the American Society for Engineering Management, Chatanooga, TN, October 1991.
6. R Hodgson. The X-Model: A process model for object-oriented software development, Proceedings Toulouse '91 International Conference On Software Engineering And Its Application, 1991, pp. 713-728.

See the full article online at:

[https://web.archive.org/web/20140329210059/http://alistair.cockburn.us/Unraveling+incremental+development]

1997: Managing Increments and Iterations with VW Staging (Slides).

These are the slides from a talk. I offer them without annotation, as the slides say everything explicitly. The content is similar to the previous article, but with a few shifts that might help you anchor the ideas.

Managing Increments and Iterations with "V-W" Staging

Alistair Cockburn
Human and Technology
arc@acm.org
http://Alistair.Cockburn.us

Humans and Technology Alistair Cockburn Page 1

"Every team must deliver working function every 2-4 months."

The most important statement I know to make for a project.

Humans and Technology Alistair Cockburn Page 2

How can we describe increments, iterations, and spirals using linear calendar time?

- **Givens:**

  Developer time vs. Project Manager time

  The "Validation V"

- **Techniques:**

  V's for increments & iterations

  V-W staging

  Managing by milestones and reviews

Humans and Technology — Alistair Cockburn — Page 3

The Problem (1): Developers do not live in linear time.

Artifacts grow fast, slow, even backwards!
Spiral is a good word.

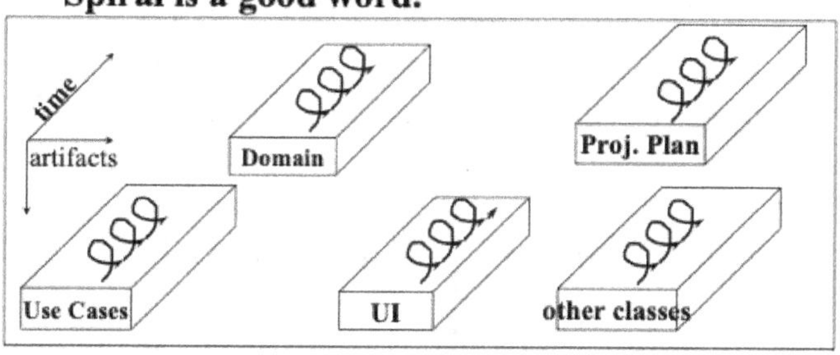

("Developer's time")

Humans and Technology — Alistair Cockburn — Page 4

The Problem (2):
Project Managers DO live in linear time.

The calendar does not show spirals.
time moves inexorably forward...

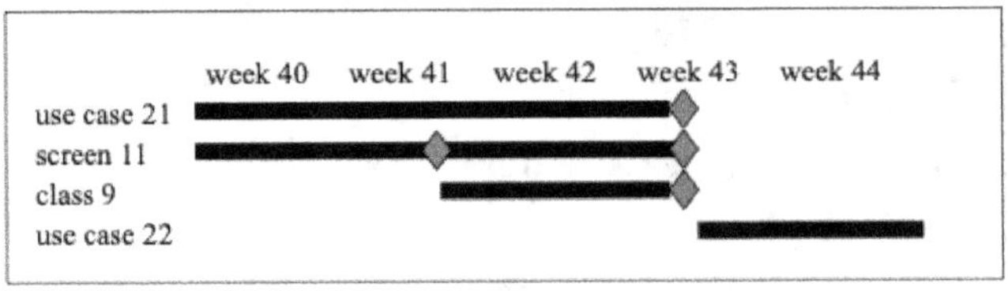

("Project Manager's time")

How do you schedule a Gestalt Round Trip?

Humans and Technology **Alistair Cockburn** **Page 5**

The 'Validation V':
Not waterfall, but a fact of life.

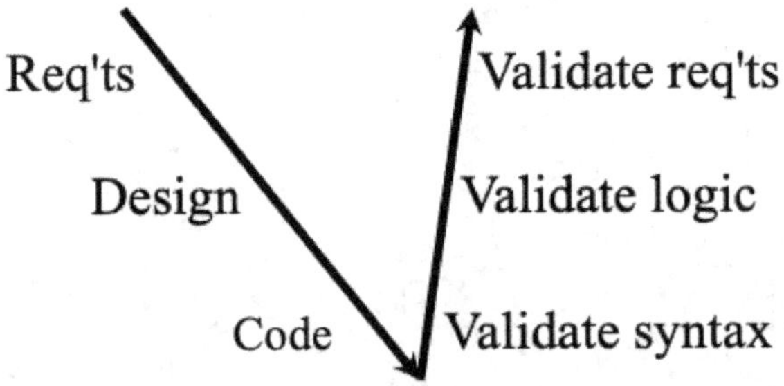

How can we use this 'fact of life'?

Humans and Technology **Alistair Cockburn** **Page 6**

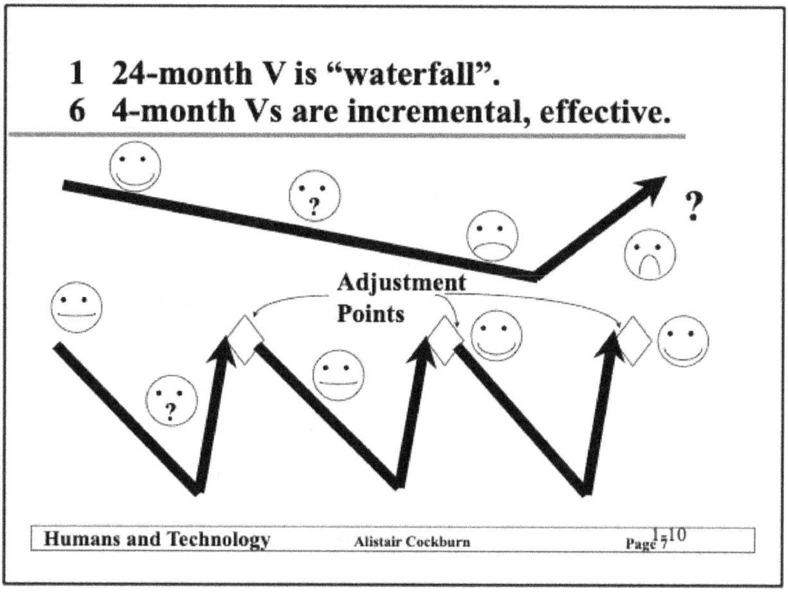
1 24-month V is "waterfall".
6 4-month Vs are incremental, effective.
?
Adjustment
Points
Humans and Technology
Alistair Cockburn
Page 7

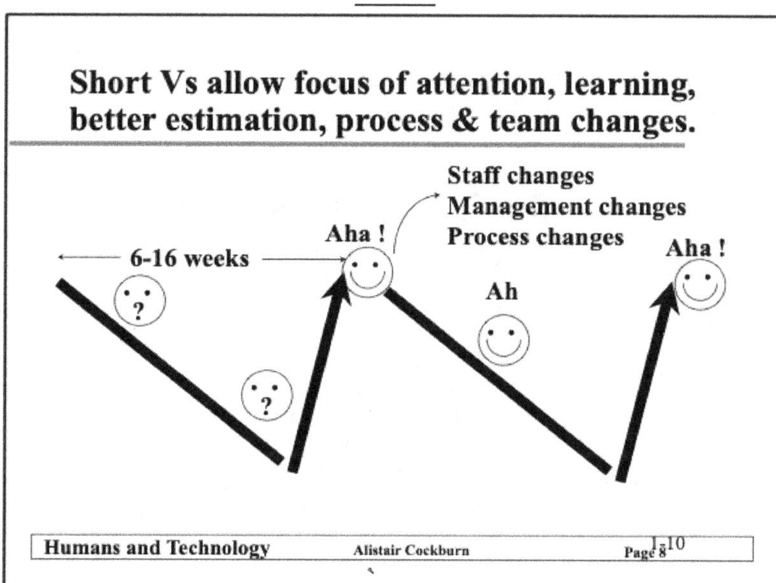
Short Vs allow focus of attention, learning, better estimation, process & team changes.
Staff changes
Management changes
Process changes
Aha !
6-16 weeks
Aha !
Ah
Humans and Technology
Alistair Cockburn
Page 8

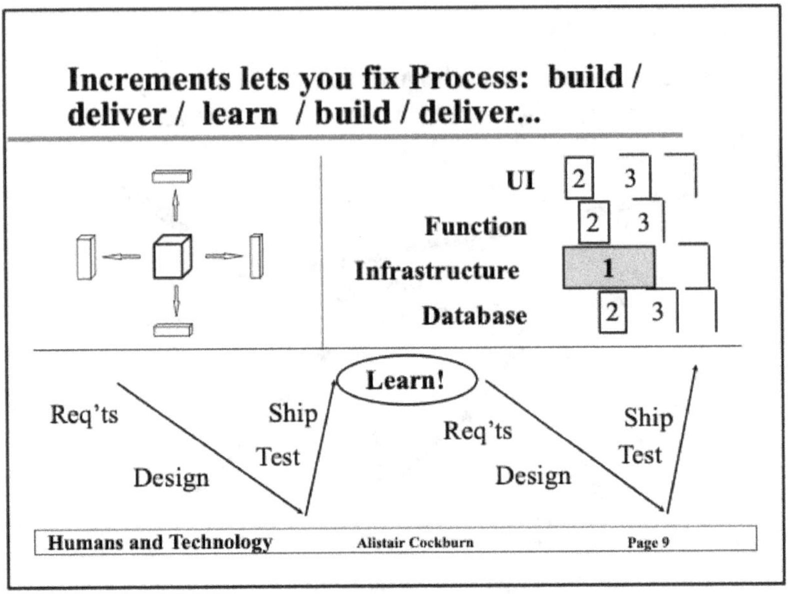
Increments lets you fix Process: build / deliver / learn / build / deliver...
UI
2
3
Function
2
3
Infrastructure
1
Database
2
3
Learn!
Req'ts
Design
Test
Ship
Req'ts
Design
Test
Ship
Humans and Technology
Alistair Cockburn
Page 9

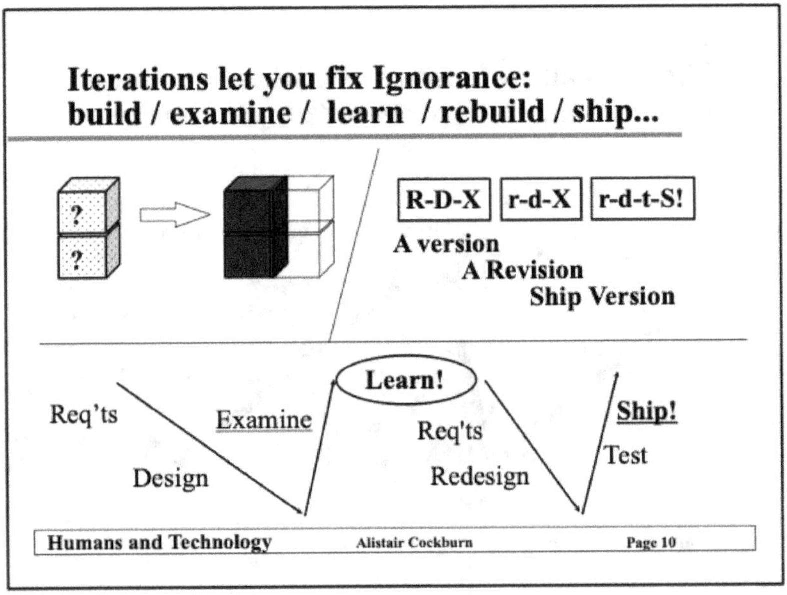
Iterations let you fix Ignorance: build / examine / learn / rebuild / ship...
?
?
R-D-X
r-d-X
r-d-t-S!
A version
A Revision
Ship Version
Learn!
Req'ts
Design
Examine
Req'ts
Redesign
Test
Ship!
Humans and Technology
Alistair Cockburn
Page 10

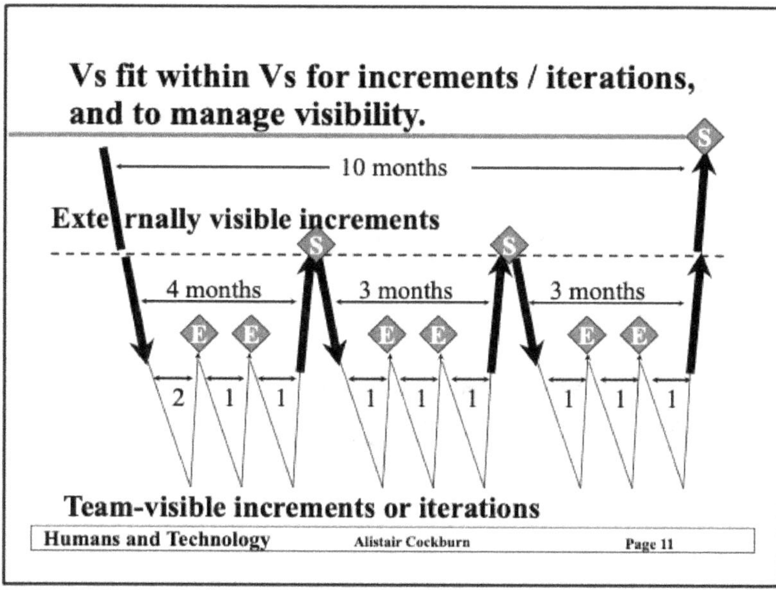
Vs fit within Vs for increments / iterations, and to manage visibility.
10 months
Externally visible increments
S
4 months
3 months
3 months
E
2
1
Team-visible increments or iterations
Humans and Technology
Alistair Cockburn
Page 11

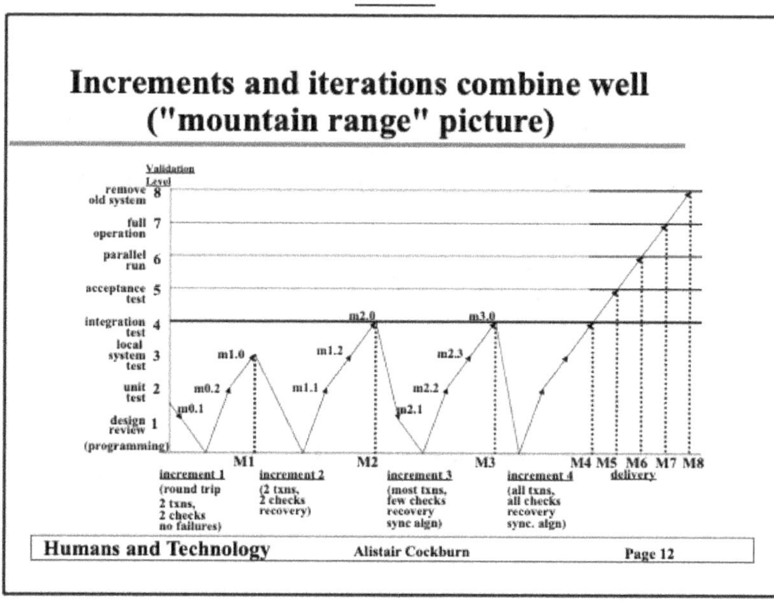
Increments and iterations combine well ("mountain range" picture)
Validation Level
remove old system 8
full operation 7
parallel run 6
acceptance test 5
integration test 4
local system test 3
unit test 2
design review 1
(programming)
m0.1
m0.2
m1.0
m1.1
m1.2
m2.0
m2.1
m2.2
m2.3
m3.0
M1
M2
M3
M4 M5 M6 M7 M8
delivery
increment 1
(round trip
2 txns,
2 checks
no failures)
increment 2
(2 txns,
2 checks
recovery)
increment 3
(most txns,
few checks
recovery
sync algn)
increment 4
(all txns,
all checks
recovery
sync. algn)
Humans and Technology
Alistair Cockburn
Page 12

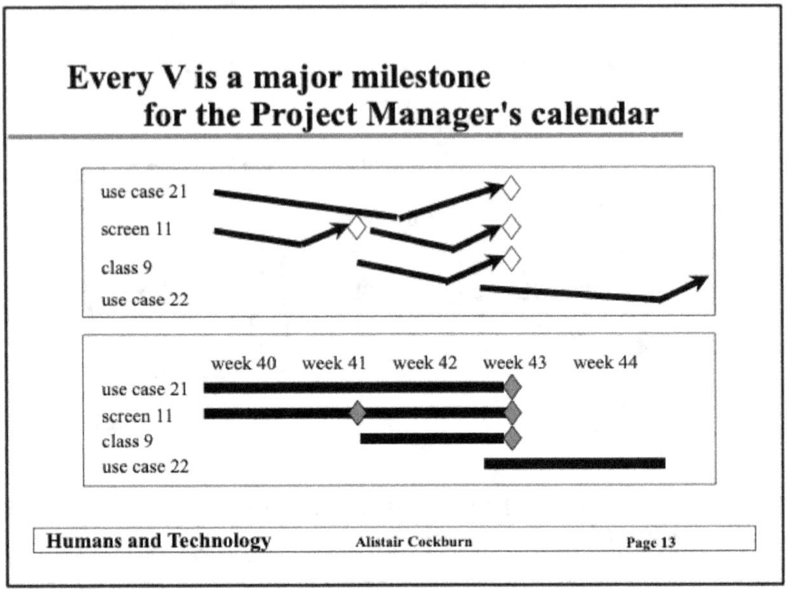
Every V is a major milestone
for the Project Manager's calendar
use case 21
screen 11
class 9
use case 22
week 40
week 41
week 42
week 43
week 44
use case 21
screen 11
class 9
use case 22
Humans and Technology
Alistair Cockburn
Page 13

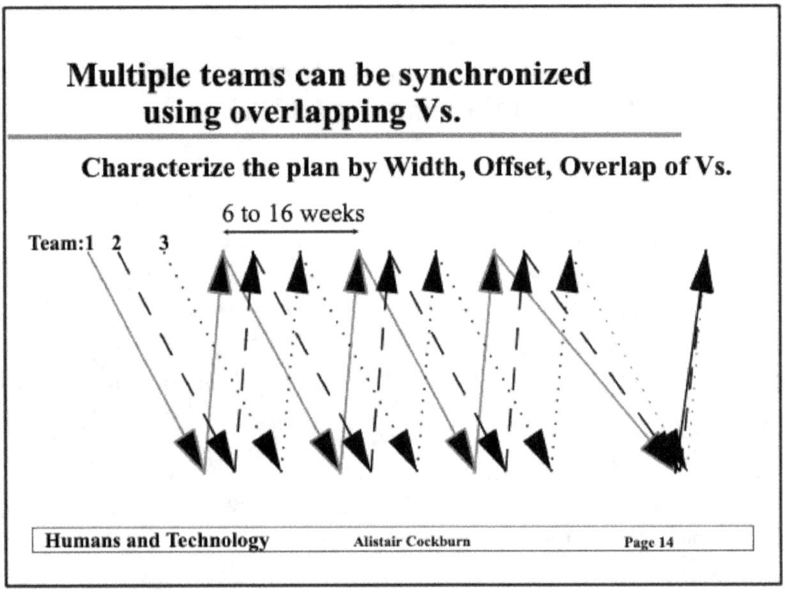
Multiple teams can be synchronized
using overlapping Vs.
Characterize the plan by Width, Offset, Overlap of Vs.
6 to 16 weeks
Team:1 2 3
Humans and Technology
Alistair Cockburn
Page 14

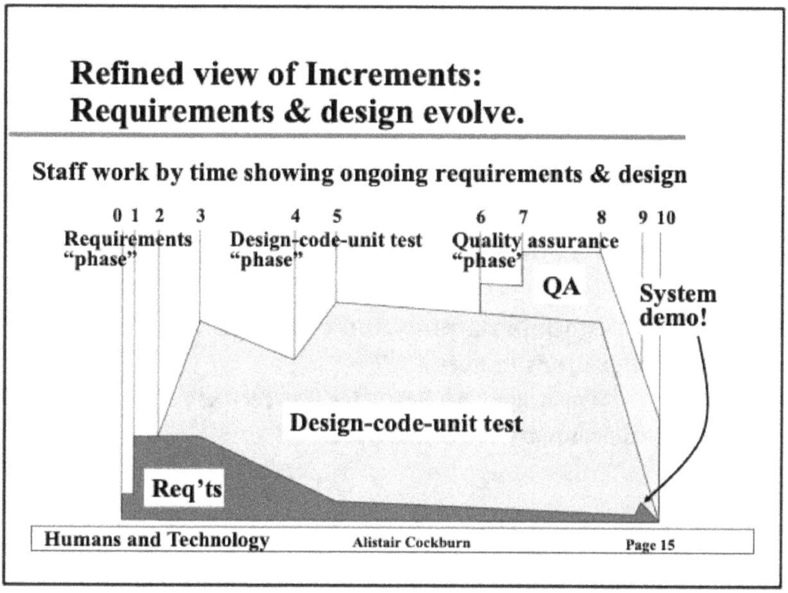
Refined view of Increments:
Requirements & design evolve.
Staff work by time showing ongoing requirements & design
0 1 2 3 4 5 6 7 8 9 10
Requirements "phase"
Design-code-unit test "phase"
Quality assurance "phase"
QA
System demo!
Design-code-unit test
Req'ts
Humans and Technology
Alistair Cockburn
Page 15

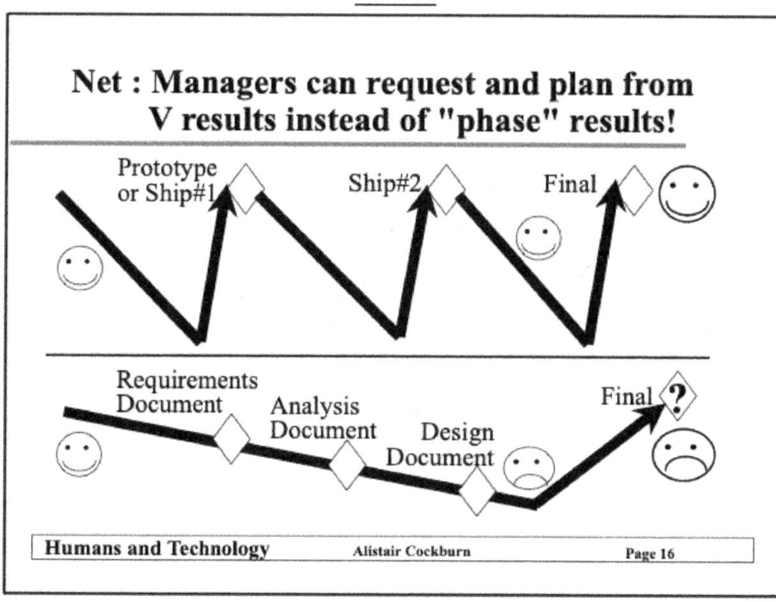
Net : Managers can request and plan from V results instead of "phase" results!
Prototype or Ship#1
Ship#2
Final
Requirements Document
Analysis Document
Design Document
Final
?
Humans and Technology
Alistair Cockburn
Page 16

Experiences (3): The "V-W" model lets people negotiate the work plan

Managers must and can write a 6-month plan.

Developers must and can iterate.

They negotiate number and duration:

- **iterations to examine**
  - » **For usage / performance / correctness**
- **increments to ship or stack**

Humans and Technology Alistair Cockburn Page 17

The V-W model lets project managers put increments / iterations on the calendar.

What this model does NOT do:

- **Does not make project managers smarter**
- **Does not improve your first estimate**
- **Does not guarantee project delivered on time**

What this model DOES do:

- **Gives a vocabulary to what we know is effective, but hard to describe.**
- **Lets project managers SCHEDULE iterations**
- **Let different people develop differently**

Humans and Technology Alistair Cockburn Page 18

Experiences (1): The "V-W" model lets developers explain what they are doing

A: 150-person project

Described the multi-team W (width /overlap /sync)

B: Dumped waterfall process

Because they could rationally explain new process

- » **They knew the waterfall was wrong, but they couldn't argue their feelings.**
- » **Moved to increments within increments**

Humans and Technology Alistair Cockburn Page 19

Experiences (2): The "V-W" model lets different people work differently

C: Released each 3 months, 3 iterations /release

(A winning strategy)

D: Released each 4 months, no iterations /release

(Iterations are hidden. An OK strategy)

E: 'V' per week, release whenever possible

(A survival strategy on, e.g., Wall Street)

F: Release each year, many iterations

(A losing strategy)

Humans and Technology Alistair Cockburn Page 20

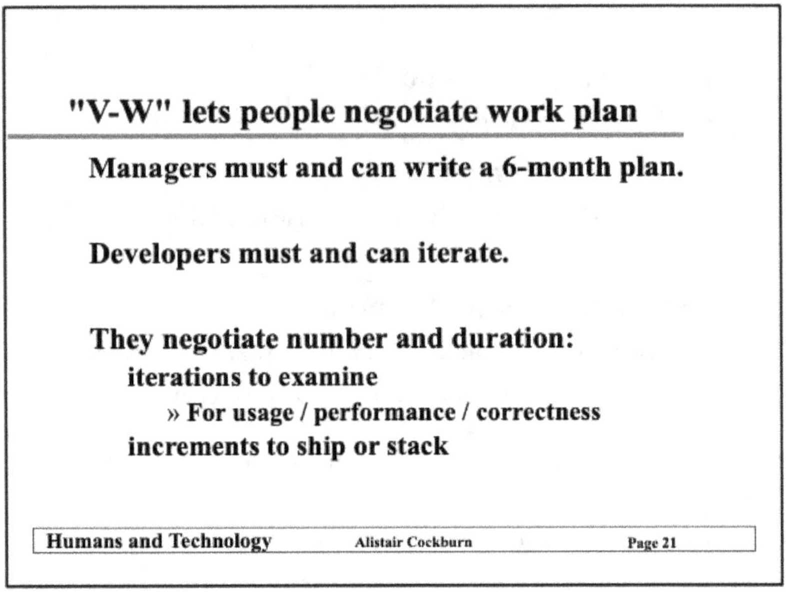

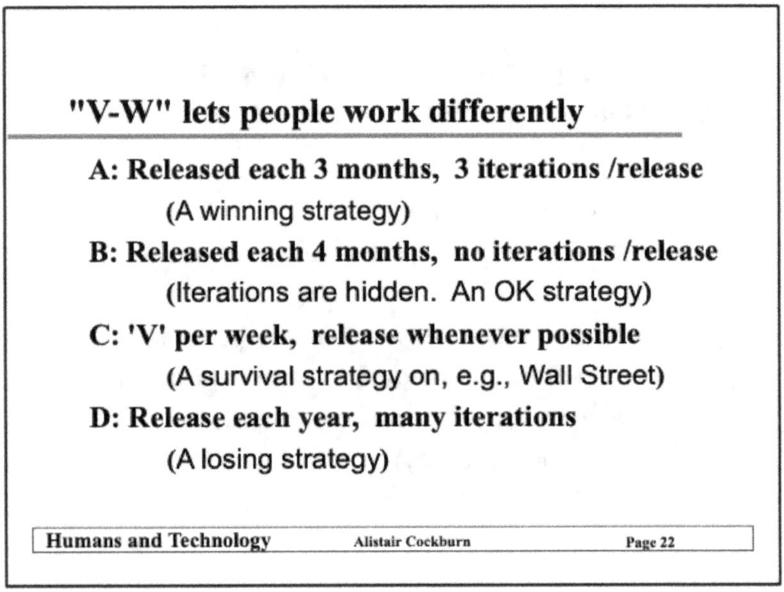

See the slides online:
[https://web.archive.org/web/20140329210317/http://alistair.cockburn.us/Managing+increments+and+iterations+with+VW+staging+030.ppt]

1997: Surviving Object-Oriented Projects

The book discussed what would be different in running a project with object-oriented (OO) programming. For most companies, that would be their first encounter with aggressive incremental and iterative strategies.

The section from the book on how incremental differs from iterative and how to run both together was given in *Chapter 7. Why Does 'Incremental' Help Improve Your Process?* That extract gives the whole argument carefully and in detail.

At the end of the book, I described a dozen strategies (called *patterns* in the pattern language community) for running these sorts of projects successfully. Here I include the first four of them, which have specifically to do with incremental-iterative development.

The section starts with a few extracts that summarize key points from the book, then continues with the four "patterns," or strategies.

Here are 4 critical success steps in creating a surviving, even thriving project.

Success in four "simple" steps:

1. Use incremental scheduling and staging.
2. Find and fix failing ideas.
3. Develop a habit of delivering.
4. Develop a good sponsor, project manager, and technical leader.

Do not confuse simple with easy. Simple often implies difficult, because simple things must be repeated daily, or require changing your work habits. Habits are a most difficult thing to change. The book reiterates those four key factors throughout.

If those are the critical success factors, I have found two key failure indicators:

Two key failure indicators

1. Absence of incremental development.
2. Use of C++ in a commercial IS department.

For the absence of incremental development, the argument is simple. If your project plan does not give you a place to recover from an initial error, you are unlikely to recover. Most of the projects I have visited have made mistakes, and the key to success was to have a way to recover.

* * * * *

10. Crib Sheet

Critical success factors:

CSF 1. Incremental scheduling and staging.

CSF 2. Willingness to find and fix failing ideas.

CSF 3. A habit of delivering.

CSF 4. Executive sponsor, project manager, technical leader.

Prime failure indicator:

PFI 1. Absence of a delivery after 8 months.

The strategies are written in a particular "pattern" form that I have found particularly useful for project management strategies. I model it on medical diagnosis or pharmaceutical prescriptions, paying attention to five elements:

-- Situation (Indications, Forces being balanced)
-- Diagnosis
-- Recommended action
-- Resulting context, with side effects of doing this action
-- Overdose effects if you do this too much

The **Thumbnail** provides the short form of the idea:

You are seeing this situation, so ... try out this action.

So that you can quote it briefly to someone else.

The **Indications** list what you might notice to tip you off you need some intervention.

The **Forces being balanced** list the probably conflicting forces that keep your immediate action from being obvious.

The **Recommended action** is exactly that.

The **Resulting context** is where you find yourself afterwards, typically with a new problem, but one that is hopefully smaller than the one you started with.

The **Overdose effect** is what happens if you do this too much.

After those, I include **Principles involved**, as in, why should we expect this to work? And **Sample Situations**, cases where it was used successfully.

I have found it useful to be very clear about the side effects and problems that come along with each strategy.

(1) Knowledge: Clear the Fog

Thumbnail:

You don't know the issues well enough to put together a sound plan, so...

Try to deliver something (almost anything); this tell you what the real issues are.

Indications:

You have to write the project plan, but you are missing key information.

You think you can write it, but you are trying out a new process / technology.

You just wrote a project plan with a first deliverable after two or more years of work.

Forces being balanced:

You need more knowledge to proceed.

You have to move forward into the project.

Factors affecting the balancing of the forces:

<This section is filled in within the specializations of the strategy.>

Recommended action:

Do something (almost anything) that is a best initial attempt to deliver some part of the system in a short period of time.

Resulting context:

As you go through that effort, you will discover what issues you need to address, their characteristics. You next need to create that project plan, fix your first effort, go on to the next part of the system, or repair your process, depending on what you learned.

Overdose effect:

If you only "clear the fog" and "clear the fog" and "clear the fog", you will not make real progress. You will have lots of little experiments and no deliverable results.

Related strategies:

Specializations:

Early and Regular Delivery - adds knowledge about your development process.

Prototype - adds knowledge about a specific decision or technology.

Microcosm - returns measurable data about process and technology.

Principles involved:

The difficulty is that you don't know what it is that you don't know. Only by making some movement can you detect what it is you don't know. Once you come to know what it is you don't know, you can pursue that information directly.

Sample situations:

A. This is your first OO project, and fills a real production need. You are unsure how similar or different OO is to your previous development. So, create a first, tiny delivery of function in 4-6 months. You will see how much is similar and how much is different. See *Early and Regular Delivery.*

B. You are trying out a relational database (or an OO database), and are worried about peak throughput. So, create a dummy database and stress it with simulated traffic loads. You will learn how it performs under load early enough to alter your design. See *Prototype.*

C. You are considering a serious project using a totally new language or technology. You don't know whether to proceed or how to size the project. So, run a carefully instrumented, mini-version of the project. Collect data on staff learning rates, productivity, technology effects. From this data, you can extrapolate the total effect to your proposed project. See *Microcosm.*

D. You want to gather your own project management strategies. You are unsure how to do it, or how it will be received by the project managers. So, gather some of those project managers together for one day, and have them write some of these strategies from their experience. You and they will learn the vocabulary of the strategies, and develop your own sense of their worth. Odds are, the people will be citing the strategies on their next project.

Reading:

Davis, A., 201 Principles of Software Development, McGraw-Hill, 1995.

MacGuire, S., Debugging the Development Process, Microsoft Press, 1994

McCarthy, J., Dynamics of Software Development, Microsoft Press, 1995, discusses daily builds.

McConnell, S., Rapid Development, Microsoft Press, 1996.

(2) Knowledge: Early and Regular Delivery

Other names:
Incremental development, Fountain / spiral/ tornado development, Staged delivery.

Thumbnail:
You don't know what problems you will encounter during development, so...
Deliver something early - discover what you don't know you don't know.

Deliver regularly - improve each time.

Indications:
You are unsure about some part of your development process.

You just wrote a project plan with a first deliverable after two or more years of work.

You want to improve and optimize your process.

Forces being balanced:
You need more knowledge to plan or set up the project.

You have to move forward into the project.

Factors affecting the balancing of the forces:

Your missing information is related to the process as well as the product.

You are already committed to producing the system.

Recommended action:
Create a delivery schedule with regular delivery dates, every 2-4 months. Let each release be determined by what can be delivered in that time frame. After each release, hold a small meeting or study group to learn what needs to be fixed or could be improved next time.

Resulting context:

If you get blindsided by an unexpected problem, you have lost no more than the delivery period (2-4 months), and at least you now know about it. If you run into minor obstacles, the period is short enough that your people can push through somehow. They can discuss afterwards what to do about that problem in the future.

If the release contents are too small to release to a final customer, create an "internal" release. Save up the internal releases until the result is large enough to release to the final customer.

You have a chance to reorganize your teams, change your process after each release. You have solid data on the working of your team over time. You can improve and tune your process.

Overdose effect:

Each increment takes some setup time, and requires regression testing of the new composite system. If the increments are too short, the scheduling, setup and test times will dominate your effort. Six weeks is usually considered a "short" time, although there are those who recommend daily (internal) releases (see McCarthy 95).

Related strategies:

Clear the Fog - the generic version of this strategy.

Prototype - the version of this for improving technical knowledge.

Principles involved:

Early delivery: Most project managers work with new technology, new people, new subject matter or new process. They really can't know what to expect, even if they have done much the same thing before. There is a strong chance that there is something they don't know that will delay them. The team's morale will improve after the first delivery.

Regular delivery: It takes common information from repetitions of a process to improve the process. With such information, you have a chance to reduce process variation, improve prediction, and attempt optimization. There is so much variation in software design from project to project that high-quality, reliable information is almost impossible to get. Multiple releases of a single project, however, provides the best possible data: the people are largely the same; the subject is the same; the technology is the same; the process is what you get to vary.

Sample situations:

A. See *Project Ingrid* and *Project Winifred* in the project histories.

B. You have been asked to run a project involving 150 people over four years. The previous project manager ran a straight waterfall process. You decide to create releases every 6 months, segmenting the project by architectural component and function.

C. You have been told by your boss that the executives only need to see a release every 10 months. You decide to create internal releases at 4-months and 7-months. This ensures that you have identified and reduced the risks for the 10-month delivery, and keeps the team's morale and confidence up.

Reading:

This entire book is centered around Early and Regular Delivery.

Boehm, Barry, Software Risk Management, IEEE Computer Society Press, 1989.

Davis, A., 201 Principles of Software Development, McGraw-Hill, 1995.

MacGuire, S., Debugging the Development Process, Microsoft Press, 1994

McCarthy, J., Dynamics of Software Development, Microsoft Press, 1995, discusses daily builds.

McConnell, S., Rapid Development, Microsoft Press, 1996.

(3) Knowledge: Prototype

Thumbnail:

You don't know how some design decision will work out, so...
Build an isolated solution - discover how it really works.

Indications:

You are designing a user interface.

You are trying a new database or network technology.

You are dependent on a new, critical algorithm.

You don't understand your project domain.

Forces being balanced:

You need more knowledge to proceed.

You have to move forward.

Factors affecting the balancing of the forces:

Your missing information is related to something about the product, not about the process.

You have a best guess you can use to move forward.

You have access to some way to evaluate the result of your best guess.

Recommended action:

Build a small system that isolates that issue, using your best current knowledge. Examine that small system to learn whether your current knowledge is correct and sufficient.

Resulting context:

You will decide that your current knowledge is or is not sufficient. If it is, incorporate that small system's design into your larger system (incorporate it entirely if it was built to production specifications). If not, decide whether you now have enough information to safely proceed, or whether you need to do another *Prototype*.

Overdose effect:

The process does not converge, the system does not deliver. Continued prototyping without convergence means that the design is constantly shifting, and the team is not learning enough to reach a conclusion. Other teams, depending on the prototyping team, do not get the stable interface they need.

Related strategies:

Clear the Fog - the generic version of this strategy.

Early and Regular Delivery - adds knowledge about your development process.

Microcosm - returns measurable data about process and technology.

Principles involved:

The risk to your project of a small, throw-away effort is a small schedule delay. The risk of making a poor technical choice is a poor product, or perhaps committing to a technology that simply will not work.

Sample situations:

A. You are trying out a relational database (or an OO database), and are worried about peak throughput. So, create a dummy database and stress it with simulated traffic loads. You will learn how it performs under load early enough to alter your design.

B. You are designing a user interface. Experience indicates that your developers probably will not get the design correct on the first try, either because the user experts did not know, did not speak correctly, or the designers did not hear correctly. So, you create a paper prototype in a few hours, or a screen prototype in a few hours or a day, or a rigged demo using fixed data. You show this to the users to discover missing information.

Reading:

There is massive literature on prototyping, rapid development, and user interface prototyping. Consider these are starters.

Boehm, Barry, Software Risk Management, IEEE Computer Society Press, 1989.

Davis, A., 201 Principles of Software Development, McGraw-Hill, 1995.

MacGuire, S., Debugging the Development Process, Microsoft Press, 1994

McCarthy, J., Dynamics of Software Development, Microsoft Press, 1995, discusses daily builds.

McConnell, S., Rapid Development, Microsoft Press, 1996.

(4) Knowledge: Microcosm

Thumbnail:

You have to create a real plan, but have never done this sort of project, so...
Run an 8-12 week instrumented pilot to get productivity and throughput data for your plan.

Indications:

You are considering whether a particular technology is for you.

You are unsure of how fast your developers will learn it.

You are unsure of how well the technology really works.

Forces being balanced:

You need more knowledge to make a decision or a plan.

You have to make a decision or a plan.

Factors affecting the balancing of the forces:

Your missing information may relate to the process as well as the product.

You are not yet committed to producing the system.

Recommended action:

Run a carefully instrumented micro-project, on the order of 8-12 weeks. Use a few of your own people plus some experts. Make sure that the micro-project is meaningfully designed to give you the data you will need. Collect data on staff learning rates, productivity, technology effects, throughput, as you need.

Resulting context:

After *Microcosm*, you will have some real data. Now you can scale up the results to your original project and decide whether it will work, or how the plan should look.

Overdose effect:

Making the *Microcosm* too short means you will not have time to get sufficient, meaningful results. Doing it too frequently means you will not make your decision or plan.

Related strategies:

Clear the Fog - the generic version of this strategy.

Early and Regular Delivery - adds knowledge about your development process.

Prototype - adds knowledge about a specific decision or technology.

Principles involved:

The principle is that of scaling. As distinct from a "proof of concept", *Microcosm* is carefully selected so that the key issues are visible and can be measured. The proof of concept only demonstrates that something small and similar can be built - no scaling data is collected in the proof of concept. On *Microcosm*, you can measure the productivity of the beginners compared to the experts, the fully loaded throughput on a simulated loading of the workstation, database or network, the memory requirements, etc. Each of these scales to give you a prediction for your real project.

I am obliged to caution that most project teams lack the discipline and care to identify the key issues and set up the project accordingly, preferring instead to create a "proof of concept". Do not confuse the two.

Sample situations:

A. The project leader ran *Microcosm* in 8 weeks for an untried database application technology. Based on the scaling data, he accepted the technology and created an 8-month project plan. The project finished within a few weeks of the plan and without major technical surprises.

B. You are considering using object technology, but are still unsure of its acceptance, code quality, ease of change, and performance. Run an 8 - 12 - week *Microcosm* and get some hard numbers to help you in your decision.

Reading:

I have not seen this technique discussed in software development.

System simulation program addresses part of the strategy, but not all.

2005: Crystal Clear: Frequent Delivery.

Chapter 3 of the book *Crystal Clear* describes the seven properties of highly successful projects. First of those is **Frequent Delivery**. Here is that section.

The single most important property of any project, large or small, agile or not, is that of delivering running, tested code to real users every few months. The advantages are so numerous that it is astonishing that any team doesn't do it:

- The sponsors get critical feedback on the rate of progress of the team.
- Users get a chance to discover whether their original request was for what they actually need and to get their discoveries fed back into development.
- Developers keep their focus, breaking deadlocks of indecision.
- The team gets to debug their development and deployment processes, and gets a morale boost through accomplishments.

All of these advantages come from one single property, **Frequent Delivery**. In my interviews, I have not seen any period longer than four months that still offers this safety. Two months is safer. Teams deploying to the web may deliver weekly.

Have you delivered running, tested and usable code at least twice to your user community in the last six months?

* * * *

Just what does "delivery" mean?

Sometimes it means that the software is deployed to the full set of users at the end of each iteration. This may be practical with web-deployed software or when the user group is relatively small.

When the users cannot accept software updates that often, the team finds itself in a quandary. If they deliver the system frequently, the user community will get annoyed with them. If they don't deliver frequently, they may miss a real problem with integration or deployment. They will encounter that problem when it is very late - at the moment of deploying the system.

The best strategy I know of in this situation is to find a friendly user who doesn't mind trying out the software, either as a courtesy or out of curiosity. Deploy to that one workstation. This allows the team to practice deployment and get useful feedback from at least one user.

If you cannot find a friendly user to deliver to, at least perform a full integration and test as though you were going to. This leaves only deployment with a potential flaw.

* * * *

The terms *integration*, *iteration, user viewing*, and *release* get mixed together these days. They have different effects on development and should be considered separately.

Frequent Integration should be the norm, happening every hour, every day, or at the worst, every week. The better teams these days have continuously running automated build-and-test scripts, so there is never more than 30 minutes from a check-in until the **Automated Test** results are posted.

Simply performing a system integration doesn't constitute an *iteration*, since an integration is often performed after any single person or subteam completes as fragment of a programming assignment. The term *iteration* refers to the team completing a section of work, integrating the system, reporting the outcome up the management chain, doing their periodic **Reflective Improvement** (I wish), and very importantly, getting emotional closure on having completed the work. The closure following an iteration is important because it sets up an emotional rhythm, something that is important to us as human beings.

In principle, an iteration can be anywhere from an hour to a quarter. In practice, they are usually two weeks to two months long.

The end date of an iteration is usually considered immovable, a practice called "time boxing." People encounter a natural temptation to extend an iteration when the team falls behind. This has generally shown itself to be a bad strategy, as it leads to longer and longer extensions to the iteration, jeopardizing the schedule and demotivating the team. Many well-intentioned managers damage a team by extending the iteration indefinitely, robbing the team of the joy and celebration around completion.

A better strategy is to fix the end date, and have the team deliver whatever they have completed at the end of the time box. With this strategy, the team learns what it can complete in that amount of time, useful feedback to the project plan. It also supplies the team with an **Early Victory**.

Fixed-length iterations allow the team to measure their speed of movement—the project's *velocity*. Fixed lengths iterations give that rhythm to the project that people describe as the project's "heartbeat."

Some people lock the requirements during an iteration or time box. This gives the team peace of mind while they develop, assuring them they will not have to change directions, but can complete *something* at least. I once encountered a group trying out XP where the Customer didn't want the trial to succeed: This Customer changed the requirements priorities every few days so that after several iterations the team still had not managed to complete any one user story. In such hostile environments, both the requirements locking and the peace-of-mind are critical. Requirements-locking is rarely needed in well-behaved environments.

The results of an iteration may or may not get released. Just how often the software should be sent out to real users is a topic for the whole team, including the sponsor, to deliberate. They may find it practical to deliver after every iteration, they may deliver every few iterations, or they may match deliveries to specific calendar dates.

Frequent Delivery is about delivering the software to users, not merely iterating. One nervous project team I visited had been iterating monthly for almost a year, but not yet delivered any release. The people were getting pretty nervous, because *the customer hadn't seen what they had been working on for the last year!* This constitutes a violation of **Frequent Delivery**.

If the team cannot deliver the system to the full user base every few months, *user viewings* become all the more critical. The team needs to arrange for users to visit the team and see the software in action, or at least on user to install and test the software. Failure to hold these user viewings easily correlates to end failure of the project, when the users finally, and too late, identify that the software does not meet their needs.

For the best effect, exercise both packaging and deployment. Install the system in as close to a real situation as possible.

2005: Unrolling Cyclic Development Processes.

Extracted from Chapter 4 of "Crystal Clear".

Crystal Clear uses nested cyclic processes of various lengths: the development episode, the iteration, the delivery period and the full project. What people do at any moment depends on where they are in each of the cycles.

This chapter linearizes the cycles to the extent possible and points out some of their interactions. [This extract contains only the illustration of the unrolling.]

Most of the development processes described from 1970 through 2000 were described as sequences of steps, even when the process recommended iterations and increments. This always caused confusion among readers. The text appeared to dictate a "waterfall" process, while the authors kept asserting it was not.

These linear-looking process descriptions suffer from two problems. The first is that they really describe the dependency graph between work products, the *workflow*. A dependency graph should be read in back-to-front order: The team cannot deliver the system until it is integrated and runs. They cannot integrate and test the code until it is written and running. They can't design and write the code until they learn what the requirements are (and so on). The workflow graph does not mandate a waterfall process; it simply reflects dependencies.

When a process is described by a work-flow dependency graph, people mentally treat the dependency graph picture as encouragement to complete each mentioned work product before starting on the next work product in the graph. This is rarely a good strategy in software development. When looking at a workflow dependency graph, the relevant questions to ask are these:

How many requirements, *at what level of completion* are needed before design can usefully get started? (The answers are "relatively few" and "relatively low", respectively.)

How much of the system must be designed and programmed before useful integration and testing can be done? (The answer is "relatively little.")

How much of the system, at what level of correctness, is needed before being useful to the users or suitable for user review? (The answers are "relatively little" and "relatively low," respectively.)

The low levels of each actually needed comes as a surprise to many people.

Concurrent development is the name given when work proceeds in parallel on dependent work products. In concurrent development, many or all activities are in play at the same time. People trade notes continually to keep abreast of the changing state of each part. Concurrent development is not new, either to software development or project management in general. It is done by almost every project team I visit, although few have noticed they do it.

Concurrent development is described at length in Agile Software Development, in the ***Gold Rush*** strategy in *Surviving Object-Oriented Projects*, and is generally presupposed in most of my writings. Therefore, I won't try to describe concurrent development here, nor the dependency graph in Crystal Clear (that should be quite obvious). Removing these two topics allows me to describe other interesting aspects of the process.

The second problem plaguing linear descriptions of process is that the processes they are trying to describe are cyclic, using multiple cycles of differing lengths.

I notice seven cycles in play on most projects:

- The project (a unit of funding, which could be any duration)
- The delivery cycle (a unit of delivery, one week to three months)
- The iteration (a unit of estimation, development and celebration, one week to three months)
- The work week

- The integration period (a unit of development, integration and system testing, 30 minutes to three days)
- The work day
- The development episode (developing and checking in a section of code, taking a few minutes to a few hours)

Crystal Clear requires multiple deliveries per project, but not multiple iterations per delivery. I will repeat this point several times, but I wish to draw your attention to it right away.

Teams using short iteration periods inside a long delivery cycle sometimes add a "supercycle" of perhaps four or six iterations, to provide an intermediate rhythm. They use this supercycle to reflect on their process, to celebrate, to unwind. I will not elaborate much on the supercycle in this chapter. Teams can derive what elements of the iteration and delivery cycles to move to the supercycle.

Each cycle has its own sequencing, its own rhythm. In any given day, different activities will be in play from the various cycles. The activities change from hour to hour, day to day and week to week. This makes a complete linear description of the process virtually impossible.

The following figures show various ways of unrolling these cycles. These simple sketches have to omit some of the interactions between cycles, a few of which I'll point out shortly. Notice that episodes, days, and integration periods can nest inside an iteration in various ways; there are other valid combinations even more difficult to draw.

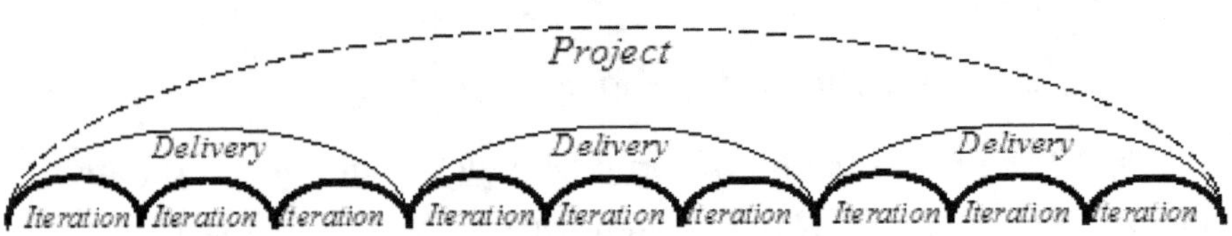

Figure 77, Part 3. Iteration and delivery cycles within a project.

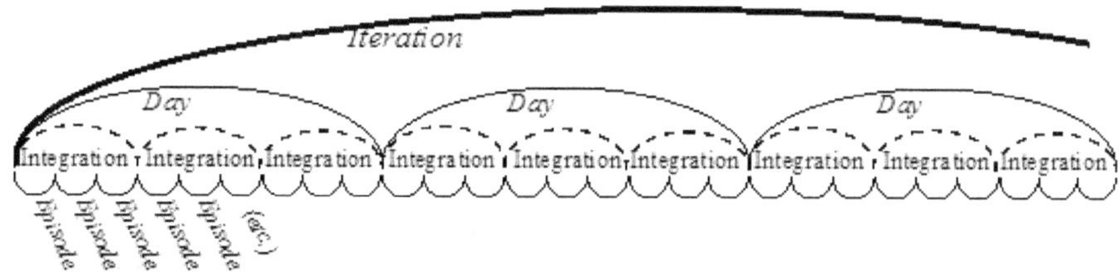

Figure 78, Part 3. An iteration cycle, integrating multiple times per day.

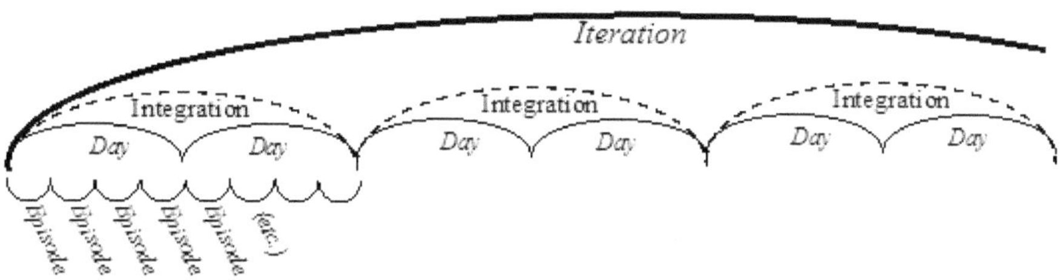

Figure 79, Part 3. An iteration cycle with multiple days per integration.

The following figures show the expansion of each cycle separately, listing specific activities that occur specifically for that cycle type.

Figure 80 shows them in increasing magnification.

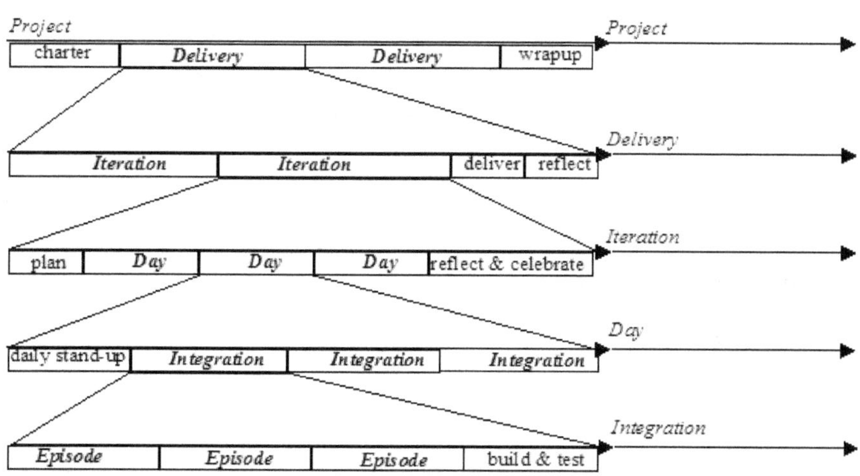

Figure 80, Part 3. The cycles expanded to show specific activities.

Project	Iteration	Day	Integration	Episode
Charter				
	Plan			
		Daily standup		
				Design & Check-in
				Design & Check-in
			Build and test	
				Design & Check-in
				Design & Check-in
			Build and test	
		Daily standup		
				Design & Check-in
				Design & Check-in
			Build and test	
				Design & Check-in
				Design & Check-in
			Build and test	
	Deliver			
	Reflect and celebrate			
	Plan			
	(etc.)			
Wrapup				

Figure 81, Part 3. The activities in a plausible vertical sequence.

Figure 81 shows activities in a plausible time sequence vertically down the page.

Finally, in *Figure 82*, I unrolled all the cycles and shaded the cycles in different ways so the activity can be connected to its cycle. The capital and small letters stand for project Chartering, iteration planning, daily standup, development, check-in, integration, Reflection workshop, Delivery, and project Wrap-up. Of course, I had to choose one particular relationship between the daily cycle and the integration cycle for this particular unrolling.

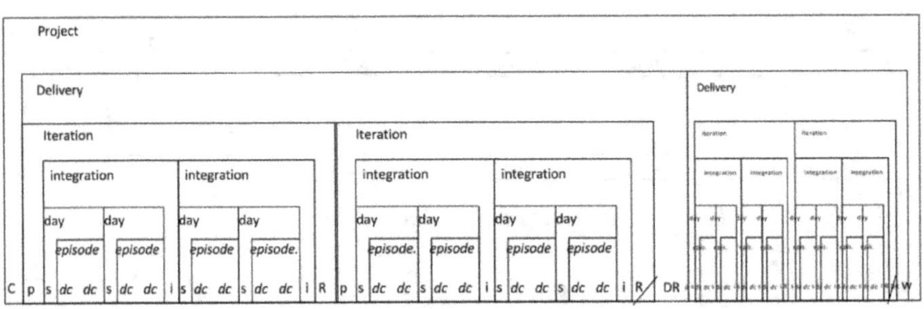

Figure 82, Part 3. The cycles unrolled all the way to show daily activities.

People interested in detail will notice that there is a line drawn through the R at the end of the last iteration of a delivery cycle. That indicates that team does not "reflect, deliver, reflect again," but rather, more naturally waits until after the actual delivery, then reflects just once.

Another detail is that the planning session in the first iteration of a delivery cycle is likely to have two parts: adjusting the coarse-grained project plan and creating a fine-grained iteration plan.

These are the sorts of minor process adjustments that most teams make naturally, but make cyclic process so hard to describe explicitly.

See online:

[https://web.archive.org/web/20140329203415/http://alistair.cockburn.us/Unrolling+cyclic+development+processes]

2007: Incremental versus Iterative Development.

Fifteen years later, yet another go at getting these two concepts described. You should recognize most of these words by now :).

Just a small reminder to show they are not the same.

I've noticed people lately yet again getting wrapped around the axle of "incremental" development versus "iterative" development. RUP and the OMG didn't help matters any by calling everything "iterations" and "iterative development". They're different, have to be managed differently, have to be thought of differently. It happens that most project teams do both at the same time, usually without thinking about it. Then someone starts thinking about it, gets clever, and does one without the other. Bad things ensue.

Incremental development defined

By "incremental development", I specifically mean

> **staging and scheduling strategy** "in which the various parts of the system are developed at different times or rates, and integrated as they are completed.

It neither implies, requires nor precludes iterative development or waterfall development – both of those are rework strategies. The alternative to incremental development is to develop the entire system with a "big bang" integration.

"Incremental" development helps you improve your **process.** Each time around the process, you get to change and improve your work habits.

Iterative development defined

By "iterative development", I specifically wish to mean a

> **rework scheduling strategy** "in which time is set aside to revise and improve parts of the system."

It does not presuppose incremental development, but works very well with it. As shown in the figures, the difference is that an increment may actually ship, whereas an iteration is examined for modification.

"Iterative" development helps you improve your **product.** Each time around the process you get to change and improve the product itself (and maybe some of your work habits)

These definitions were written back in 1992, when they were still separate terms and people wanted to know their meanings. Then, as above, RUP and the OMG people mushed the two together and we've been having trouble ever since.

Those definitions are still pretty good, 15 years later. Sit on them, hatch them, think about what it means to do them separately and together. Think about how your project strategies might vary as you needed to manage more of one, and then more of the other. Good things should happen inside your brain.

How did we go wrong?

Back in 1992, we were still fighting waterfall development (as if we aren't still today!). I came in from the outside, into application development from IBM Research, and was told to investigate modern (1990s style) software development. I noticed these two things, asked people what they meant by them, and wrote down those definitions.

What I noticed, and you will of course notice, is that

- in **waterfall** development, you do "requirements" only once; then you do "design" only once; then you do "programming" only once (ha! ha! fooled you – of course you do the programming over and over and over, but don't tell your PM that!); you "test" only once (ha! ha! of course not! but that's the theory); you "integrate" only once; you "deliver" only once (that part may be true);
- in **incremental** development, you do each of activity multiple times , that is, you go around the requirements – design – programming – testing – integration – delivery cycle **multiple**

times. You "iterate" through that cycle multiple times. ("iterate" – get it? sigh…)

in **iterative** development, you also do each of those activities multiple times … you go around the requirements – design – programming – testing – integration – delivery cycle **multiple times.** You "iterate" through that cycle multiple times. By Gummy! Both of those are "iterative" development! WOW!

Of course, the $200,000 question is, do you repeat the cycle

- on the same part of the system you just got done with, or
- on a new part of the system?

How you answer that question yields very different results on what happens next on your project.

I have always kept them separate, with good results. What stunned me, back in around 1994, was that the pundits and authors at the time seem to have gotten so excited at the thought of repeating the cycle "at all" that they lumped the two together and never saw the difference in what happened on the project based on whether you were **revising old** stuff or **getting onto new** stuff!

Baffled me, but as Martin Fowler told me around 1995 —- "You lost, Alistair."

Indeed I did, and so did a lot of projects. I visited a 200-person project team, where, as one manager put it when he finally saw the difference, "We're iterating when we should be incrementing!!" You can imagine the feeling of helplessness on that project as the developers saw the same requirements coming at them over and over again in slightly different forms, and no plan for making progress through the requirements set. At that time, the lesson was: be sure to increment; yes you will iterate anyway.

More recently, on XP/agile projects, we see them incrementing like wildfire, but never putting time into the schedule to iterate. Now the quality suffers.

Note – "Iterative" development was a particularly bad choice of words, and remains a troublesome phrase. Any sponsor hearing,

"We're going to do "iterative" development" immediately hears, "We're going to do a lot of rework"! (Ouch, my wallet!)

At least with "incremental development" they get to think, "We're going to do step-wise growth." Their funding reflexes twitch differently (much more scared ((and rightfully so)) with iterative).

Remember,

> **Incremental** fundamentally means **add onto**.
> Incremental development helps you improve your **process.**
>
> **Iterative** fundamentally means **revise**.
> Iterative development helps you improve your **product.**

Both call for improvement. Create your staging, integration and rework strategies accordingly.

See online:

[https://web.archive.org/web/20140329203252/http://alistair.cockburn.us/Incremental+versus+iterative+development]

2008: Using Both Incremental and Iterative Development (the CrossTalk Article).

Published in CrossTalk, May 2008.

Incremental development is distinctly different from iterative development, in its purpose and also from its management implications. Teams get into trouble by doing one and not the other, or by trying to manage them the same way. This article illustrates their differences and how to use them together.

Incremental and iterative development predate the agile movement – I first ran into them while doing research for the IBM Consulting Group in 1991 [1, 2, 3]. At that time I learned how different they are in purpose and nature, and eventually, how to manage them. Those differences seem to have gotten forgotten in the intervening years. I now see would-be-agile teams suffering from doing only incremental development, where I used to see waterfall-type projects suffering from doing neither or only iterative development.

Both are needed. People need to learn to use them separately as well as together.

Definitions, please!

Briefly,

- **Incremental** development is a staging and scheduling strategy in which various parts of the system are developed at different times or rates, and integrated as they are completed.

The alternative strategy to incremental development is to develop the entire system with a "big bang" integration at the end.

- **Iterative** development is a rework scheduling strategy in which time is set aside to revise and improve parts of the system.

The alternative strategy to iterative development is to plan to get everything right the first time.

It is important to notice that neither strategy presupposes, requires or implies the other. It is possible to do either alone, both, or neither.

In practice, it is advisable to do both, in different quantities. If you only increment, there tends to be an unpleasant surprise at the end when the quality is not good enough. If you iterate the entire system, ripple effects of the changes easily get out of control.

It's not waterfall

First of all, we need to get past the "It looks like waterfall!" trap.

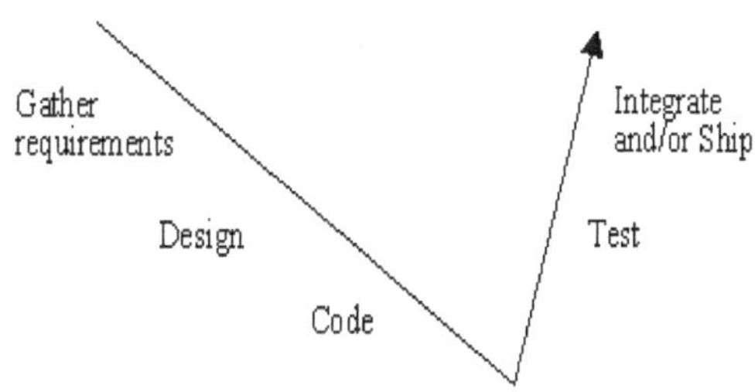

Figure 83, Part 3. The validation V is a fact of life.

In all development, whether prototype, agile, tornado, or waterfall, we first decide what to build. We then design and program something. Only after doing some programming (however much we decide to program), are we in a position to debug the system. Only after the system is running can we validate that what we built is the right thing to build, built correctly. This sequence is shown in *Figure 83*.

Figure 83 should really be read backwards, as a dependency diagram: we can't ship till we debug and validate; we can't debug till we code; we can't code till we design, we can't design till we have decided what to design.

In other words, the "Validation V" is a simple fact of life, and we shall have to deal with it in both incremental and iterative development.

Incremental development

In incremental development, we break up the work into smaller pieces, schedule them to be developed over time, and integrated as they get completed. The following figures illustrate.

Imagine that the top sheet of blocks represents various user interface components, the middle sheet represents middle ware, and the bottom sheet represents back end or database components.

Figure 84 shows that in the first increment, a full piece of functionality is built from UI through to back end (and in this case, additional pieces of the UI are also built).

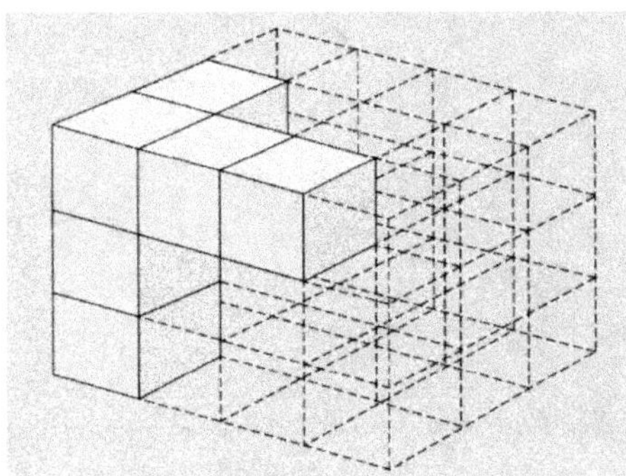

Figure 84, Part 3. Incremental development, stage 1.

In the second increment (*Figure 85*), we see that additional functionality is added across all layers of the system. This may be a sufficient point to deploy the system-as-it-is-so-far to real users and start accruing business benefit.

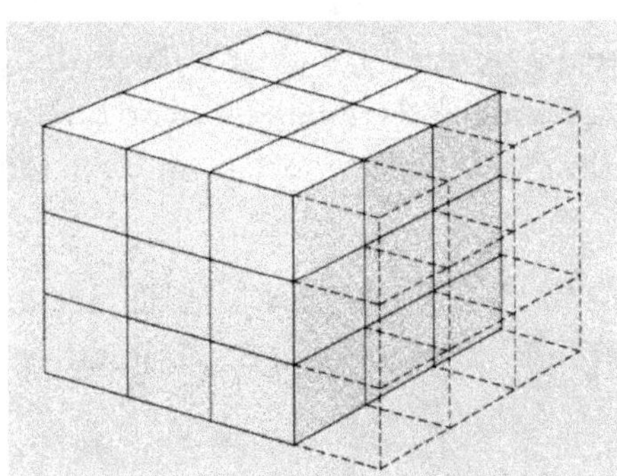

Figure 85, Part 3. Incremental development, stage 2.

In the third increment (*Figure 86*), the rest of the system is completed and incremented.

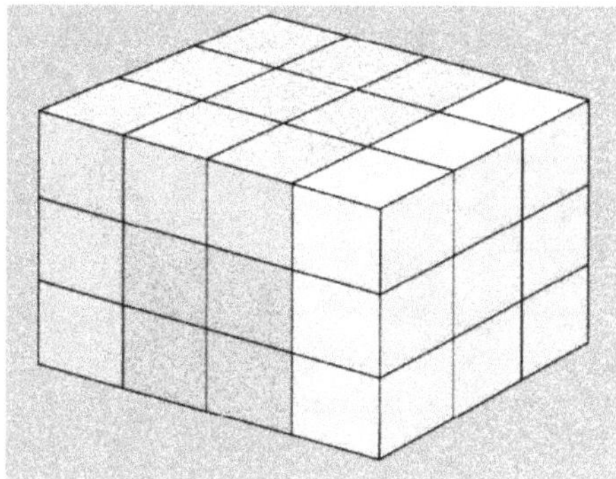

Figure 86, Part 3. Incremental development, stage 3.

The pattern just described is the one used by most modern projects, agile or not. It is a staging strategy with a long history of success.

The mistake people make these days is they forget to iterate. They don't plan in the time to learn what they misunderstood when they decided what to build at the very beginning, and what needs to be improved in the design.

This mistake results in the old failure of delivering what people don't want. I wish to highlight that even many agile project teams make this mistake.

The correcting strategy is iterative development.

Iterative development

In iterative development, we set aside time to improve what we have.

Requirements and user interfaces are the most notorious places where we historically have had to revise our work, but they are not the only ones. Technology, architecture and algorithms are also likely to need inspection and revision. Performance-under-load is often misguessed in the early stages of design, requiring a major architectural revision.

In terms of the validation V, the difference is that instead of integrating and perhaps shipping the software at the end of the cycle, we *examine* it from various standpoints: Was it the right thing to develop? Do the users like the way it works? Does it work fast enough?

Figure 87 shows the validation V for an iterative development cycle.

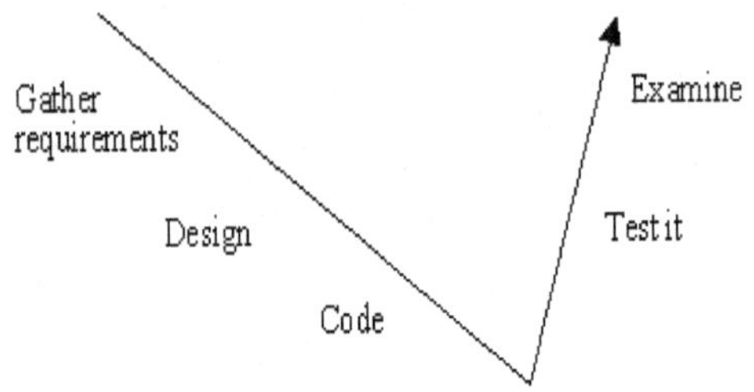

Figure 87, Part 3. The Validation V for an iterative cycle.

There are two particular, specialized rework strategies:

- Develop the system as well as possible, in the thinking that if it is done sufficiently well, the changes will be relatively minor and can be incorporated quickly.
- Develop the least amount possible before sending out for evaluation, in the thinking that less work will be wasted when the new information arrives.

There are afficionados of both approaches. Indeed, both work well under certain circumstances. A project manager must learn to use both.

Here is an effective use of the first strategy:

> ***A musician and a photographer were making a DVD together. The musician recorded the four-minute track in its entirety. The photographer noticed that a small sequence of slide transitions didn't match the music. The musician re-recorded just those bars, and spliced them into the music track.***

To show an effective use of the second strategy, I adjust Jeff Patton's example of the painting of the Mona Lisa [4], imagining the discussion between Leonardo and his patron (*Figure 88*).

Figure 88, Part 3. Iterative development of the Mona Lisa.

> *Leonardo draws a sketch of what he intends to do (left drawing) and goes to the patron, asking, "How's this going to work for you?"*
>
> *The patron says, "No, no, no. Sshe can't be looking right, she has to be looking left!" Fortunately, Leonardo hasn't done too much work yet, so this is easy to change.*
>
> *Leonardo goes away, reverses the picture and does some color and detail (center drawing). He goes back to the patron:*
>
> *"By cost, I'm about one-third done. What do you think now?".*
>
> *The patron says, ""No, you can't make her head look that big! Make it look more balanced with her body size." (Yes, they had the equivalent of PhotoShop and airbrushing back then. It was called "Leonardo").*
>
> *Leonardo goes away and finishes the painting (right drawing) and turns in his bill.*
>
> *The patron says, "Really, I'd rather have her eyes bigger, but OK, for the money I've paid, let's call it done."*

What I wish to highlight is that both strategies are valid and both fit the *iterative* tag. In both cases, rework was done on an existing part of the system.

Blending the two

Incremental and iterative development fit well with each other. Taking advantage of the validation-V, we can arrange to alternate "incremental" Vs with "iterative" Vs in various ways to get any number of composite iterative / incremental strategies. *Figure 89* illustrates.

Figure 89 shows a strategy in which each incremental section of the system is given two examination / rework periods before being integrated and staged for delivery. The figure shows three incremental development periods, each increment staged as it gets completed, the whole then shipped as a package.

This is one – but only one! – of the possible ways to blend the two. As long as they are clearly marked "examine" and "stage" (or even better, "ship"), the Vs can be mixed in almost any combination.

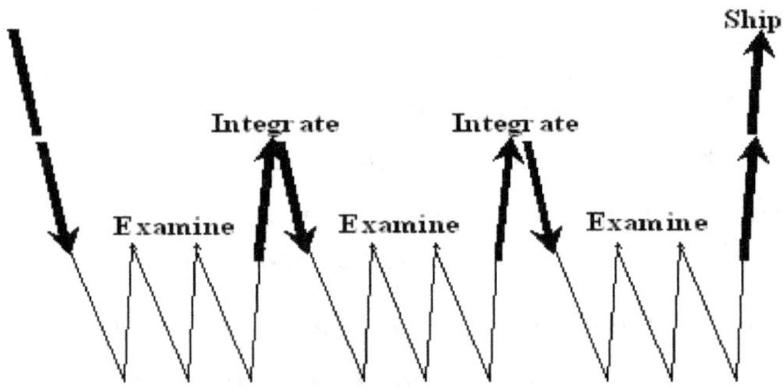

Figure 89, Part 3. Iterative and incremental development fit together.

Figure 89 shows one added benefit of describing increments and iterations with Vs: the resulting diagram maps easily to a calendar. Each examine-, integrate-, or ship marker is a milestone in the project manager's project plan. This allows the project manager to preview and monitor the time spent revising. In this way, we put the validation V "fact of life" to good use in showing our incremental-iterative development strategy.

Managing them

Superficially the two look very similar. However, they need to be managed differently.

Increments are easy to spot, easy to separate, relatively easy to estimate, and easy to schedule. The entire strategy can be summarized in two steps:

- Divide the system into complete, useful slices of functionality, or according to some other useful decomposition you may choose.
- Do them one after the other.

Iterations are considerably more difficult. They are hard to separate, hard to estimate, and hard to schedule. Of course, being hard doesn't mean you don't have to do all those things. You still have to do them.

The three questions are these:

- Which items need to get rework periods scheduled?
- How many rework periods does each need?
- How long should each rework period be?

Although there is no simple, reliable answer to those questions, there is a simple starting strategy, from which you can derive a version that fits your project [5].

- Plan to revise the user interface for sure, plan time to add or revise requirements as the end users start to use the system, and suspect that the performance-under-load architecture will need to be revised.
- Allocate two revision periods for the user interface design, and one each for requirements drift and performance re-architecture.
- Allocate for the first revision one third of the initial development time, and for the second revision one half of that.

You will need to develop and test your own numbers, but those might not be bad starting numbers for the first estimate.

If you are doing agile development with Scrum or XP, make sure every user story or backlog card passes through the Scrum sprint backlog three times, with those multipliers on them as work size estimates for the subsequent passes.

Three stories

Finally, I offer three stories of incremental / iterative development done poorly and done well.

The first one, project *Baker*, shows iterative confused with incremental: They iterated when they should have incremented.

> *Project Baker was a fixed-price, fixed-scope project, with 200 people. They worked in month-long cycles (an incremental development strategy).*
>
> *The teams were separated, working in pipeline fashion, so that the requirements writers wrote requirements for some features for a month, passed them along at the start of the next month to the designers. A month later the designers passed the designs along to the programmers, who programmed for a month. At the end the testers were given pieces of code to test and integrate.*
>
> *Misunderstanding the term "iterative development", they then gave everyone instructions that requirements and design could be changed at any time (this was their iterative development strategy).*
>
> *The pandemonium that ensued is just what you might expect: Each month the requirements writers revised any part of the requirements document, which changed any amount of design and programming. By the third month, it was obvious to the programmers that they were programming a system that had already been changed by the designers, who were simultaneously aware that they were designing a system that had already been changed by the requirements writers. The testers never got anything that fit together.*

> *Project Baker was in trouble from the start, partly due to the pipelining strategy, but even more to the uncontrolled iteration.*

The second one, Project *Laddie*, shows the problem of modern agile projects incrementing without iterating.

> *Project Laddie was using an agile approach, with two-week iterations. All user stories were put into a long list and developed to completion each iteration (their incremental development strategy).*
>
> *At the end of each iteration, the customer was shown what had gotten built during those two weeks. Of course, since two weeks is a very short time, there was never time to show the customer what was being designed, and so there generally were corrections to be made.*
>
> *The customer person had to choose whether to delay work on new user stories in order to correct the mistakes made, or to push the corrections to the back of the work queue. (This was their iterative development strategy – not a very nice one from the customer's perspective.)*
>
> *The customer complained after a while that he felt he had to get things right the first time, since the choices given to him about how and when to fix mistakes were not very pleasant. This, he correctly felt, violated the very spirit of agile development [6].*

Let's end with a happy story. The final one, Project *Winifred*, shows them done well (for one configuration of "done well").

> *Project Winifred [7] was a fixed-price, fixed-scope, fixed-time project of 18 months, using about 45 people at its peak. The basic development cycle was three months, resulting in deployment after each cycle. (This was the incremental strategy)*
>
> *There was no particular incremental strategy required within each development cycle – the teams got to develop features in any sequence they wanted. However, every team had to show their ongoing work to real users at least twice within each cycle, so that the users could change or correct what was being built (their iterative strategy). It had to be real software, from user interface to database, not just screen mock-ups.*

> *Typically, each team showed the users what they were building after 6 weeks of work and again after 8 weeks of work. In the first user viewing, perhaps 60-80% of the functionality was complete. The users were given the right to change anything they didn't like about what they saw, including "I know that's what I said I wanted, but now that I see it, it's actually not what I want at all."*
>
> *By the second viewing, perhaps 90-95% of the functionality was complete, and the users were only allowed to correct egregious mistakes and make fine-tuning corrections. This permitted both requirements and user interface correction while still making sense for a fixed-price contract.*
>
> *Project Winifred deployed successfully, and the users got more or less what they wanted. The system is still in use and being maintained a decade later, which is a fair indicator of success.*

Note that project *Winifred's* incremental-iterative strategy combination followed the style of the Mona Lisa story earlier.

Summary

The word *increment* fundamentally means *add onto.*

The word *iterate* fundamentally means *revise.*

Sadly, *iterative development* has come to mean either incremental or iterative, indiscriminately. That was an unfortunate turn for our industry, since they serve different purposes and need to be managed differently.

Incremental development gives you opportunities to improve your development process, as well as adjust the requirements to the changing world.

Iterative development helps you improve your product quality. Yes, it is rework, and yes, you probably need to do some rework to make your product shine.

Development process, feature set, product quality, all need constant improvement. Use an *incremental* strategy, with reflection, to improve the first two. Use an *iterative* strategy, with reflection, to improve the third,

References

Cockburn, A., "The Impact of Object Orientation on Application Development", IBM Systems Journal, Nov. 1993.

Cockburn, A., "Unraveling Incremental Development," online at http://alistair.cockburn.us/index.php/Unraveling_incremental_development

Cockburn, A., "Using VW Staging to Clarify Spiral Development", online at http://alistair.cockburn.us/index.php/Using VW staging to clarify spiral development

Patton, J., "The Neglected Practice of Iteration", StickyMinds, Dec 2007, online at http://www.stickyminds.com/sitewide.asp?Function=edetail&ObjectType=COL&ObjectId=13178

Cockburn, A., "Three Cards for User Rights", online at http://alistair.cockburn.us/index.php/Three_cards_for_user_rights

Cockburn, "Are Iterations Hazardous to Your Project?", online at http://alistair.cockburn.us/index.php/Are_iterations_hazardous_to_your_project?

Cockburn, A. *Surviving Object-Oriented Projects*, Addison-Wesley, 1997.

See on the archive of my old site:

[https://web.archive.org/web/20140329203138/http://alistair.cockburn.us/Using+both+incremental+and+iterative+development]

See on the archive of the CrossTalk site:

[https://web.archive.org/web/20120611174441/http:/www.crosstalkonline.org/storage/issue-archives/2008/200805/200805-Cockburn.pdf].

2008: Incremental Means Adding, Iterative Means Reworking.

Blog post, 2008. This is my favorite article by far, blending art and software.

"Incrementally" means *adding onto,* "Iteratively" means *reworking*. This little article illustrates using paintings as a basis.

I was planning on extending Jeff Patton's modification of John Armitage's example (see further reading) and write a made-up story about Leonardo dialoguing with his patron for the Mona Lisa using incremental and iterative strategies.

... but The Mona Lisa is too simple a painting for the *incremental* side of the story to be convincing, so I changed to van Bruegel the elder's "Peasant Wedding." They are complex enough so that it would make sense to apply both iterative and incremental development to them …

Figure 90, Part 3. Van Breugel, the Peasant Wedding.

... but then I ran across two excellent documents about Michelangelo painting the Sistine chapel and using clay models for drafts, and saw that he already had executed almost the very strategies I was going to invent for van Bruegel.

The Sistine chapel ceiling

The Sistine chapel ceiling is large – 5,200 square feet (almost 60 square meters). It took Michelangelo 4 years of work. He used throw-away prototypes, he did a little revision (iterative development) and he worked in increments. I didn't find evidence of him doing serious iterative development (meaning: revision or refactoring), but OK, he's recognized as a genius for a reason.

Figure 91, Part 3. The Sistine Chapel.

Prototyping and the Sistine chapel

Before doing any real painting, Michelangelo created several sorts of disposable prototypes.

One was what they called a *cartoon.* It was a full-size but simplified version of the whole thing, serving probably to show which elements fit into which sections of the ceiling. No cartoons of the Sistine chapel ceiling survive to this day.

> *"No full-sized fresco cartoons for the Sistine Chapel ceiling have survived. Vasari suggests that Michelangelo burned the cartoons. Perhaps this was not as absurd as it sounds — if the fresco cartoons were indeed as minimalistic as I suggest, and that the best drawing work was confined to the small (red chalk) drawings"*
>
> [https://karlzipser.com/michelangelo.html]

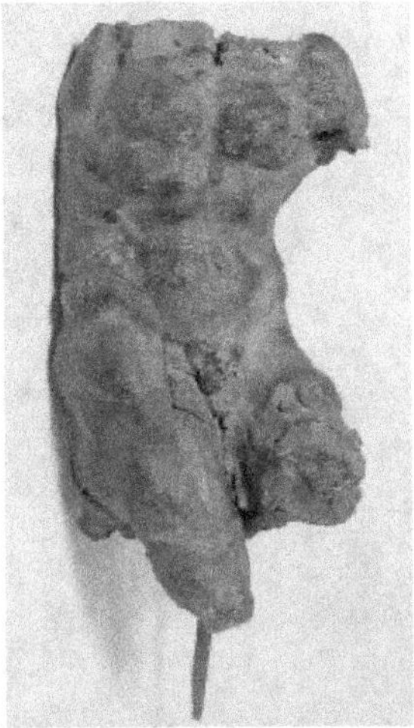

Figure 92, Part 3. Sculpture used to get shadows right.

Another sort of prototype was a 3D sculpture of a person's torso that he might want to use, onto which he could arrange appropriate lighting to mimic the lighting the would be available on the ceiling.

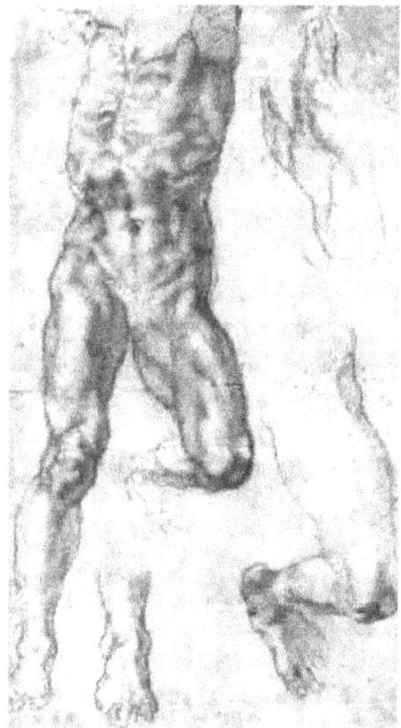

Figure 93, Part 3. Sketches of those sculptures.

A third sort of prototype would be the detailed sketches of those sculptures, with the shadows and details he wanted. These he could carry up the scaffold with him.

These are **disposable prototypes**, exactly as used in spike investigations and certain kinds of load testing.

Iterative development and the Sistine chapel

I didn't find much talk of Michelangelo **revising his work** (which is what iterative development is), except at the very beginning, when they were still learning how to mix the plaster that would be painted on/in. However, this did happen at least once:

> ***He had one more major setback before the work would progress. The first layer of plaster began to mold because it was too wet. So Michelangelo had to remove it and start again.'***

[http://www.twingroves.district96.k12.il.us/renaissance/SistineChapel/Michelangelo/Ceiling.html. (Link broken in 2026, sorry)]

This was not *intentional* iterative development; it was an *oops.* He didn't want to iterate, because he wanted to get done. Trying to get done in good time, it was important that he didn't go back and revise a lot.

In software development, and in the apocryphal stories about Leonardo or van Bruegel, we can arrange for a meaningful version of iterative development to show up.

Incremental development and the Sistine chapel

Michelangelo worked **incrementally** ... that is, he worked on and completed a small section at a time, and then *moved on.* Working in plaster, he would only put fresh plaster on as much of the ceiling as he could complete in one day:

> *"Each morning, an assistant, Jacopo l'Indaco, would apply a thin layer of a special plaster called "intomaco" to the area of the ceiling which was to be painted that day.*
>
> *"Next, the "cartoon" or drawing was secured in place and the design transferred to the wet plaster by scoring along the lines with a hard slate point.*
>
> *"Before the plaster was dry, the Michelangelo would apply the basic colors using a thick brush. The outline was repainted then darker tones were added for shading and white was added to create highlights. "*

[http://www.twingroves.district96.k12.il.us/renaissance/SistineChapel/Michelangelo/Ceiling.html. (Link broken in 2026, sorry)]

That was Michelangelo demonstrating excellent **incremental development** technique with the Sistine chapel.

van Bruegel the elder

Now let's look at a made-up story about how van Bruegel the elder might have used **iterative** and **incremental** development together to paint the wedding picture.

(*Unrelated note* – I really wanted to write about his *Dulle Griet* (*Mad Meg*) picture, because then I could write little notes about how he foreshadowed Salvador Dali by 400 years :). I really wanted to do that. I just couldn't manage to get my little incremental / iterative story to work out with the Mad Meg painting the way I wanted to (I'm sure it *can* be done, but it would be even more stretched. Shucks.)

Figure 94, Part 3. Van Breugel's Dulle Griet (Mad Meg).

Figure 95, Part 3. One of Salvador Dali's paintings.

... But back to van Bruegel the elder

Imagine for a moment that van Bruegel was painting this picture for a patron, Sam. (He wasn't painting it for a patron, because it is a picture of a peasant wedding, but never mind, I need Sam the patron for the story). The end painting is in *Figure 96*, but how did he get there?

Figure 96, Part 3. Van Breugel, the Peasant Wedding (again).

Incremental development and van Bruegel

Sam goes to van Bruegel and wants an approximate cost estimate for the painting (Sam is paying time and materials, and wants to steer the costs…)

Van Bruegel paints this section (*Figure 97*):

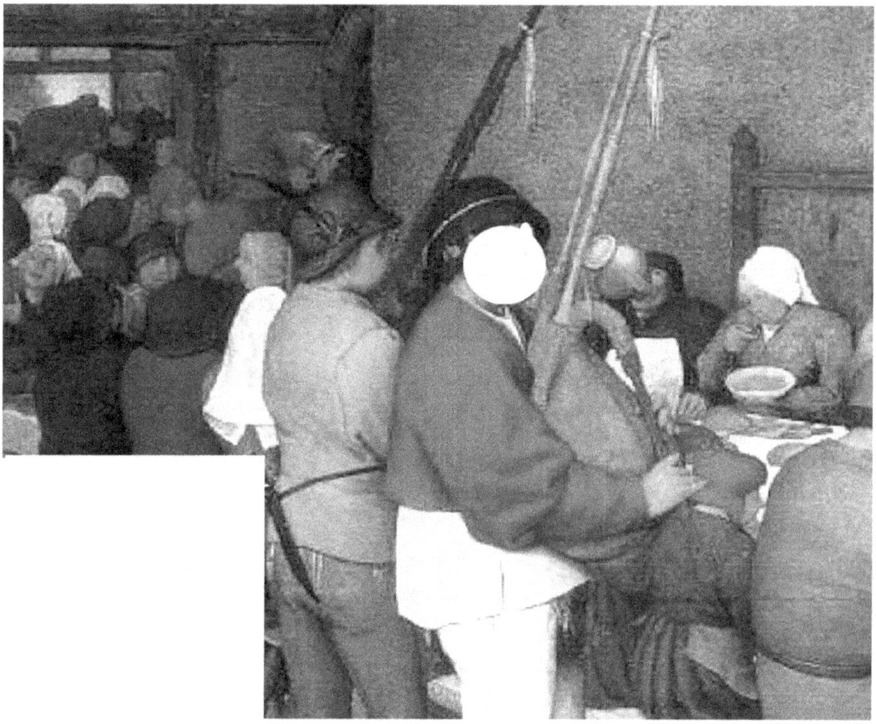

Figure 97, Part 3. Van Breugel, one section, the son's face left out.

He multiplies this by the time and materials taken, and presents the schedule and cost estimate to Sam.

Sam says, "That's too expensive … cut some costs. Don't repaint the bit you already have, leave it in, but put in fewer people in the other sections."

Iterative development and van Bruegel

Van Bruegel continues, but he is worried about one man in the picture (the one with the whited-out face in *Figure 97*, because that is Sam's son, Marc, and he wants to make Sam happy with Marc in the picture, so that Sam will be happy to pay for it.

First, van Bruegel makes some **disposable prototypes** to see how Sam reacts (disposable prototypes are a form of iterative development), as in *Figure 98*:

Figure 98, Part 3. Disposable prototype drawings.
[http://commons.wikimedia.org/wiki/File:Beggars_and_Cripples.jpg]

Sam picks out some that he likes and some that he doesn't, and both van Bruegel and Sam are happy, because van Bruegel didn't waste too much time painting them in full color.

Van Bruegel paints all the rest of the picture, but leaves Sam's son's face blank until the very end, and **he budgets time to do three completely full versions of Sam's son's face**, because he is pretty sure by now that Sam will want a little Photoshop work done on the son's visage to make him look good for posterity.

Sure enough, when Sam sees the first version of Marc's face, he says, "You have him in full silhouette! I need to see his face!"

So van Bruegel repaints the face. Sam says, "No, no, no! You can't show his childhood scars! Clean them up so he looks more attractive!"

Van Bruegel gets it right on the third try, and Sam agrees to pay for the painting.

It was a good thing van Bruegel **budgeted for 3 rounds** on Marc's face. That is *planned iterative development* in action.

Van Bruegel ("the savvy", as we might call him) used **disposable prototypes** (a form of **iterative** development) as well as well-scheduled **iterative** and **incremental** development to deliver a satisfactory painting to his patron, for about as low a cost and time as was possible.

Summary

Are we clear yet on what is **iterative development** and what is **incremental development**?

> **Increment** fundamentally means *"add onto."*
>
> **Iterate** fundamentally means *"change."*

See the article online:

[https://web.archive.org/web/20140329205707/http://alistair.cockburn.us/Incremental+means+adding,+iterative+means+reworking]

2008: Design as Knowledge Acquisition.

This is the article that shifted my entire way of thinking. It resolved the riddle I couldn't explain in 1993 about how to schedule risk-based project management, which was a complete mystery to me back then.

alias: Knowledge acquisition v. business value creation
alias: Design as Knowledge acquisition
alias: Trim the Tail
alias: Pay to learn

Design as knowledge creation

Several people have written about design as knowledge creation. Donald Reinertsen in his excellent book *Managing the Design Factory* discusses that a key output of design work is the knowledge that is gained. Philip Armour writes that what we really learn when we deliver the software is how to build the software we just delivered. A quick Google even turns up a company Knowledge Evolution, Inc. (which has a nearly empty website, sadly) whose sole purpose is to support this line of inquiry.

In any team design activity, we are working with a problem we don't yet understand, creating a solution we don't yet understand, and expressing our ideas in languages and technologies we generally don't yet understand – and all of them keep changing out from under us.

As we work, we learn more about the problem, about the technologies, about the proposed solution … and eventually, usually *just after* we've shipped the system, we wake up and go, "Oh! That's how it works", or "Oh! That's how we should have done it".

What's missing is advice as to how to make use of all the above.

Late knowledge creation in big-bang integration

Figure 99 shows the problem with big-bang integration in terms of knowledge.

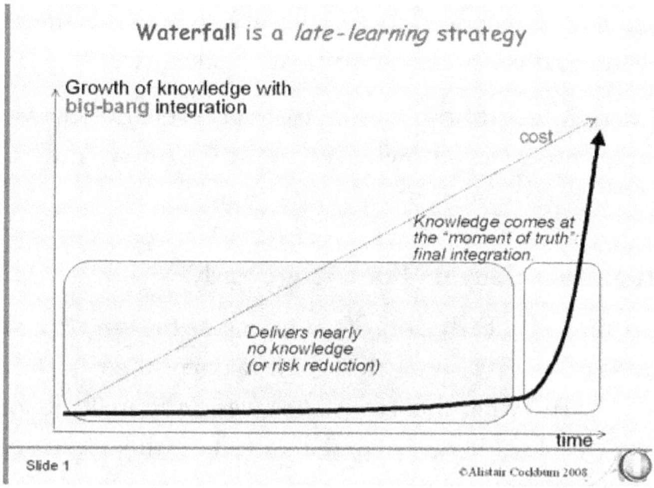

Figure 99, Part 3. Waterfall is a late-learning strategy.

In the early stages, everyone is designing away, making decisions, even writing code. But since the code of the various teams haven't been tested against each other, they contain lots of errors. In lean terms, since *the unit of inventory in design activities is the unvalidated decision (discussion: Re: What engineering has in common with manufacturing and why it matters)*, there is a lot of inventory.

In knowledge creation terms, there are lots of decisions hanging out there, but not yet a matching amount of knowledge about them. This is evidenced each time the managers and sponsors ask the tech leads, "You sure this will integrate properly, (please, please)?"

In the meantime, as the graph show, costs are mounting up. Costs are running considerably ahead of the knowledge.

It doesn't have to be this way, and we'll see that shortly.

In any case, getting back to the big-bang integration, finally the moment of truth comes, and the big-bang integration starts. What is not of concern here is whether or not it works – sometimes it does, sometimes it doesn't. And that's just the point – there is a *surprise* factor there. And surprise = learning. I.e., when we finally do the integration, and more, when we finally get the integration to work, **at that point** we have gained knowledge (about what was present in the design just before the integration, and how to finally make it work).

In terms of **risk reduction**, we see that this scenario leaves a big risk until the end, produces knowledge late in the story, and is generally neither fun to live through nor a pretty sight.

Early integration delivers knowledge early

Teams that integrate early and often take that big surprise and split it over many sessions. By doing this, they discover their mistakes earlier, that is they "learn" what those mistakes were, and make it so that later integrations are less likely to fail badly, i.e., the "learning" factor becomes smaller over time.

This is a good thing.

Notice in this curve (*Figure 100*) that the learning outstrips the spending early on, which is also a good thing.

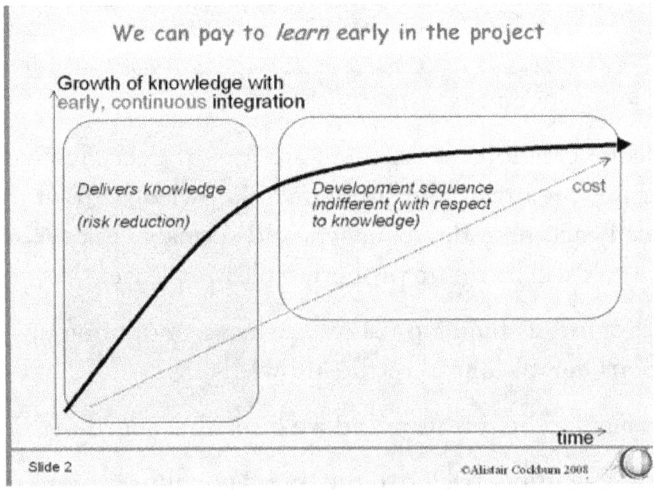

Figure 100, Part 3. Early integration delivers knowledge early.

Finally, notice that once the system risks are put to rest, the actual sequence of development becomes nearly irrelevant in terms of "learning". That is, the team can develop in any order, including, particularly, "highest business value first."

What the curve can't show is just what constitutes "learning items" a.k.a. "risk reduction items."

Rather than asking people on the project what are the "risk items", ask instead, "What worries you?" or "What scares you?" The answer is likely to be some piece of technical work that they are unsure of – i.e., needs learning about. Once they have learned that, then they are less worried or scared.

The only thing that is odd is that the items that worry or scare people are unlikely to show up in any tidy sequence … that is, if you work on the scary items early, it may not look like working in an architectural sequence, or a business-value sequence, or any other sequence – except the sequence that increases knowledge the fastest for the money spent, the sequence that reduces the project risk the most.

A nice characteristic about growing along this curve is that "worriedness" diminishes with time.

Develop for business value once risks are down

Once the knowledge curve starts to flatten, then is a good time to develop the features in a business-value-first sequence (as shown in *Figure 101*). This matches the normal agile recommendation. Notice that, in principle, business value was always being developed during the knowledge-acquisition-intensive period, so it's not as though you weren't gaining business value, it's just that gaining business value wasn't the dominant driver.

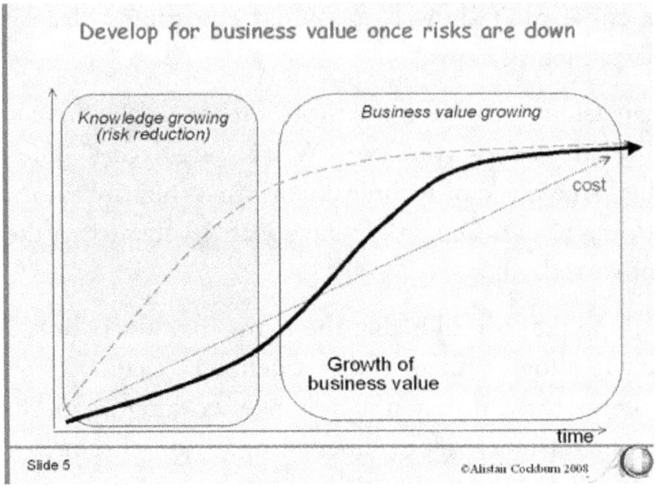

Figure 101, Part 3. Develop business value once risks are down.

Trim the tail of the feature set

There is one pleasant surprise left. At the right hand side of the curve (magnified in *Figure 102*), both the knowledge creation and the business value being developed flatten out.

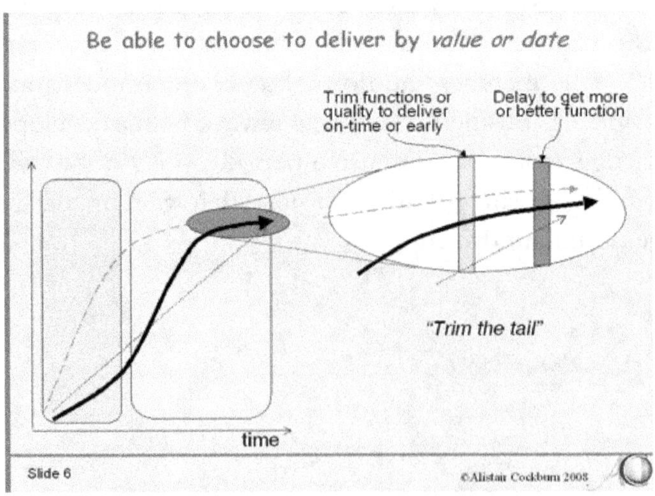

Figure 102, Part 3. Trim the tail of the feature set

This is an opportunity for the project sponsor.

Quite often the project is running late and the sponsor is being forced to decide what to do. When the design team works in a big-architectural, top-down fashion (even without a big-bang integration at the end), they quite easily end up in a situation that they literally *cannot* cut off a remaining section of functionality in order to deliver earlier. This is because they have designed the framework or feature set in an entirety so that it can't be *thinned* (see Feature thinning (discussion: Re: Feature thinning). The sponsor has only one choice: wait. Actually, two choices: wait a short time and get the full feature set thrown together and full of bugs, or wait a longer time and get the full feature set with fewer bugs. What's missing is the choice to get a reduced feature set without bugs sooner.

Jeff Patton is the champion of Feature thinning. In Jeff Patton and the ABCs of Quality and Kano and quality, I describe a bit about how he tunes the feature requests (and hopes the programmers follow suit with the program design) so that they *can* be thinned.

The point is, once the knowledge- and business-value curves flatten out, the sponsor is in a position to deliver on-time (or early! to match a competitor's move) with a thinned feature set, or to deliver later with the fuller feature set. The choice is where it belongs, in the sponsors hands.

Don't confuse knowledge acquisition with BDUF

There is a hazard in the interpretation of the above graphs, that working in the knowledge creation period means the old habit of sitting at the desk and drawing up a big, fancy, full-scale design (BDUF = "big design up front"). In most cases, the bigger the design that is done in the beginning, the more the unvalidated decisions produced, i.e. no "knowledge" is produced, only hypothesis, which is inventory). Of course, there are times when sitting and thinking allows one to investigate alternatives and rule out weaker ones, or to create "interesting" hypotheses, which then need to get tested.

Most of the time, knowledge acquisition comes from writing code to test a hypothesis, or writing code to see if it really is as difficult as it scarily seems to be.

The point of this article is to give a viable alternative to creating business value, by creating knowledge about how to build the system. Ideally, either knowledge or business value increases each day.

Examples

I have done the above explicitly on two projects.

Muffinland content management system

A tiny project, just me and one programmer – we're making a new content management system to replace the Media Wiki engine currently running this site (date stamp: late 2007). I start with a couple of pages of use cases and work items listing all the things we should do.

Since I'm paying out of my own pocket, I really care that we spend my money in the best way.

Here are (in approximate sequence) what we implemented.

1. Start from empty everything.
2. Implement from SQL database through to HTML on browser "View a muffin" (a muffin is a piece of content of any media format) for a simple text muffin ("Hi, there"). This created the Walking skeleton) for us, high initial business value (viewing muffins is what the site is all about), and high knowledge gain (everything hooks together properly).
3. We specifically never mocked up any sensible UI before starting. Nate (the programmer) convinced me, by showing me examples on the web, that I could have whatever I want in JavaScript and CSS, so there was no risk here. In other words, when we got started, we simply threw everything onto the

screen in "some" HTML, knowing it would all be changed later. Visually ugly, but near zero cost.

4. Implement a couple of other formats to make sure they work: jpg, pdf, YouTube. JPG in particular because it involves a callback, PDF because it calls an external program for viewing, YouTube to prove that we could have a video muffin, also YouTube involves wrapping a URL. We didn't bother implementing any other image formats or PPT, DOC, XLS because those involve mechanisms already debugged. I.e., low knowledge gain.

5. Implement comments on muffins. Comments are also muffins, so there is a recursion here. High business value since I want this to be a place, like Media Wiki, where people can hang out and comment. It also changes the domain model, proves we can get comments on comments, have them reuse the same plumbing as we have for all other muffins.

6. Implement muffin versioning. This changed the database quite a bit, and we debated over things like whether muffins can change formats in different versions, if we can delete versions, etc.

7. I can't recall at this instant what it was, but I then decided we should make everything conceivable a muffin. It proved a mistake. We programmed it all up one morning, then started getting lost in the reflection, and the next day threw the whole thing out.

Nice try. Knowledge gained early, but of course no business value.

8. At one point I felt that the markup language would prove difficult or unknown, so I put that on the day's work.

   Nate doesn't much care for text processing assignments, so we contracted that one out to a friend.

   And then 15 minutes later found an open-source .NET implementation of Textile markup, 15 minutes later had it hooked in and working. Canceled the outsource contract to the friend.

This changed my internal format from Media Wiki markup to Textile markup.

9. Collections and categories.

   We spent one whole morning staring at and comparing different possible designs for collections and categories.

   In this particular case I didn't want to program anything at all until we understood our choices. Collections and categories is essentially an unbounded problem, and the simple, naive implementations involve masses of code and code copying.

   I.e. once we go down the wrong path, it becomes relatively expensive to reverse directions.

   Hence a morning spent comparing designs. The winning design is to decide that a "collection" is only way of viewing a muffin, it is not a distinct and different thing on its own.

   The next day (we only work in 1/2 day shifts), we implemented the selected design in about half an hour, adding only few dozen lines of code.

The half-day of thinking paid off handsomely.

10. Now getting close to deployment, we go over the use cases to make sure we are implementing the minimal required functionality for all use cases sufficient to replace my current (this one, if you're reading it in April 2008) site. Security, users, comments, versioning, etc.

While I travel, Nate goes through and adds low-risk items on our list (such as more formats: png, bmp, gif, ppt, doc, ...), cleans up code, pokes around doing research on frameworks we might use to simplify our work.

An example of the payoff of our design … I want to have cascading style sheets available so poems look different from articles from blogs and so on. We find we can make a CSS a muffin, since we have versioning available, etc. A few lines of code later Nate shows me CSS working from muffins.

You get the point. ***Almost ready to deploy, and we still have no UI***. However, that's a decision of a day. We have the use cases broken out with work items (see Examples of ultralight use cases: [https://web.archive.org/web/20140329202950/http:/alistair.cockburn.us/Re%3a+Examples+of+ultra-light+use+cases])

This way, I can always see what item is going to add the most knowledge and/or the most business value, and trim back everything not needed for going live.

I will comment that it is a bit freaky describing the development of a system we haven't deployed yet. And notice that "freaky" implies "lack of knowledge".

We've looked at it with real content, but without having an interesting subset of the 800 pages of actual content I currently have, and without having the CSS and JavaScript in place, I'm still nervous (ref again "lack of knowledge"). And yet, short of actually deploying, I can't see what else to do to reduce that risk. What possible goof is waiting out there for us that I don't yet know that will make a mess of our plans?

(**Postscript:** Just found one. In converting the Media Wiki content, we learned that the Microsoft server engine IIS was originally built to store things in files, and so it doesn't allow any characters that aren't legal MS file name characters! Holy punctuation, Batman! That means the punctuation characters I have littered throughout my website page names are all disallowed! That's a fine example of late learning. At this instant, we have no solution to this problem, so we're stopped dead on deployment, although there are potential clumsy workarounds. It's interesting to imagine rolling back time and asking how we could have learned this earlier, and what different decision we might have made (not using .NET at all? Out very first decision!))

I'll add to this section when we finish deployment and I learn the last little bits.

Norges Bank transaction tracking system

In 1997-98 I was technical coordinator for a project at the Central Bank of Norway that tracks all bank-to-bank transactions. There was already a system that did that, but it did it at half-hour intervals. The new project was to allow real-time updates for very large transfers. The system was classic banking: COBOL, LU 6.2, assembler, CICS. I know nothing about those technologies, but I was in charge of technical sequencing.

After interviewing the 3 developers involved, who fortunately were already used to incremental development, I learned that there were a few high-risk items, including that end-to-end service guarantees and rollback were not well studied and there was a potential race condition in the database. Our schedule included:

Implement a single transaction throughout the whole system Walking skeleton, ignoring all validations and errors.

Do a load test on the transactions

Implement the piece that ran over the potential race conditions in the database.

Implement the rest of the transactions in any preferred order, implement the validations in any preferred order.

The programmers were OK with working incrementally, using the Walking skeleton, but were very uneasy about deferring transaction validations until late in the project. As it turned out, because those were easy, they would implement them whenever they had a bit of extra time. This of course is fine, according to the knowledge acquisition / business value theory … since it didn't much when they did those, as long as doing them didn't get in the way of the major milestones, it was just fine.

I should mention that this project looks simple according to the above list, but in fact took 9 months to implement.

And indeed, it was quite good to have used that order, because we found a hole in the end-to-end service guaranteed, found a CICS memory leak in the load testing, and found a bad race condition in the database. The project was originally scheduled to take 15 work weeks to implement, but at one point so many things were going wrong and cropping up that we lost 2 work weeks per day for 6 weeks! We ended at about 180 work weeks for the project —- but this date stabilized by 1/3 of the way through the project and never had to be changed again after that. It illustrated "better bad news early than bad news late."

In the end the project delivered at the 180 work week mark, quite amusingly interfacing with a system developed using a full waterfall approach (which slipped schedule the same amount our system did!), went live and was considered successful.

The sponsors were happy because they had never had an IT project declare an accurate end date as early as 1/3 of the way through the project (most would just go on indefinitely, the standard problem).

Chapter 2 of the Story, 2010

In 2010 I had the opportunity to work briefly with a project, whose assignment was a set of subprojects they were pretty sure they couldn't get through in the next 3 months. I found myself expanding on the TtT idea by making explicit the 3 stages of a feature, MFF, or assignment, namely, that there is a Knowledge Acquisition or risk aspect to take care of, then a growth of business value aspect, and finally a trimmable tail aspect.

Putting these together gives a nifty table, which allows this team to select their execution strategy carefully to maximize the value delivered to the business for whenever they ran out of time.

It is not a given that they will attack their work in row order, or column order, or a funny diagonal slicing; this table allows them to choose any strategy, and make that strategy explicit and visible.

I find this exciting and would like to hear back from anyone who tries this out on their project.

Feature area	Risk aspect	Value aspect	Tail aspect
section 1	whatever 1	whatever 6	whatever
section 2	whatever 2	whatever etc.	whatever
section 3	whatever 3	whatever	whatever
section 4	whatever 4	whatever	whatever
section 5	whatever 5	whatever	whatever

Figure 103, Part 3. Learning-Value-Tail table (again).

Here is the drawing to match it, another description for agile in tables.

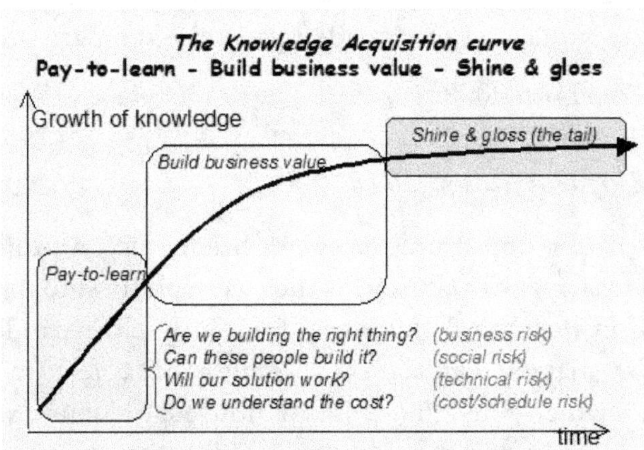

Figure 104, Part 3. Learning-Value-Tail curve (again).

Alistair (currently Australia, June 2011)

See also:

- The A-B work split
- Agile in tables
- Nonakas knowledge assets categories
- and the figures:
- Knowledge acquisition curve.png

- Early integration delivers knowledge early.png
- Knowledge acquisition curve.png
- Nonakas 4 categories of knowledge assets.png
- 3 stages of feature development.png

P.S. Do *trim the tail*, but don't trim the tail too much!.

Standard agile canon has it to develop highest business value first. There are indeed good reasons to do this – but there are also reasons to blend the business value climb with deliberate moves of "knowledge acquisition". Here I'll look at how to create "knowledge", when to switch over to business value creation, and the magical ability agile teams have to "trim the tail" of the feature set to deliver the optimal result at the optimal time. (Caution: Just Don't trim the tail too much!)

See online:

[https://web.archive.org/web/20140329202950/http://alistair.cockburn.us/Design+as+Knowledge+Acquisition]

Epilogue: See Chapter 5, "*Disciplined Learning*" for how I eventually developed these thoughts from those early blog posts and articles into my current way of describing things.

Reflections and Key Points

Reflections

Reading those articles 20-30 years later, I find my favorite thoughts are:

> *"absence of an incremental process was a good predictor of failure."* (is still true)
>
> *"**How much** of the system, at **what level of correctness**, is needed before being useful to the users or suitable for user review? (The answers are "relatively little" and "relatively low," respectively.)"*
>
> *"The Validation V is a fact of life."* → I have tried since 1991 not to advocate anything I'll have to recant. I've done pretty well. Of all the changes, AI changes this V. It's now cheaper to vibe code and show to get feedback. Requirements can to a certain extent come **after** shipping running-not-tested code.

Did you catch these key points?

1993: The impact of object-orientation on application development

"the terms incremental and iterative / are used almost interchangeably by some people."

"The intent of an *incremental* strategy is to develop a system piece by piece and to permit additions to the requirements, improvements to the development process, or changes to the scheduling."

"The intent of an *iterative* strategy is to allow correction of mistakes and product improvements based upon user feed-back, performance tuning, or maintenance criteria, and to allow it in a controlled manner.

"*In truth, iteration is rework*"

"A **disposable prototype** is one not intended for production and thus possibly not meeting production quality standards. An

evolutionary prototype is one incomplete in scope but intended for eventual production.'

1994: Unraveling incremental development

"*absence of an incremental process was a good predictor of failure.*"

"changing work habits is among the hardest thing you can ask people to do."

"*a person's skill improves dramatically at the end of a development V.*"

"the same team does analysis, design, code, and test, so there is no hand-off or retraining to prepare for (note, the team needs to include a qualified analyst, designer, coder, and tester!)."

"The Vs are short and self-sufficient enough that their end results adequately indicate the rate of completion."

"synchronization of teams. A team commits to a section of design, and delivers production code to other teams at predictable times."

"With the consecutive Vs, the project develops its own internal history, a history that is as similar and accurate as can be hoped for."

"it is difficult to put into practice the first time. It requires a noticeable change of habits for the project managers."

1997: Managing increments and iterations with VW staging

"Every team must deliver working function every 2-4 months. The most important statement I know to make for a project."

"Developers do not live in linear time. Project managers do live in linear time."

"The Validation V is a fact of life." → (I have tried since 1991 not to advocate anything I'll have to recant. I've done pretty well. Of all the changes, AI changes this V. It's now cheaper to vibe code and show to get feedback. Requirements can come (to some extent) AFTER shipping running-not-tested code.)

"Increments let you fix process: build-deliver-learn-build-deliver…"

"Iterations let you fix ignorance: build-examine-learn-rebuild-ship…"

"Managers can request and plan from V results instead of phase results."

"The V-W model lets different people work differently."

2004: Unrolling cyclic development processes

"Crystal Clear uses nested cyclic processes of various lengths: the development episode, the iteration, the delivery period and the full project."

"*How many* requirements, *at what level of completion* are needed before design can usefully get started? (The answers are "relatively few" and "relatively low", respectively.)"

"*How much of the system* must be designed and programmed before useful integration and testing can be done? (The answer is "relatively little.")"

"*How much of the system, at what level of correctness,* is needed before being useful to the users or suitable for user review? (The answers are "relatively little" and "relatively low," respectively.)"

2007: Incremental versus iterative development

"the pundits and authors at the time seem to have gotten so excited at the thought of repeating the cycle "at all" that they lumped the two together and never saw the difference in what happened on the project based on whether you were **revising old** stuff or **getting onto new** stuff!"

"when he finally saw the difference, 'We're iterating when we should be incrementing!!'"

"immediately hears, "We're going to do a lot of rework"! (Ouch, my wallet!)"

2008: Using both incremental and iterative development

"Both are needed. People need to learn to use them separately as well as together."

"in the old failure of delivering what people don't want. / The correcting strategy is iterative development."

"they need to be managed differently."

"How many rework periods does each need?"

"Allocate two revision periods for the user interface design, and one each for requirements drift and performance re-architecture."

"Yes, it is rework, and yes, you probably need to do some rework to make your product shine."

2008: Incremental means adding, iterative means reworking

"The Mona Lisa is too simple a painting for the *incremental* side of the story to be convincing."

"Before doing any real painting, Michelangelo created several sorts of disposable prototypes."

"Michelangelo worked **incrementally** ... that is, he worked on and completed a small section at a time, and then *moved on*."

"I really wanted to write about his Dulle Griet (Mad Meg) picture, because then I could write little notes about how he foreshadowed Salvador Dali by 400 years :)."

"It was a good thing van Bruegel **budgeted for 3 rounds** on Marc's face. That is *planned iterative development* in action."

2008: Design as knowledge acquisition.

"we are working with a problem we don't yet understand, creating a solution we don't yet understand, and expressing our ideas in languages and technologies we generally don't yet understand – and all of them keep changing out from under us."

"there are lots of decisions hanging out there, but not yet a matching amount of knowledge about them."

"Early integration delivers knowledge early"

"We can pay to learn early in a project"

"business value was always being developed during the knowledge-acquisition-intensive period, so it's not as though you weren't gaining business value"

"the items that worry or scare people are unlikely to show up in any tidy sequence."

"Once the knowledge curve starts to flatten, then is a good time to develop the features in a business-value-first sequence."

"choose to deliver by *value* or *date*."

"Trim the Tail"

"Pay to learn / Build business value / Shine & glass (trim the tail)"

It took me all these years to get to:
Pay to learn/ Grow business value/ Shine & gloss or trim the tail.

Part 4. Epilogue

Key Phrases from the Chapters

For the book as a whole:

Your organization operates from *decisions.*

Your organization is a conveyor belt of decisions. Surprisingly, that decision flow is just like parts flow in manufacturing, so we can learn and borrow from decades of manufacturing lessons.

Unvalidated decisions are your enemy.

Unvalidated decisions are those that have not yet proved themselves correct with the outside world. Your favorite initiative contains thousands to millions of them. They are your internal inventory. As they back up, your organization moves slower and mistakes get more expensive to fix.

Seek *bad news early.*

The sooner you find a decision has a mistake, the more time you have to recover. And it's cheaper to change.

Think *small bites.* A bit at a time, the smallest possible.

Get feedback on those *small bites* from the outside world. The outside world thinks differently from whatever you imagine. Put it out there. ASAP.

Work this way:

Pay to learn.
Grow business value.
Trim the tail or Shine & gloss.

Pop Quiz:

I heard this statement on a failing project. Can you diagnose it now?

"We were iterating when we should have been incrementing!"

Hint, see the article 2007: Incremental versus Iterative Development.

Chapter 1. What

Incremental means ***add onto****. It helps improve the* process.

Iterative means ***revise****. It helps improve the* product.

Neither requires the other, but they work great together.

Chapter 2. Why: The Executive's Version

> *Prefer staged over single delivery. It lets you capture value sooner, and find and fix errors sooner and cheaper.*

"the day after you deliver, your brand-new call center gets swamped with calls about errors."

"you start earning money from the moment of the earliest delivery."

"Gain value earlier; Discover and fix errors earlier."

"We live in a rapid-changing world. The odds that you guessed correctly what your users and customers would need, and also how the world would shift over the duration of the project, are slim, probably zero."

"decisions become your internal inventory in mental/social work"

"unvalidated decisions create drag on your organization."

Chapter 3. Why Decisions Matter

> ***Unvalidated decisions*** *are your internal inventory. The more they are stacked up, the slower your organization moves and the more expensive it is to fix mistakes. Find ways to move decisions through your organization in the smallest batches possible.*

"You can't know if the decision is a good one until it is delivered and in use."

"To the extent that it is not earning value in the business, each decision loses value and quality with time ... the requirement is waste"

"people wait on each other for decisions ... decisions stacking up at some particular work group. That stack creates a *botteneck*, limiting the speed of the overall team"

"There is no ideal software process any more than there is any ideal manufacturing process"

"The more decisions stuck inside the pipeline, the more decaying "inventory" the organization is carrying."

"move small amounts, continuously"

"Large internal inventory makes it hard to change directions... [and] for late discovery of mistakes."

"In mental work, it is impossible to avoid rework"

"Every decision in the requirements document gets compounded by thousands of work-hours put in developing it."

"big-batch transfer makes movement lumpy and the timing unpredictable. Combining that with constant revision means that you *cannot say when the final product will come out.*"

This should be the scariest sentence in the entire book!

Chapter 4. From Slicing to Growing

We "slice" an initiative into smaller ones, but we "grow" the solution. Slice thinly when breaking down a large problem. Look for growth stages when growing the solution.

"having just a slice of ham doesn't give us a sandwich, any more than having just a user interface gives us a running application. When we ask for a *slice*, we demand that all the layers be integrated."

"if they want a car and you show up with a skateboard, you'll be fired. They want a car."

"A better metaphor is growing the system."

"first put in place an armature or skeleton; add layers of paper and glue, making a continually 'better elephant'."

"look for *growth stages*, things we can show or ship, intermediate stages that are directionally like the elephant, always getting to a better elephant."

Chapter 5. Disciplined Learning

Learn early, learn often. Validate or break decisions as soon as possible. We now have strategies to help do that.

"Upgrade project planning from failure-avoidance to success-seeking. Not 'fail early, fail often,' but 'learn early, learn often.' "

"A development team has four critical things to learn:
What they should really be building,
How their people might best work together,
Where their technical ideas are flawed,
How much it will cost to develop."

"attention is given to what can be omitted at the discretion of the business, the 'tail.' … Trim the tail."

"Every feature being developed has a learning period, a value period and a tail."

"Disciplined learning with trim-the-tail is one of the few approaches equally available to very small and very large projects, fixed-price and floating-price projects."

Chapter 6. The Elephant Carpaccio Exercise

This exercise shows both why to deliver soon and small, and how to do that, justified entirely from a business perspective.

"do the full exercise, so that you feel it under your fingertips."

"when the money coming in equals the money going out – that's when the project is *self-funding*."

"You can start earning money after delivering to just one state", and set up the call center, check the user interface, tax compliance, and your business model.

"the cost of retyping the formula is small compared to the value produced by the early delivery."

"That MVP allows to change your business model at the earliest possible moment."

"I never shy away from discussions about rework… discuss which will be adequately paid for by early business value."

Chapter 7. Why Does 'Incremental' Help Improve Your Process?

You have to finish the gestalt round trip and find the boogeyman to improve your process properly.

"Any part of your process that you don't go through fully is likely to contain a problem that you can't foresee."

"The boogeyman is What You Don't Know You Don't Know"

"The early parts of your project have two goals, and one of them is to find the boogey-man (learn WYDKYDK). If you do not take care of this, he will indeed jump out at you when you least expect it"

"Establish the architecture, deliver one function, find the Boogeyman

- Only after you deliver can you accurately reflect on how the different parts of your process interact (the gestalt round trip)."

"The purpose of the first increment is to:

1. Establish an architecture for the software,
2. Deliver feedback to the project sponsors and users,
3. Develop good patterns of programming and designing,
4. Find the boogeyman and learn WYDKYDK."

"The purpose of the second increment is to:

1. Repair the major mistakes discovered in the first increment,
2. Establish or tune the software architecture,
3. Create a process and teaming that works for you,
4. Settle on good development habits.
5. Deliver more function to the users. "

"Each increment produces a chunk of the system you could deliver if you chose to."

"Burn Some Pancakes"

Chapter 8. The business person version

Construct fine-grained growth stages from use cases while developing and deploying.

Use cases "capture all the usage pathways your development team will need to consider; They are easily read, understood, and passed around the organization."

"spy trouble spots early without going into too many details too soon"

"what we are after: the least writing, the fewest unvalidated decisions, the easiest to scan, that allows us to find value and risk."

"if you write them all at once, you have spent a huge amount of time creating a terrible stack of unvalidated decisions, blocking early delivery of value and filling your organization with internal inventory."

"A Walking Skeleton is a tiny implementation of a process or system that supports a small end-to-end function."

"take the thinnest path through the most important sea-level use cases you will develop. That will make the *walking skeleton* of the use case."

"what is the *least* we can develop that will produce a functioning machine? … we now have a functioning machine, we've reduced risk and opened feedback on all our decisions"

"Idea 1. Find and develop the use case's Walking Skeleton.
Idea 2: Separate out each sentence and each extension.
Idea 3: Implement just part of a step as its own slice.
Idea 4. Some sentences can be done in different ways.
Idea 5. Slice your data, business rules, etc. similarly.
Idea 6. Split knowledge-acquisition from implementation."

"it is quick, fun, and easy to list all the possibilities. You then can decide which to implement now and which to defer."

Chapter 9. The Programmer Version

Slice even more finely while programming to implement the Hexagonal Architecture in test-driven nano-increments.

Hexagonal ("Ports & Adapters") Architecture is briefly stated as: "The app cannot know anything about the external technology," so it can "equally be driven by users, programs, automated test or batch scripts, and to be developed and tested in isolation from its eventual run-time devices and databases."

The development sequence is:

Test-to-test: Test cases driving, test doubles as driven actors.
Real-to-test: Real UI driving, test doubles as driven actors.
Test-to-real: Test cases driving, real systems on the driven side.
Real-to-real: All real external systems, driving and driven.

"program the fewest decisions at any time and to validate (or break and fix) them as soon as possible."

After two nano-increments: "*Congratulations! You have now implemented the Ports & Adapters architecture!* Your system has its first configurator, driving port, driving actor, driven port, driven actor, and the app itself correctly interacts with all of them. From here on, you can evolve the system in any direction you like."

"Looking to validate (or break) the fewest number of decisions at a time, you have two in the first nano-increment and four in the second nano-increment. Any mistakes you make in either of these should be easy to find, and once you have them in place, they are solid for the future."

Chapter 10. The Project Manager Version

Visualize what is happening on the project with burn charts. Show status on complex projects with fox-and-rabbit charts.

Earned-Value and Burn Charts

"They have a natural mapping to earned-value charts."

"They reveal the strategy being used, show the progress made against predictions, and open discussions about how best to proceed."

"Find "interesting" and clear intermediate milestones. … In software, those milestones are the delivery of running, tested code."

"The *Iceberg List.* The "above water" part lists all the items that can be delivered in the current delivery cycle. The "below water" part lists every that will be delivered in later delivery cycles. / The *Iceberg List* is useful in hostile environments, where the sponsors change the requirements and priorities on a daily basis and without warning"

"you get no credits for any item that does not result in running, tested code." p142

"it is *bad news detected early*, as opposed to *bad news detected too late to do anything about it!*"

"It shows both the status and rate of progress ("velocity") in a way that is both clear and easy to discuss."

"Burn-down charts provide emotional motivation."

"project scope does in fact change over time. / raising and lowering of the ceiling, or 100% mark, as the project progresses."

A Governance Model For Incremental, Concurrent or Agile Projects

"Ron Jeffries neatly calls these Running, Tested, Features, or RTF."

"A team that can't deploy its system to live users every few months can *pretend* to deploy the system / test, integrate and deploy the system to the computer of one or two "friendly" but real users."

"Intention-completion markers show the expected and the actual current accomplishment, and the alarm level."

"Intention-completion bars are created for each component and for each intersection of application-dependent components."

"use the intention-completion bars to show progress within each specialty, whether the team is using a sequential (waterfall) strategy or a concurrent strategy."

"it allows different teams to choose different strategies and report on them, all in the same format."

Using burn charts in practice

"The intention-completion graphic is so important because it allows different teams to choose different strategies and report on them, all in the same format."

"tasks are not the interesting unit of completions."

"Tasks such as writing a spec, writing a design document, writing tests, writing code only *add decisions* to your internal inventory. / The only way to cancel that debt is to validate or break and fix those errors. Until the code is tested and integrated, it is all speculation."

"puts all the 1D charts on the wall in front of their office."

"it shows a fox or a greyhound chasing a rabbit."

Chapter 11. The Product Manager Version

Slice your product features according to Kano's subjective quality elements. Fit those into the Learning-Value-Tail curve.

Jeff Patton and the ABCs of Quality

"Kano's Theory of Attractive Quality and Packaging" (1984)."

"you can have 'a little bit of a lot more things than you otherwise were going to get, and you get to choose the amount of each."

Agile in tables

"The Learning-Value-Tail table shows a set of features against their risk or knowledge-acquisition aspect, their value aspect and their tail or gloss aspect."

"allowing the team to tackle them in any order they might prefer – column-first, row-first, or some funny diagonal. / and maps to the trim the tail."

"four knowledge acquisition areas: Business risk, Social risk, Technical risk, Cost/schedule risk."

" 'What are we trying to learn right now?', which is quickly followed by, 'What is the cheapest, fastest way to get that information?' "

"Feature Grade Table / use the time available to get the important features up to B or A as desired. / this delivers the highest "perceived" quality of the final product."

"Hexagonal architecture micro-increment table: developing features in three stages:

1. Test harness functionality loopback in lieu of database
2. Real UI functionality loopback in lieu of database
3. Real UI functionality real database"

"This yields, as with the Risk-Value-Tail table, a rich set of possibilities for sequences in which the feature set might be implemented."

Reflection on the use of tables

"Tables create a map of the project. They give it a parts inventory."

"*thinning* the feature elements and adding minor improvements in competition with new features/ balance time against quality at a fine-grained level to get the maximum net *value* for the time spent."

Kano and quality

"Baseline – Linear – Exciters – Avoid"

"Exciters fade over time."

"things move from the must-have to the sliding (linear) dimension."

Fitting Kano into the Knowledge Acquisition Curve

"the *Learning-Value-Tail* curve is a more appropriate name"

"The absolute minimum set of mandatory items plus one delighter for each stakeholder."

Reflection on Kano and fine-grained incremental work

"Organize your project around Learning-Value-Tail."

"add in a fine-graine manner until you run out of time or money, then deliver."

"one delighter per key stakeholder to make your first delivery pop."

"Use the Patton–Derbier grading method ABCEF to grow feature and system quality to fit schedule and budget."

Chapter 12. How big should slices be?

Smaller is generally better, but your mileage may vary, so learn how to choose.

"Quarters make great units of delivery at the executive level."

"If you can't actually deliver to users each quarter, for some reason, have a fire-drill practice deployment."

"1-week "planning horizon," which might not close out any particular development item, but is used to track what is happening."

"Programmers: 15 minutes to 2 days."

Part 3. Learning over time

It took me all these years to get to:

- Pay to learn
- Grow business value
-Shine & gloss or Trim the tail.

1993: The impact of object-orientation on application development

"the terms incremental and iterative / are used almost interchangeably by some people."

"The intent of an *incremental* strategy is to develop a system piece by piece and to permit additions to the requirements, improvements to the development process, or changes to the scheduling."

"The intent of an *iterative* strategy is to allow correction of mistakes and product improvements based upon user feed-back, performance tuning, or maintenance criteria, and to allow it in a controlled manner.

"*In truth, iteration is rework*"

"A **disposable prototype** is one not intended for production and thus possibly not meeting production quality standards. An **evolutionary prototype** is one incomplete in scope but intended for eventual production.'

1994: In search of methodology

"a methodology is more likely to be used as it is simple, clearly effective, and small in terms of required work products."

"Incremental development was key to the success of so many projects that I was able to use it as a predictor in the interviews (its absence was a good predictor of failure)."

"that incremental development affects the work habits of project managers"

"Incremental development is so important that it deserves an entire article to itself."

"1994: Unraveling incremental development

"*absence of an incremental process was a good predictor of failure.*"

"changing work habits is among the hardest thing you can ask people to do."

"*a person's skill improves dramatically at the end of a development V.*"

"the same team does analysis, design, code, and test, so there is no hand-off or retraining to prepare for (note, the team needs to include a qualified analyst, designer, coder, and tester!)."

"The Vs are short and self-sufficient enough that their end results adequately indicate the rate of completion."

"synchronization of teams. A team commits to a section of design, and delivers production code to other teams at predictable times."

"With the consecutive Vs, the project develops its own internal history, a history that is as similar and accurate as can be hoped for."

"it is difficult to put into practice the first time. It requires a noticeable change of habits for the project managers."

1997: Managing increments and iterations with VW staging

"Every team must deliver working function every 2-4 months. The most important statement I know to make for a project."

"Developers do not live in linear time. Project managers do live in linear time."

"The Validation V is a fact of life."

> *(I have tried since 1991 not to advocate anything I'll have to recant. I've done pretty well. Of all the changes, AI changes this V. It's now cheaper to vibe code and show to get feedback. Requirements can come (to some extent) <u>after</u> shipping running-not-tested code.)*

"Increments let you fix process: build-deliver-learn-build-deliver…"

"Iterations let you fix ignorance: build-examine-learn-rebuild-ship…"

"Managers can request and plan from V results instead of phase results."

"he V-W model lets different people work differently."

2004: Unrolling cyclic development processes

"Crystal Clear uses nested cyclic processes of various lengths: the development episode, the iteration, the delivery period and the full project."

"*How many* requirements, *at what level of completion* are needed before design can usefully get started? (The answers are "relatively few" and "relatively low", respectively.)"

"*How much of the system* must be designed and programmed before useful integration and testing can be done? (The answer is "relatively little.")"

"*How much of the system, at what level of correctness,* is needed before being useful to the users or suitable for user review? (The answers are "relatively little" and "relatively low," respectively.)"

2005: Crystal Clear

"The single most important property of any project, large or small, agile or not, is that of delivering running, tested code to real users every few months."

"The advantages are so numerous that it is astonishing that any team doesn't do it."

"Fixed-length iterations allow the team to measure their speed of movement."

"The people were getting pretty nervous, because *the customer hadn't seen what they had been working on for the last year!*"

2007: Incremental versus iterative development

"the pundits and authors at the time seem to have gotten so excited at the thought of repeating the cycle "at all" that they lumped the two together and never saw the difference in what happened on the project based on whether you were **revising old** stuff or **getting onto new** stuff!"

"when he finally saw the difference, 'We're iterating when we should be incrementing!!'"

"immediately hears, "We're going to do a lot of rework"! (Ouch, my wallet!)"

2008: Using both incremental and iterative development

"Both are needed. People need to learn to use them separately as well as together."

"in the old failure of delivering what people don't want. / The correcting strategy is iterative development."

"they need to be managed differently."

"How many rework periods does each need?"

"Allocate two revision periods for the user interface design, and one each for requirements drift and performance re-architecture."

"Yes, it is rework, and yes, you probably need to do some rework to make your product shine."

2008: Incremental means adding, iterative means reworking

"The Mona Lisa is too simple a painting for the *incremental* side of the story to be convincing."

"Before doing any real painting, Michelangelo created several sorts of disposable prototypes."

"Michelangelo worked **incrementally** ... that is, he worked on and completed a small section at a time, and then *moved on.*"

"I really wanted to write about his Dulle Griet (Mad Meg) picture, because then I could write little notes about how he foreshadowed Salvador Dali by 400 years :)."

"It was a good thing van Bruegel **budgeted for 3 rounds** on Marc's face. That is *planned iterative development* in action."

2008: Design as knowledge acquisition.

"we are working with a problem we don't yet understand, creating a solution we don't yet understand, and expressing our ideas in languages and technologies we generally don't yet understand – and all of them keep changing out from under us."

"there are lots of decisions hanging out there, but not yet a matching amount of knowledge about them."

"Early integration delivers knowledge early"

"We can pay to learn early in a project"

"the items that worry or scare people are unlikely to show up in any tidy sequence."

"Once the knowledge curve starts to flatten, then is a good time to develop the features in a business-value-first sequence."

"business value was always being developed during the knowledge-acquisition-intensive period, so it's not as though you weren't gaining business value"

"choose to deliver by *value* or *date*."

"Trim the Tail"

"Pay to learn / Build business value / Shine & glass (trim the tail)"

AI Hits

Figure 105, Epilogue. Cognitive load is the new bottleneck.

In 2026, there is so much dust in the air around AI that I see no trustworthy pattern. Many people post that they have the answer, but further practice nullifies their results and then the LLM vendors come out with new capabilities and we start over.

At this moment, I have two thoughts:

- The new bottleneck is cognitive load. That is, the LLMs generate so much output so fast that we cannot even evaluate what they produced: not the specs they produced, nor the user stories, nor the plan, nor the code, nor the final product. In the terms of this book, they close so many *decisions* so fast that we, as humans, can't handle the sheer volume of decisions we are to validate.
- As a result, we are still dealing with the same question as before:

How many decisions are in play at one time?

Some people use a single shot with the LLM and tune from there. This works well for one-off, internal applications, but not for production systems, so it is out of the scope of this book.

A second approach is to write a full product requirements document and have the LLM build from there. The problem with this is the same as it ever was: It is full of unvalidated decisions. Every generated artifact the errors in that document. As Jeff Patton used to say about large requirements documents: "You can't know that much this soon."

A third approach, matching the experience in this book, is to use very fine-grained requests (carpaccio) and try to grow the code with as few off-track moments as possible. Fine-grained incremental development helps the AI system from generating too much noise.

The people I am watching closely treat AI agents as hostile, or at least aberrant partners: Not that agents are malicious, they just don't have a basis to care if they do something you might not like. These people create different agents to write specs, tests and code, to run the tests, to audit the code, to audit the check-in history to see if agents have been altering the code or the tests in unauthorized ways, and so on.

The best approach I've seen to date applies all the ideas from software engineering approaches documented over the last 50 years. This includes particularly:

- Use cases for overall behavior description;
- Cut to user stories for the nano-increments; then expand each user story to its own use case to build a spec for the agent;
- Hexagonal Architecture for boundary protection;
- Automated regression test suites to protect those boundaries;
- Test-driven development or similar to create the tests along with the code;
- Elephant Carpaccio nano-increments to shrink the number of decisions in play at any time and to catch errors as soon as possible;
- Agents evaluate classical complexity and run lint and style exams over the code;
- Frequent reflection with the agent on level of trust, quality discussions and the like.

High-ceremony, high-discipline methods such as these have been really difficult for humans to carry out consistently over the decades, but they work well with agents, who actually benefit from the extra precision being called for.

Additionally, it appears that working in nano-increments uses fewer tokens than working in big chunks, so there is a financial benefit.

Back to the cartoon. AI systems output more than we can cognitively handle, even for small systems. Whether the agent writes the 200-page product requirements document or 200 user stories, we, as humans, don't know what's there.

Nano-increments are the only path I see to keep control of both the quality of the output and our knowledge of what's in there.

Repeating here *Figure 7*: "Learn early, Learn often.": Fine-grained incremental development is still key. The slices may be different sizes, but the thinking is very similar.

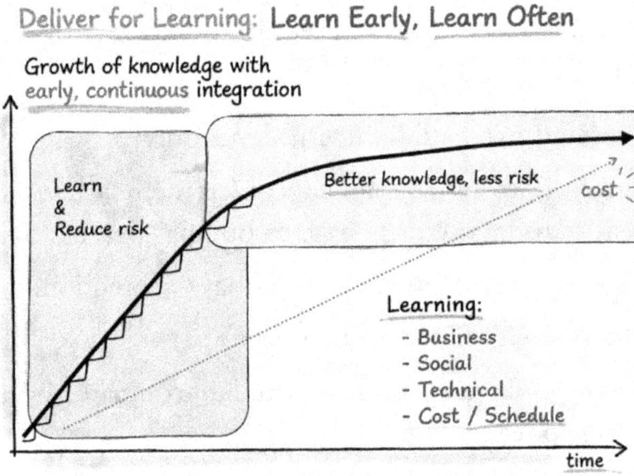

Learn Early, Learn Often !

Fin

AI, nicely done. Image creation: Isabel Grosser.

Practice it. Get used to seeing all initiatives split this way. You can slice finely, as I have, or you might choose fatter slices. Once you know *how* to do it, you can choose whatever thickness suits your situation.

Start to see unvalidated decisions flowing through your organization as *exposure* that you have to catch and get rid of as soon as possible.

Check out the book list for other texts that may be of interest to you.

Alistair

About the Author

Dr. Alistair Cockburn (pronounced CO-BURN), known for his wild hair photo, was named as one of the "42 Greatest Software Professionals of All Times" in 2020, as a world expert on project management, software architecture, use cases, and agile development.

Besides co-authoring the Agile Manifesto, he wrote the award-winning books *Writing Effective Use Cases* and *Agile Software Development: The Cooperative Game.*

In 2015, he created the *Heart of Agile* concept to be used in every kind of initiative, including social impact projects, governments, and families. For his latest work, see https://alistaircockburn.com/

He is most likely to show up in your workshop looking like this.

Or maybe like this:

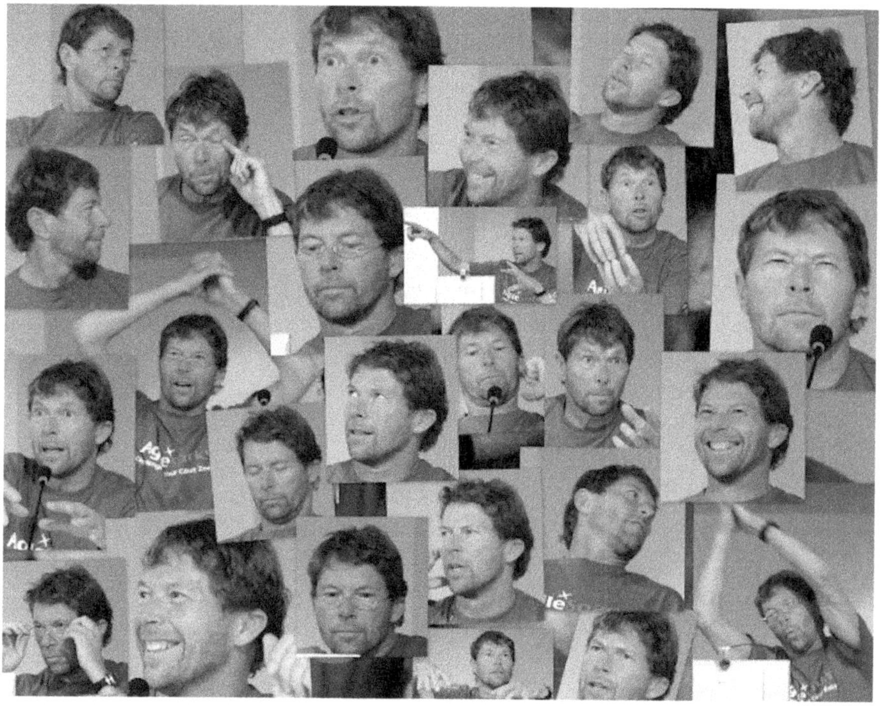

Books by Alistair Cockburn

Surviving Object Oriented Projects	1997
Writing Effective Use Cases	2000
Agile Software Development (1st ed)	2001
Patterns for Effective Use Cases	2002
People and Methodologies in Software Development *(Dr. Philos. dissertation)*	2003
Crystal Clear: *A human-powered methodology for small teams*	2004
Agile Software Development: *The cooperative game (2nd ed)*	2006
Design in Object Technology: *Class of 1994*	2021
Design in Object Technology: *The Annotated Class of 1994*	2022
Love Trio Trio del Amor (selected poems)	2022
Unifying User Stories, Use Cases, Story Maps	2024, 2025
Hexagonal Architecture Explained: *How the Ports & Adapters architecture simplifies your life, and how to implement it*	2024,` 2025
Collaboration Cards: *The Dance of Collaboration*	2025
The Mini-Book on Use Cases	2025
Simplifying Software Design: *The genius of bureaucracies, or how not-my-job sharpens your design*	2026
Guest Leadership: *What happens when the guests take the lead?*	2026
Slice the Problem Grow the Solution *A Practical Guide to Fine-Grained Incremental Development*	2026

See the full list at https://alistaircockburn.com/Books

www.ingramcontent.com/pod-product-compliance
Lightning Source LLC
LaVergne TN
LVHW052225200926
848481LV00001B/217
* 9 7 9 8 9 9 6 8 9 7 6 1 2 *